The Old English Verse Saints' Lives

A Study in Direct Discourse and the Iconography of Style

Critics have traditionally treated the Old English poems about saints – *Guthlac A, Guthlac B, Juliana, Elene, Andreas* – as individual, autonomous works, relating but little to one another except in a broadly generic way. Robert Bjork challenges this traditional view with an examination of the major structural feature that all the poems share: direct discourse.

Syntactical and rhetorical analyses of the five poems reveal a consistent use of speech in creating stylistic norms or ideals – stylistic icons – in spiritually perfect figures. In all the poems the speech of the saints is formal, rhetorical, and balanced, the stylistic analogue both of their immutable faith and of the Christ-saint figural connection. The speech of all other characters is measured against this standard; their ability or inability to meet the saintly ideal in language reflects their level of spiritual awareness.

The consistency with which these patterns appear sheds new light on the conventions of Old English poetic hagiography.

ROBERT E. BJORK is a member of the Department of English, Arizona State University.

MCMASTER OLD ENGLISH STUDIES AND TEXTS 4

Alvin A. Lee (General Editor)

Laurel Braswell

Maureen Halsall

Prudence Tracy (University of Toronto Press)

The Old English Verse Saints' Lives

A Study in Direct Discourse and the Iconography of Style

ROBERT E. BJORK

UNIVERSITY OF TORONTO PRESS

Toronto Buffalo London

© University of Toronto Press 1985
Toronto Buffalo London
Printed in Canada
ISBN 0-8020-2569-2

Canadian Cataloguing in Publication Data

Bjork, Robert E., 1949–
    The Old English verse saints' lives

    (McMaster Old English studies and texts; 4)
    Bibliography: p.
    Includes index.
    ISBN 0-8020-2569-2

    1. Anglo-Saxon poetry – History and criticism.
    2. Direct discourse in literature.   3. Hagiography.
    I. Title.   II. Series.

PR203.B57 1985   821'.1   c85-098937-x

Publication of this book was made possible
by grants from McMaster University
and from the Publications Fund of
University of Toronto Press.

TO DANIEL G. CALDER

boca gleaw, larum leoþufæst

Quid enim mutabilitas nisi mors quædam est?

Gregory *Moralia* xii, xxxiii, 38

        Social charmers daren't invite comment
And a chatterbox doesn't; in
Speech, if true, true deeds begin.

W.H. Auden 'A Short Ode to a Philologist'

Contents

Preface

This book has a dual purpose: to provide an approach to Old English poetic hagiography, showing unified conception and technique in the five verse lives, and to advance the new field of stylistic analysis of Old English, showing how such analysis illuminates the poetry. Two assumptions underlie my argument, and I freely admit them here. First, though the Old English verse saints' lives do not always reach the highest literary plateaus, I assume that they are always carefully crafted because of their status as religious artifacts. While they may seem tedious, naïve, primitive, or in some other way unsatisfactorily conceived, they are seldom unsatisfactorily executed. And second, even though direct discourse in the lives has until now received negligible critical attention, I assume that each life invests it with considerable meaning. The device looms large in all the poems, and its sheer bulk, like the monsters' in *Beowulf*, argues for its importance;[1] my study elaborates that importance, showing ultimately that *oratio recta* in the Old English verse lives is a major hagiographic convention and plays a much more functional, more thematically crucial, and less ornamental role than such critics as Andreas Heusler,[2] Walter M. Hart,[3] Adeline Courtney Bartlett,[4] and N.F. Blake[5] have allowed.

In organizing the book I have entertained three decreasingly tenable systems of arrangement, none supporting a coherent thesis, though all happily coinciding in some respects. The first is chronology: I have addressed the five poems in what scholars generally feel was the order of their composition.[6] The second is developmental order, the underlying assumption being that direct discourse waxes and wanes in use: it seems tentatively and abstractly exploited in *Guthlac A*, brought to full power in *Juliana, Elene,* and *Guthlac B*, and then becomes relatively lifeless and inexact in *Andreas*. And the third is typology. Each life figurally represents one aspect of

Christ's life, from his trials in the desert to his Passion; the figural essence of the lives alluringly suggests the existence of a saint's life cycle, comparable to the late medieval cycle plays that present Christ's typological history through his earthly mediums. But we simply do not have a sufficient number of lives nor sufficient corroborative evidence to support such a conclusion, attractive and provocative though it may be.[7] Neither do we have sufficient evidence to fix the poems' chronology and so cannot assume or construe development in any aspect of their composition. I have structured the book, therefore, mindful of the first two possibilities. But I have not lost sight of the arbitrary in the ostensibly reasonable. The chapters remain free and separate discussions of individual poems, united only through a focus on direct discourse and generic likeness.

I would like to add more than a word here about those who have helped me to bring this book into being. Professor Daniel G. Calder, under whose tutelage I first learned Old English, encouraged me tremendously at every stage of composition; Professors Edward I. Condren and Henry A. Kelly offered me sound advice at crucial points in the writing and publication process; and Dr Carol P. Hartzog greatly helped me to give shape and direction to the book's introduction. I would like to thank, too, Professor Stanley B. Greenfield for reading the pre-publication draft of the book and pointing out many errors, inconsistencies, and infelicitous phrases that all other eyes had missed; Ms Theresa Tinkle for providing skilful research assistance and for compiling the indexes; and the Bodleian Library, Oxford, for allowing me to reproduce pages 3, 16, and 17 of ms Junius XI. Finally, my gratitude goes to the editorial board of the McMaster Old English Studies and Texts series. The board and its counterpart at the University of Toronto Press painstakingly reviewed my work, making numerous and welcome suggestions for its improvement. I thank all these people even as I accept full responsibility for any errors, misperceptions, and stylistic failures still clinging, alas, to this book.

The Old English Verse Saints' Lives

Introduction

Saints' lives, insistently didactic and erected on a fixed set of conventions, have fared poorly in modern criticism. Considered too simplistic, they escaped serious notice in English before 1916[1] and even then were studied from an historical, not an artistic, perspective. Critics have lately reconsidered the Old English vernacular lives, however, with illuminating results. Daniel G. Calder, for example, has demonstrated the legitimate art of *Juliana, Guthlac A,* and *Guthlac B;*[2] Jackson J. Campbell has shown that Cynewulf skilfully manipulates traditional symbolism to create a unified *Elene,*[3] while other critics such as John Gardner have delineated the poem's structure;[4] and David Hamilton has detailed the thematic relevance of word repetition and dramatic irony in *Andreas.*[5] In these essays and all the others on vernacular saints' lives published in the last fifteen years, a tacit assumption of the poem's artistic unity has proven fruitful; we now better apprehend the workings of the individual Old English lives and can re-examine old presuppositions about their merits.

The same respect shown to the individual poems can now be effectively given to the genre as a whole. In the past, if we looked for generic similarity at all in these lives, we merely saw the crude and predictable features of every other saint's life, inconsistently and incompletely used: the *imitatio Christi* tradition, creating in all saintly characters the endlessly repeated image of Christ; the lulling review of a life replete with virtue and discipline but devoid of vice; the fantastic list of miracles and marvels; and the recording of a virtuous, often excruciating, death.[6] The tendency of the Old English lives, however, to select only some of these features – and never the same ones – has traditionally caused them to be viewed as individual, autonomous works of art, differing as much among themselves as from their continental progenitors. But they do share at least one characteristic.

Direct discourse, frequently amplified to twice or more its original length, commands attention. By concentrating on the speeches in the poems, setting them in thematic context, and scrutinizing their stylistic peculiarities and affinities, we can see that poetic hagiography in England developed its own set of conventions related to but distinct from the Latin tradition. Those conventions begin in style – the word – and end in the typological identification of the saint and Christ.

Studying style in the saints' lives is almost a mandatory enterprise. The style's relative simplicity makes the poems extremely accessible and becomes a dominant characteristic, totally appropriate for such a didactic mode. That characteristic has marked affinities with *sermo humilis*, the biblical low style through which Augustine eventually saw eternal truth. At first disdainful of the crudeness of Scripture in comparison with Cicero's stately periodic style,[7] Augustine turned to other sources of knowledge, other avenues of spiritual growth, but to no avail. Once he was converted, however, he began to understand his former blindness. Scripture, far from lacking the beauty and intricacy of Cicero and classical literature, exceeds both in its subtle combination of a sublimity of subject-matter with an apparent lowliness of presentation.[8] The scholarly, erudite reader can approach Scripture confident that it contains profound mysteries, while the common man can enjoy its treasures because of the simple style. The saints' lives, then, gain power from the low style and operate in its spirit, which the subject-matter implicitly contains: an ordinary individual typically becomes exalted as a saint, and the saint's life typically has its roots in an everyday kind of realism that makes it accessible to all men even while its seeming simplicity approaches a sublime sophistication.[9]

Augustine's view of rhetoric and Scripture permeates the thought of the Middle Ages. Bede, for example, arguing that the secular masters of eloquence cannot surpass the beauty of scriptural poetry and prose, uses biblical in place of classical quotations in his *Liber de schematibus et tropis*. He states his position in this way:

> Sed ut cognoscas, dilectissime fili, cognoscant omnes qui haec legere uoluerint quia sancta Scriptura ceteris omnibus scripturis non solum auctoritate, quia diuina est, uel utilitate, quia ad uitam ducit aeternam, sed et antiquitate et ipsa praeeminet positione dicendi, placuit mihi collectis de ipsa exemplis ostendere quia nihil huiusmodi schematum siue troporum ualent praetendere saecularis eloquentiae magistri, quod non in illa praecesserit.

> But, my beloved child, in order that you and all who wish to read this work may know that Holy Writ surpasses all other writings not

merely in authority because it is divine, or in usefulness because it leads to eternal life, but also for its age and artistic composition, I have chosen to demonstrate by means of examples collected from Holy Writ that teachers of secular eloquence in any age have not been able to furnish us with any of these figures and tropes which did not appear first in Holy Writ.[10]

The great encyclopaedists popular at the time, such as Isidore of Seville and Cassiodorus, likewise subordinated rhetoric and learning to ecclesiastical ends while unmistakably including both in those ends. Isidore, whose *Origines* or *Etymologia* was a standard text for the English long before the close of the seventh century,[11] states that 'rhetorica est bene dicendi scientia in civilibus quaestionibus, [eloquentia copia] ad persuadendum iusta et bona' (rhetoric is the science of speaking well: it is a flow of eloquence on civil questions whose purpose is to persuade men to do what is just and good) and that 'coniuncta est autem Grammaticae arti Rhetorica. In Grammatica enim scientiam recte loquendi discimus; in Rhetorica vero percipimus qualiter ea, quae didicimus, proferamus' (rhetoric goes hand in hand with the art of philology. In philology we teach the science of correct speaking, while in rhetoric we show how to make sure of the knowledge we have taught).[12]

Scholars have felt for some time that the knowledge conveyed through rhetoric in Latin was conveyed in the vernacular as well. The tradition of rhetorical analysis of Old English poetry goes back to the nineteenth-century German school of generic and rhetorical criticism represented in critics such as Reinhold Merbot,[13] and moves with only minor mishaps into the twentieth century, most notably in works such as Adeline Courtney Bartlett's *The Larger Rhetorical Patterns in Anglo-Saxon Poetry*. Not until recently, however, predominantly through the work of Jackson J. Campbell,[14] have we realized how thoroughly rhetoric pervades our oldest literature. Campbell notes that 'beginning with Aldhelm in the late seventh century and Bede in the early eighth, we have good evidence of the extensive knowledge of classical learning in England, and also of the free adaptation and modification of that learning to fit the English situation.'[15] The works of such writers as Juvenal, Ovid, Persius, Priscian, Cicero, and Martianus Capella were diligently copied by scribes in the British Isles as guides for understanding sacred texts,[16] 'but during the ninth, tenth and eleventh centuries we find a great body of vernacular literature which would probably not be as it is unless its authors had studied Latin grammar and rhetoric.'[17]

The rhetorical sophistication of Old English poetry generally is not an entirely surprising phenomenon. Since English style in its written form probably moved towards emulating Latin models rather than the native spoken tongue, it would necessarily allow room for classical rhetorical effects. In addition, because rhetoric organizes language, it may have served the same function that punctuation does in modern English. Both devices help the reader to see how a passage is organized and how linguistic units relate to each other.[18] But most importantly, organizing language for instructive ends becomes a pious act. Fitting words together in an effective manner expresses the force of truth and becomes a manifestation of power;[19] by manipulating style and rhetoric one emulates the Creator himself, praises him, and becomes part of his everlasting body. The creative force of rhetoric expressed through symmetry, harmony, and balance thus mimes the similar features of the unchanging Ptolemaic universe above the circle of the moon. St Ambrose in his *Hexaemeron* – another popular and influential work in the Old English period[20] – draws the analogy between God and artist rather firmly in his discussion of various arts, theoretical and practical:

> Aliae hujusmodi, ut, cessante quoque operationis officio operis munus appareat, ut aedificatio atque textura quae etiam tacente artifice, peritiam ejus ostendunt, ut operatori operis sui testimonium suffragetur. Similiter hic mundus divinae majestatis insigne est, ut per ipsum Dei spaientia manifestetur.

> There are other arts of such nature that, even when the processes of operation cease, the handiwork remains visible. As an example of this we have buildings or woven material which, even when the craftsman is silent, still exhibit his skill, so that testimony is presented of the craftsman's own work. In a similar way, this work is a distinctive mark of divine majesty from which the wisdom of God is made manifest.[21]

The Old English verse lives, four of which almost certainly derive from Latin sources, just as certainly must have been influenced by the rhetorical tradition. For example, they fall into an essentially rhetorical mode exemplifying as they do the venerable practice of paraphrase. Paraphrase was first used in Latin renditions of books of the Bible, recast in hexameters. The Spaniard Juvencus, the Egyptian Nonnus, and the Ligurian Arator all used it, and the procedure could even be applied to the lives of the saints, as Paulinus of Périgueux and Fortunatus both discovered. The same procedure could also be reversed so that a piece of prose turned into poetry could be turned back into prose once more. Aldhelm, Bede, and Alcuin all followed this practice.²² Thus, by transforming the original sources, elaborating and contracting the accounts to fit modified concepts (and by choosing a new medium – poetry), the Old English scops performed a traditional rhetorical act.

Apart from using paraphrase, the Old English verse lives also make use of topoi, another large building-block of traditional rhetoric. Both Cicero's *Topica* and Boethius's *De topicis differentiis* were known to the Anglo-Saxons,²³ and both provided practical advice on what topics or commonplaces fitted what situations and audiences. Topoi (*loci communes* in Latin) are basic plans, outlines, or formulae that one can use to create many different arguments or observations differing in detail and substance but not in structure. Several of them appear in the Old English lives. The prologue to *Guthlac A*, for example, contains what Curtius calls the 'World Upside-down' topos,²⁴ and a major structural feature of *Guthlac B* depends on the topos of death as a separation of soul and body. While some topoi occur in the Latin source, the death-as-separation topos represents a marked change in the narrative of *Guthlac B*.²⁵ Topoi in the other poems are likewise often unmistakable additions made specifically for rhetorical effect. In *Juliana* Cynewulf adds the 'Praise of Rulers' topos,²⁶ putting it in the mouth of Affricanus to heighten our sense of his obsequiousness to Eleusius and his weakness in the context of the poem (see below, pages 49–50). And the *Andreas* poet injects the *puer-senex* topos into Andreas's dialogue when he praises Christ the Steersman. The addition helps to emphasize Andreas's perceptivity in recognizing divine wisdom when it seems to come from a mere mortal.²⁷

Although, as Joshua Bonner and Luke Reinsma point out,²⁸ we perhaps should not argue too strongly for Latin influence on Old English poetry, Campbell and others nevertheless alert us to the skilful artifice of the verse. Its deliberate artistry has become an established tenet of its criticism, since the poetry clearly depends on a mode of thought that is in essence ordered, harmonious, rhetorical.²⁹ The verse itself testifies most convincingly to its own importance as artifact and to its creators' importance as skilled and intelligent men. A famous passage from *Beowulf* provides a good example:

> Hwilum cyninges þegn,
> guma gilphlæden, gidda gemyndig,
> se ðe ealfela ealdgesegena
870 worn gemunde, word oþer fand
> soðe gebunden; secg eft ongan
> sið Beowulfes snyttrum styrian,
> ond on sped wrecan spel gerade,

wordum wrixlan.[30]

> At times the king's thane, the man covered with glory, mindful of
> songs, he who remembered a great many of the old sagas, found
> other words truly bound; the warrior again began to recite wisely
> Beowulf's undertaking and to utter successfully the story with skill,
> to vary his words.

The importance of style, then, or the ability wordum wrixlan, inheres in
the poet's own view of his world; that view, together with *sermo humilis*
and the Anglo-Saxon interest in rhetoric, justifies its study. What remains
now is to define what we mean by 'style' and to outline a method for isolating its salient features and effects. As used here, the term implies the
relationship between meaning or message or purpose on the one hand and
verse form, rhetoric, and syntax on the other. The message of the saints'
lives happily raises little debate; through close scrutiny of their technical
features we make more profound, more delicate, a moral already commonly
accessible.

My basic approach to the stylistic analysis of the five verse lives derives
from recent stylistic theory, especially that of Michael Riffaterre,[31] who
demonstrates that formal features of language can reinforce meaning in a
text.[32] Thus, to take an example from rhetoric, a trope can buttress the se-
mantic level of a poem. Polyptoton, for instance (the repetition of the same
root word with different endings after some intervening words), can be
used to argue for or against change. Shakespeare employs the device in
Sonnet 116 when he defines love's stability: 'Love is not love / Which alters when it alteration finds, / Or bends with the remover to remove.'
Chiasmus (an *abba* crossing structure) can be used as a figure of the Cross
in poems on the Cross, such as *The Dream of the Rood*, while synchisis, or
confused word order in a sentence, can reflect the confusion or disorder of
the person using it.

In Old English, formal features of poetry and language imply meaning
by creating patterns of expectation, then disrupting those patterns at thematically or aesthetically crucial points. The norm or the pattern of expectations against which the disruptions or deviations gain value exists in the
language as a whole but grows most significantly from the context of the
individual poem, from the pattern of norm and deviation within the poem
itself.[33] Although the notion of norms and thwarted expectations is relatively simple, the method of analysis it implies requires complex execution,
demanding a rigorous attention to the function of each word, phrase, and
syntactic and rhetorical pattern in the work being considered. And that exe-

cution necessitates our knowing something about 'normal' Old English usage and the expectations it creates. Two norms are especially relevant to this study, particularly to my treatment of *Juliana* and *Elene*. The first concerns word order, the second how words relate to each other in a verse line.

Central to the study of Old English verse is the 'Law of Sentence Particles' developed by Hans Kuhn[34] and expanded by A.J. Bliss,[35] D. Slay,[36] A. Campbell,[37] and especially Lydia Fakundiny.[38] Briefly, the law states:

> (1) sentence particles used in the verse dip must be proclitic to either the first or second stressed element in the verse clause, but they cannot be divided between both dip positions unless the word occupying the intervening lift is itself a sentence particle; if the sentence particle occurs later in the clause it must be stressed; (2) it follows that if the first dip position in the verse clause is occupied, one of the unstressed words in that position must be a sentence particle.[39]

Put another way, sentence particles usually remain unstressed in Old English verse, but their position in the verb clause ultimately determines their metrical value. Kuhn defines sentence particles as unstressed or weakly stressed words (such as adverbs, finite verbs, pronouns) used as independent sentence modifiers, and he applies the term 'sentence-part particles' either to unstressed words belonging to parts of the sentence or to single words (such as possessive pronouns and quantity words preceding their nouns).[40]

Bliss, Slay, and Campbell concentrate mainly on finite verbs, showing that they normally do not alliterate in Old English poetry. Fakundiny, however, deals with the sentence-part particles, 'including indefinite adjectives of quantity, possessive pronouns, demonstrative adjectives, and prepositions, in an attempt to show their use in verse composition.'[41] Among her conclusions, two have special significance: possessive pronouns and articles in Old English normally precede the words they modify; and substantives normally occupy the stressed positions in poetry.[42] Thus, in *Beowulf* lines 1703b–7a we find both principles violated, but the violations have aesthetic and rhetorical justification:

Blæd is aræred

geond widwegas,   wine min Beowulf,

1705   ðin ofer þeoda gehwylce.   Eal þu hit geþyldum healdest,
        mægen mid modes snyttrum.   Ic þe sceal *mine* gelæstan
        freode, swa wit furðum spræcon.

Glory is raised up through the wide ways, my friend Beowulf, *yours* over each of nations. You will hold it all steadily, strength with wisdom of mind. I shall fulfil *my* friendship with you, as we agreed a short time ago [my italics].

Fakundiny observes that the separation of the pronoun 'ðin' from the noun 'blæd' envelops and so expresses the sentence's meaning. Stress on the pronoun 'underlines its importance and effects the transition from the normal two-beat verse to the hypermetric series in such a way that sense and rhythm are perfectly co-ordinated.' Displacement of the other pronoun, 'mine,' also calls attention to itself 'so that reciprocation is established between Beowulf's fame, "blæd ... ðin" (resulting from his brave services to Hroðgar), and the king's friendship, "mine ... freode." '[43]

Also central to the study of Old English verse is the notion, formulated by Randolph Quirk[44] and developed by Richard A. Lewis,[45] of lexical and alliterative collocations. In discussing the formula as 'a habitual collocation, metrically defined,' Quirk observes:

> [It] is thus a stylization of something which is fundamental to linguistic expression, namely the expectation that a sequence of words will show lexical congruity, together with (and as a condition of) lexical and grammatical complementarity. It may be said of 'wide' and 'way', for example, that in Old English they set up a reciprocal expectancy of each other, which may operate strictly within the 'half-line' structure (as in 'wegas ofer widland', *Andreas* 198), but equally across halflines (as in 'Wærun wegas ðine · on widne sæ', *Paris Psalter* 76, 16), and also of course in prose: 'þæt geat ys swyðe wid, and se weg ys swyðe rum', Matt. 7. 13. An example with a thematically more powerful connexion (and in consequence one still more widely exploited) is the pair *mod* and *mægen*, perhaps most familiarly contrasted in Byrhtwold's words, 'mod sceal þe mare, · þe ure mægen lytlað' (*Maldon* 313).[46]

In Old English verse, then, an expectation of lexical congruity exists, and often the alliterative pairings interanimate one another. The name Grendel, for instance, is frequently linked 'with words congruently indicative of fierceness.'[47]

Such conventional yoking of like to like obviously sets up norms which are pleasurable in themselves but which the poets can also break with telling effect. Again *Beowulf* serves as a good example. Quirk points out that the word 'sæl' (joy, happiness) appears three times in the poem (lines 607, 632, 1170) in 'a congruent context'[48] before Hrothgar uses it incongruently following the attack by Grendel's mother. Hrothgar replies to Beowulf: 'Ne frin þu æfter sælum; / Sorh is geniwod // Denigea leodum. / Dead is Æschere.' (Ask not about joy; sorrow is renewed for the Danish people. Æschere is dead [1322–3]). The incongruity here reflects the upheaval that the murderous attack has wrought.

Through such examples Quirk demonstrates how Old English poets 'achieve a disturbing and richly suggestive poetry'[49] within the verse line. Lewis, by contrast, begins with the notion of lexical congruity and the thematic content it can bear, then combines it with John Leyerle's hypothesis about interlace design in Old English poetry.[50] What he achieves is a provocative essay that shows, contra R.B. LePage,[51] that lexical congruity can exist across whole verse paragraphs, producing an integrative interlace structure of syntax, alliteration, and meaning. Lewis offers several examples, but one from *Andreas* seems especially appropriate here. In these lines 'we notice a contextual and to some extent lexical continuity of items alliterating on *h* (six of the 12 lines alliterate on *h*) and also a number of items alliterating on *d*.'[52]

```
        Geseh he hæþenra      hloð ætgædere,
        fore hlindura      hyrdas standan,
        seofone ætsomne.      Ealle swylt fornam,
995     druron domlease.      Deaðræs forfeng
        hæleð heorodreorige.      Ða se halga gebæd
        bilwytne fæder,      breostgehygdum
        herede on hehðo      heofoncyninges þrym,
        godes dryhtendom.      Duru sona onarn
1000    þurh handhrine      haliges gastes,
        ond þær in eode,      elnes gemyndig,
        hæle hildedeor.      Hæðene swæfon,
        dreore druncne,      deaðwang rudon.
```

He saw the band of heathens together before the door, guards standing, seven together. Death took them all; they died bereft of glory. The death rush seized the blood-stained men. Then the saint besought the gracious Father; in his breast-thoughts he praised the glory of the heavenly King on high, the majesty of God. The doors immediately burst open through the hand-touch of the Holy Spirit, and mindful of courage, the brave hero walked in there. The heathen slept, drunk with blood, stained the death-place.

'Such passages,' Lewis claims, 'show an integration of syntax and alliteration which is well expressed in the concept of structural interlace.' He concludes:

This is not to say that the poet consciously calculated the interspers-
ing of 'alliterative strands.' It is certainly not to say that the arrangement of poetic items was as dexterously and precisely handled
as zoomorphic figures. It is to see in such integration a sense of design that combined one axis of word coordination with another. The
more we appreciate the role of alliteration as an axis of word corre-
spondence, the more we will recognize and appreciate its recurrence
as an axis of narrative continuity.[53]

The work of the foregoing scholars teaches us how important the basic
laws of stress, word order, and alliterative collocation are and how deviations from those norms can reinforce meaning in a poem. With these two
points in mind, we may now return to a practical application of our method
as a prolegomenon to a broader study of the verse saints' lives. The broader
study will first focus on the larger structural features of whole speeches
(are they balanced or unbalanced? bipartite or tripartite or neither?), and
will then shift attention to syntax, rhetorical figures, and diction, all means
of isolating the differences among the characters' dialogue. The focus at
this point, however, does not require such breadth; we need only illustrate
the potential usefulness of a basic methodology.
The passage I wish to consider is one which Stanley B. Greenfield has
analysed admirably before. It is a famous one from *The Wanderer*:

     Swa ic modsefan   minne sceolde,
20   oft earmcearig,   eðle bidæled,
     freomægum feor   feterum sælan,
     siþþan geara iu   goldwine minne
     hrusan heolster biwrah,   ond ic hean þonan
     wod wintercearig   ofer waþema gebind,
25   sohte sele dreorig   sinces bryttan,
     hwær ic feor oþþe neah   findan meahte
     þone þe in meoduhealle   minne myne wisse,
     oþþe mec freondleasne   frefran wolde,
     wenian mid wynnum.

So I, often full of sorrows, separated from my native land, far from
friendly kinsmen, had to shut my mind in fetters, since many years
ago the darkness of earth covered my gold-friend, and I wretched
thence travelled full of the cares of winter over the frozen waves,
sought drearily the hall of a giver of treasure, where I far or near
might find one who in the meadhall might know my thought, or
would comfort me friendless, entertain me with joys.[54]

The intricacy of this sentence, with its complex of clauses, is 'a vital element in conveying the sense of movement and frustration felt by the speaker.'[55] As subject to the main clause and the 'ic hean' (I wretched) and 'hwær ic feor' (where I far) clauses, the speaker indicates his past self-reliance in his state of exile; as object of the last two clauses ('minne myne wisse,' might know my thought; and 'mec freondleasne frefran wolde,' would comfort me friendless), he signals his shift in outlook 'to that devoutly-to-be-wished-for state wherein he can depend upon another, have a lord to care for him':

> In a very real sense, this formal, syntactic arrangement here anticipates the later happy dream of submissive dependence upon his former lord and the rude awakening to the reality of independent insecurity that will ultimately lead to the statement at the end of the poem about the only real security lying in God.[56]

At the pivotal point in the sentence, the speaker is neither subject nor object of the action ('siþþan geara iu / goldwine minne // hrusan heolster biwrah,' since many years ago the darkness of earth covered my gold-friend) and the poem's theme is foreshadowed: darkness covering the twin values of gold and friendship points to 'the transience of all earthly values.'[57] The placement of 'biwrah' at the end of the a-verse, one of only nine such placements in the poem, gives the clause added emphasis, as well as contributing to the sense of motion in the sentence. The initial appearance of 'wod' (travelled) and 'sohte' (sought) in the succeeding two a-verses, a feature also rare in this poem, contributes further to that sense.

Other features increase the sentence's majesty. The triple modification of 'ic' ('oft earmcearig, /eðle bidæled, // freomægum feor,' often full of sorrows, separated from my native land, far from friendly kinsmen) in lines 20–1a reflects the larger structures of the sentence. Lines 19–21 stress the speaker's state of mind ('earmcearig'); 23b–25 his movement into a new land ('eðle bidæled'); 26–9, in their concentration on the idea of a search for a new lord, the idea of absence from kinsmen.[58] And finally, the single modification 'freondleasne' in the last clause 'reinforces the threefold repetitions of the earlier segments of the sentence, but [in its] very singularity allows the hope that the last clause implies to filter through.'[59]

Although Greenfield does not integrate Fakundiny's and Quirk's findings into his analysis, they do support his point and deserve mention. First, we should notice that 'minne' in line 19b is metrically dominant, concentrating our attention on the speaker and his inner world. Second, and more tenuous, is the possibly incongruent pairing of 'earmcearig' with 'eðle' in line 20. Since we have only one other instance of the word earmcearig in Old

English poetry,[60] we cannot definitely establish incongruity here. But the association of the word with 'eðle' does recreate the psychological focal point of the sentence, and a disruption of lexical expectation would nicely coincide with the speaker's sense of a disjointed world.

One other point is important both here and in the chapters that follow. Old English poets generally seem to favour syntactic disjunction as a stylistic principle,[61] showing no reluctance to separate words logically belonging together. Thus the separation of the modal auxiliary 'sceolde' (had to) from its infinitive 'sælan' (shut) in lines 19–21 of The Wanderer is far from unusual. In context, however, the device stands out as a deviation: in no other place does the poet so widely separate the two parts of a verb.[62] And in no other place could such a separation serve a dual purpose. The disjointed words at once reflect the division of the speaker from his homeland and create a syntactic analogue to his 'mind-fetters' by enclosing the other constituents of this first major clause. We will see the same device used with similar impact in Guthlac B.

The concepts of context, norm, and deviation will be important in determining how the Old English poets manipulate their verse for didactic ends. But they will also be important from a larger perspective, for the verse lives function within other traditions besides the linguistic and rhetorical. We can best understand the lives' significance by looking briefly at their native heroic, their hagiographic, and their iconographic contexts.

We begin with direct discourse and again focus on Beowulf, where we find the device playing a major role.[63] The first dramatic moment of the poem is the Beowulf – coast-guard exchange (lines 237–85). The weard Scildinga descends from his watch to find out who Beowulf and his men are and why they have come to Denmark. Beowulf answers the guard's carefully structured and formal words in a speech just as carefully structured and just as formal. To the guard's direct question 'Hwæt syndon ge?' (Who are you?), he answers directly, 'We synt gumcynnes / Geata leode' (We are of the race of the Geatish nation [260]). This is followed by six lines of explanatory digression before the speech returns to the present:

267   We þurh holdne hige   hlaford þinne,
       sunu Healfdenes   secean cwomon,
       leodgebyrgean.

With friendly heart, we come to seek your lord, the son of Healf-dane, the protector of the people.

Beowulf thus flatters the guard by miming the structure of his speech, which also has an initial six-line digression, and he ensures the Dane's trust by giving him his own: 'Wes þu us larena god' (Be good to us in your counsel [269b]). The guard's judgment about Beowulf's motives and capabilities may influence the fate of the Danish people.

In his next two speeches Beowulf displays similar tact and control, raising the level of his discourse as the situation demands. He matches the formality and skill of both Wulfgar (lines 333–55) and Hrothgar (407–90) but takes care not to exceed their abilities. When he meets Unferth, however, a noticeable shift in style occurs. While Unferth's speech is aggressively simple and direct, consisting predominantly of short clauses, Beowulf's is noticeably more subtle and complex, making use of a number of subordinate clauses, most of which begin with 'þæt' (see 555b–57a, for example). Unferth, however, does not use one þæt clause. We may thus take syntax 'as something of the measure of the man.'[64]

This small sampling of heroic dialogue forces two conclusions upon us. First, speech is action in *Beowulf*, so a man's worth coincides with the power of his discourse. The coast guard's reaction to Beowulf's speech has paramount importance here, for he does not differentiate at all between Beowulf's words and deeds:

> Weard maþelode,   ðær on wicge sæt,
> ombeht unforht: 'Æghwæþres sceal
> scearp scyldwiga   gescad witan,
> worda ond worca,   se þe wel þenceð.
> 290 Ic þæt gehyre,   þæt þis is hold weorod
> frean Scyldinga.'

The guard spoke, sitting there on his horse, the officer unafraid: 'Any keen shield-warrior must be a judge of words and deeds, he who thinks well. That I hear, that this is a troop loyal to the lord of the Scyldings.'

Beowulf's words, which constitute the only 'deeds' the guard has witnessed, convince him of the Geat's heroic stature.[65] Throughout the poem the poet emphasizes the necessity of significant words matching imposing deeds (see also 1830b and following), implying that 'integrity of thought, word and deed constitutes the whole man. The interplay of states of mind, speech and action is a principal narrative concern.'[66] The second conclusion we may draw from this sampling of heroic dialogue is that Beowulf tailors his discourse to situational demands. He gauges his audience before he speaks and thus displays an adaptability characteristic of heroes in the early epics.[67]

We may draw similar conclusions from a much later poem, *The Battle of*

Maldon, a poem with marked epic features[68] as well as, for some critics, definite hagiographic ones.[69] Here too the words-deeds theme plays a crucial role. It is not accidental, for instance, that one of the dramatic highlights of the poem is the initial flyting between Byrhtnoth and the Viking messenger.[70] The exchange becomes part of the battle itself, with words equalling weapons.[71] Earl R. Anderson elaborates:

> The close relationship between actions and words, expressed through style in *Maldon*, might best be illustrated by the poet's introduction to Byrhtnoth's speech.
>
> —Byrhtnoð maþelode,   bord hafenode,
>   wand wacne æsc,   wordum mælde (42–3.)
>
> ... Byrhtnoth, who *rad and rædde* (18a) instructing his men, proves to be a resolute leader in words and deeds. As Byrhtnoth raises his shield, the homoeoteleuton *maþelode / hafenode* and the chiastic arrangement of his speech and action suggest through style an intertwining of action and speech which could only have been a conscious act of artistry.[72]

Levels of discourse also manifest themselves, even though Byrhtnoth has a limited number of speeches in the poem. In his first he sarcastically addresses the Viking messenger, refusing to pay ransom to avoid battle:

```
45    Gehyrst þu, sælida,    hwæt þis folc segeð?
      Hi willað eow to gafole    garas syllan,
      ættrynne ord    and ealde swurd,
      þa heregeatu    þe eow æt hilde ne deah.
      Brimmanna boda,    abeod eft ongean,
50    sege þinum leodum    miccle laþre spell,
      þæt her stynt unforcuð    eorl mid his werode,
      þe wile gealgean    eþel þysne,
      Æþelredes eard,    ealdres mines,
      folc and foldan.    Feallan sceolon
55    hæþene æt hilde.    To heanlic me þinceð
      þæt ge mid urum sceattum    to scype gangon
      unbefohtene,    nu ge þus feor hider
      on urne eard    in becomon.
      Ne sceole ge swa softe    sinc gegangan;
60    us sceal ord and ecg    ær geseman,
      grim guðplega,    ær we gofol syllon.[73]
```

Do you hear, Viking, what this people says? They wish to give you spears for tribute, poisoned points and old swords, the war-gear that does not avail you at battle. Messenger of the sea-wanderers, announce once again, say to your people a much more hateful message that here stands an undaunted earl with his army who will defend this country, Æþelred's homeland, the people and earth of my lord; the heathen shall fall at battle. It seems too disgraceful to me that you should go with our tribute unfought to ship, now that you have come thus far into our land. Nor shall you obtain the teasure so softly; point and edge shall first reconcile us, grim battle-play, before we give tribute.

The dominant rhetorical strategy here is deliberate and ironic echoing of the Viking's words. 'Gafole' (tribute) and 'garas' (spears) in line 46 echo and invert 'garræs' (spear-rush)[74] and 'gafole' in line 32 of the messenger's speech; a similar opposition informs Byrhtnoth's concluding line ('guð-plega,' 'gofol' [61]). Other echoes, less evident, have equal ironic force. Byrhtnoth answers the Viking's 'hilde dælon' (partake of battle [33b]), for instance, with 'eow æt hilde ne deah' (does not avail you at battle [48b]) and parries 'swa hearde' (33a) with 'swa softe' (59a). Finally, he responds sarcastically to the Viking's promise that they will go to their ships 'mid þam sceattum' (with the tribute [40a]): now that they have come so far, it would be disgraceful to allow them to leave unfought 'mid urum sceattum' (with our tribute [56a]).[75]

The cumulative effect of this exchange impresses on us the sense of play – serious play, to be sure – animating both characters. Byrhtnoth meets the Viking's complex rhetorical and syntactic strategies with a strategy of irony equally complex. The situation demands a display of skill, and the Englishman rises to the challenge. As the situation changes, however, so does his discourse. The Vikings, who now apparently speak collectively, approach Byrhtnoth in a different manner:

86   ongunnon lytegian þa   laðe gystas,
      bædon þæt hi upgang   agan moston,
      ofer þone ford faran,   feþan lædan.

The hated strangers then began to use guile, asked that they might have passage to travel over the ford, to lead the foot-troop.

The brief and determined collective request contrasts with that of the Viking spokesman, who showed considerable rhetorical skill and syntactic

complexity in calling for tribute. Byrhtnoth's response likewise differs from
his first speech and in the same way. Lines 93 to 95 include 'none of his
earlier biting counters to the messenger's rhetoric':[76]

> Nu eow is gerymed,   gað ricene to us,
> guman to guþe;   god ana wat
> 95   hwa þære wælstowe   wealdan mote.

> The way is now open for you. Come quickly to us, men to battle;
> God alone knows who might govern the battlefield there.

Matching discourse to situation, words to deeds, Byrhtnoth fits decidedly
into his heroic role.

The words-deeds theme naturally belongs to a people who viewed words
as acts, who considered the beot as a reflection of self-knowledge, and the
poets of the saints' lives accord the theme an importance equalling and even
exceeding the importance that the *Beowulf* and *Maldon* poets give it. That
importance probably derives from at least two theological sources: the notion of Christ as Logos and the notion that the saints are part of Christ's
body. The power of the Logos was known to both pagan and Jewish antiquity. Heraclitus saw it as the universal reason that governs and permeates
the world, and in the Old Testament, as an extension of God, it takes on
creative as well as communicative powers, eventually assuming an almost
independent existence (Wisdom 18:14–16; 2 Samuel 15:10; Isaiah 55:11;
Jeremiah 23:29).[77] In the New Testament the Logos becomes God, the creative Word, and thus is synonymous with the Messiah himself. The prologue to the Gospel of John makes the identification clear: 'In principio erat
Verbum, Et Verbum erat apud Deum, Et Deus erat Verbum' (In the beginning was the Word, and the Word was with God, and the Word was God
[John 1:1]).[78] The very shape of this passage embraces the theological
premise it states. 'Principio' is a play on 'princeps,' so that the beginning,
the Prince, the Word, and God all become one.

The coincidence of words and deeds in the person of Christ is an important Christian concept, one that every emulator of Christ had to understand. The Apostle Paul emphasizes it in Colossians 3:17: 'Omne,
quodcumque facitis in verbo aut in opere, omnia in nomine Domini Iesu
Christi, gratias agentes Deo et Patri per ipsum' (Whatever you do in word
or in work, do all in the name of the Lord Jesus, giving thanks to God the
Father through him). The Church Fathers were not slow to rephrase and
re-emphasize this exhortation. Addressing a council of bishops in Carthage
on 5 May 418, Augustine, for example, enjoined: 'Laudemus Dominum,
fratres, vita et lingua, corde et ore, vocibus et moribus' (Let us praise the

Lord, Brothers, by our lives and our speech, with our hearts and our mouths, with our utterances and our ways).[79] By quite early in the Middle Ages, then, the doctrine of the Logos had taken on central theological – and epistemological – importance, as Marcia Colish attests:

> The ineffable God had revealed himself to a man in Christ. Christ had taken on human nature and human faculties. By his life, death, and resurrection, he had renewed and restored these human faculties, reenabling them to become Godlike. Medieval thinkers drew an important epistemological corollary from this doctrine. In the Christian dispensation, human modes of thought and expression, although still limited by the human condition, could now worthily take on the tasks assigned to them by God. Human language, reborn through the Incarnation, could now assist God in spreading the effects of the Incarnation to the world. The medieval confidence that Babel had been redeemed in the gift of tongues was the immediate context in which men of this period judged, understood, and pressed into service the symbolic forms of human discourse.[80]

The importance of the Logos and the Christian dispensation that allows us – indeed, compels us – to use language in the service of God gives rise to the central premise of the present study: if Christians generally gave considerable attention to 'the symbolic forms of human discourse' as they strove to serve God, it stands to reason that saints or representations of saints had to give still fuller attention to every aspect of language. All saints transcend the world; all are identified with Christ. As part of Christ's body, they are alike in all their essential features, a fact that explains the extreme conventionality of hagiography: in the communion of saints all things are common, all characteristics Christ's.[81] Since one of Christ's major characteristics is his identification with the Logos, the Word, his saints should reflect that identification, something they can do in hagiography through their use of direct discourse. This study will demonstrate that in the Old English verse lives, the words-deeds theme is the underlying literary and theological principle governing the use of speech. It defines the structure of *Guthlac A* and is specifically referred to in *Juliana* (line 57), *Guthlac B* (948b–50a), and *Andreas* (596b).

One other theological premise helps to clarify the state of words in the verse lives: the Christian view of man as changeable and of God as an immutable, unchanging reality. The dualistic idea comes from classical Greek metaphysics and carries over into the Middle Ages and the entire Christian tradition. In Old English poetry it frequently determines word choice and even syntax. In *Christ II*, for instance, God 'had sung' (*sungen* [line 619])

in his anger, showing that order, harmony, and unchangeableness characterize even his wrath; in *Beowulf* clauses with God as their subject show
relatively uniform and stable syntax, while clauses relating to Beowulf himself do not show such consistency.[82] For medieval man, then, everything in
heaven functions perfectly in symmetrical, harmonious uniformity. The
sanctified can achieve heaven and immutability through Christ, but the unsanctified cannot. More importantly for our purposes, saints can achieve the
unchangeable state while still on earth because they already form part of
Christ. Gregory the Great makes this point clear in commenting on Job
33:38:

> Qui per naturam omnes in semetipsis propriam mutabilitatem ha-
> bent; se dum immutabili veritati studiose semper inhærere desider-
> ant, inhærendo agunt, ut immutabiles fiant. Cumque ad hanc toto
> affectu se tenent, quandoque accipiunt ut super semetipsos ducti vin-
> cant hoc quod in semetipsis mutabiles exstiterunt. Quid enim muta-
> bilitas nisi mors quædam est?[83]

> [The saints] by nature have in themselves an appropriate mutability;
> but while they always assiduously desire to cleave to the immutable
> truth, by cleaving they bring it about that they become immutable.
> Whenever they hold themselves to this with total affection, then
> they find that being led above themselves, they overcome this, that
> mutable things were manifested in themselves. For what is mutabil-
> ity but a kind of death?

Just as the saints' lives can be expected to manifest interest in the words-
deeds theme, so can they be expected to show an appropriate immutability
in the saints they depict. As we have seen, words often equal the man in
heroic poems, and the man displays heroic flexibility, modifying the level
of his discourse when he must. In the saints' lives, by contrast, no such
flexibility obtains, and dialogue takes on a predictable uniformity not seen
in that of *Beowulf* and *Maldon*. Heroes are humanity writ large; saints are
humanity transcended. Beyond life, they rise above the mutable world, becoming one with the imperishable, unchanging body of Christ, and their
immutable discourse becomes the stylistic analogue of their spiritual state.

Using discourse as a character-index in this way fits into a pattern of linguistic manipulation typifying other Old English hagiographic texts. Ælfric,
for example, uses aspectual features of verbs as theological metaphors, allowing verb qualities to symbolize the spiritual states of his characters.[84] In
'The Nativity of Our Lord Jesus Christ' he clearly differentiates among the
soulless things, men and angels, and God in terms of aspect,[85] and in the

life of St Eugenia he gives the pagans' verbs complex aspectual features –
active, punctual, imperative, durative – while he graces the Christians'
verbs with simple, non-temporal qualities.[86] The mutable and the immutable, the bad and the good, thus manifest themselves in the written and spoken word.

But if the Old English scops function within the same pattern of thought,
they adapt that pattern to their own vision. The fixed, stable quality of
saintly discourse, discourse obviously elaborated over the Latin original, appears to be peculiar to the verse lives, as an examination of some representative texts suggests. Again Ælfric, the measure of excellence in Old
English prose, serves as our example. At one point in the life of St Oswald
we hear the saint speak these words as he raises a cross before going into
battle with the wicked Cadwalla:

> Uton feallan to ðære rode
> and þone ælmihtigan biddan þæt he us ahredde
> wið þone modigan feond þe us afyllan wile,
> god sylf wat geare þæt we winnað rihtlice
> wið þysne reðan cyning to ahredenne ure leode.

> Let us fall down before the cross,
> and pray the Almighty that He will save us
> against the proud enemy who desires to kill us.
> God Himself knoweth well that we fight justly
> against this cruel king, to deliver our people.[87]

This is a fairly literal translation of Bede's original, showing only some
elaboration, addition, or deletion. The Latin reads:

> Flectamus omnes genua, et Deum omnipotentem uiuum ac uerum in
> commune deprecemur, ut nos ab hoste superbo ac feroca sua misera-
> tione defendat; scit enim ipse quia iusta pro salute gentis nostrae
> bella suscepimus.

> Let us all kneel together and pray the almighty, everliving, and true
> God to defend us in His mercy from the proud and fierce enemy;
> for He knows that we are fighting in a just cause for the preserva-
> tion of our whole race.[88]

In its relative faithfulness, Ælfric's translation contrasts markedly with
other parts of the life where discourse appears. Bede opens his version, for
instance, with Willibrord speaking directly, but Ælfric turns that speech

into indirect discourse. And elsewhere in the life the speeches of characters other than the saint himself are either contracted or changed to indirect discourse.[89] The same pattern marks all of Ælfric's lives. In the life of St Æthelthryth, Ælfric almost totally ignores direct discourse, giving the only instance of it to the saint herself.[90] And in the lives of St Julian and St Cecilia the good characters speak directly, while the bad characters generally have their speeches reported for them.[91] Ælfric tends, then, to use direct discourse as a means of focusing attention on the saint. When discourse does serve as an index of character, whether a character speaks at all has more importance than what specific stylistic and rhetorical form the utterance takes.

A random sampling shows that authors of other Old English prose do not make even the simple distinctions that Ælfric does. The life of St Christopher in the *Beowulf* codex and *Apollonius of Tyre*, for example, are both very literal translations of the Latin sources, with only minor changes, the great majority of which do not occur in discourse.[92] And in the Old English verse paraphrases of Scripture, which are close in rhetorical purpose to the verse lives, we find alterations made for aesthetic effect. But those alterations generally do not focus on discourse. In *Daniel*, for instance, the poet considerably elaborates his source but does so to emphasize themes embedded in the overall structure of the poem, not in its dialogue. He in fact contracts or eliminates dialogue at crucial points.[93] Discourse thus is less important to the prose authors and to the *Daniel* poet than it is to Ælfric and certainly to the authors of *Guthlac A, Juliana, Elene, Guthlac B*, and *Andreas*.

This brief review of Old English prose and poetry suggests what an exhaustive study may well prove: the Old English verse saints' lives use dialogue uniquely, investing more in direct discourse than do some other contemporary hagiographical works and giving it thematic and structural status that it usually does not have. Whether or not that statement can be validated, we can say now that the verse lives operate in a distinctly rhetorical tradition and have appropriated aspects of theology and of hagiography to advance their particular vision of transcendent reality. We may further say that discourse seems to be an unusual feature of these lives, becoming in its stability a structural analogue of the saints' spiritual state. That stability also becomes the stylistic analogue of iconography, the last mode of thought we need to consider before turning to the lives themselves.

Word and image are complementary in iconography. In fact, the term itself literally means 'writing in images,'[94] a point we can see worked out in the Cædmon manuscript of Anglo-Saxon poetry (see Plates 1–3). There the concept of an immutable God and a mutable world takes visible form in

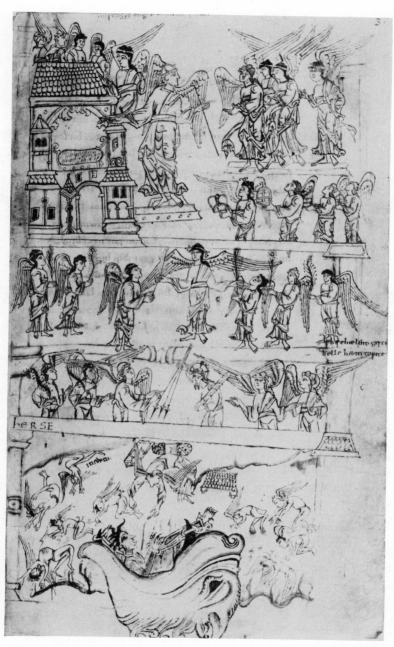

Plate 1   Ms Junius xi, page 3

ealra moðrum mæst. swa deð monna gehwilc þe
wið his waldend winnan onginneð. mid mane wið
þone mæran drihten. þa wearð yrre god se
bolgen. hehsta heofones waldend. wearp hine
of þan hean selde. hete hæfde he æt his hearran
gewunnen. hyldo hæfde his forlorene.
gram wearð him se goda on his mode. forþon
he sceolde grund gesecan. heardes hellewites.
þæs þe he wann wið heofnes waldend. acwæð hine
þa fram his hyldo and hine on helle wearp. on
þa deopan dala. þær he to deofle wearð. se
feond mid his geferum eallum. feollon þa ufon
of heofnum. þurh longe swa þreo niht and da-
gas. þa englas of heofnum on helle. and heo ealle
forsceop drihten to deoflum.

forðon hæfð his dæd gepond. noldon peorðian
forðon he hæfð on pynre leohc. undi ǫnðan
neoðan. ællmihtig god. fæce rigelfæce. on
þa rprintan helle. þæn hæbbað heo onæryn.
ungemet lange. ǫliria fronda ǫhpilc. ryn eð
neope. þonne cymð on uhtan. ǫur ce þne pind.
forrt ryrnum cald. rymble ryn oððe ǫar.
rum hǽrð ǫhpunc habban rcoldon. porhce
man hic him to pice. hyra. populo pær ǫe
hpynred. forman riðǫrylde helle. mid þam
and racum. hæfldon ǫnglar forð. heorron nicǫt
hehðe. þe ær gooðʃ hǽfdo gelæpron. lagon
þa oðre. rynð on þam ryne. þe ær ʃpa rela
la hærdon. gepinnǫ pið heora paldǫnd. pice
þoliað. haꞇne hǽfdo pelm. helle comiddǫ.

Plate 3   Ms Junius XI, page 17

three separate illustrations, each juxtaposing the symmetrical, harmonious dryht of heaven, depicted at the top, with the chaotic and damned dryht of hell, depicted at the bottom.[95] The analogy of art to poetry, a tradition established early in the Middle Ages and descending from classical antiquity,[96] is best exemplified in such documents and in other illuminated manuscripts of the period such as the Book of Kells, the Lindisfarne Gospels, the Durham Gospels, and the Book of Durrow. In manuscript illumination and especially in calligraphy, word and image interact and are made one.

The Old English hagiographic style also gives primacy to the word as artifact. We may actually describe it, to reverse the literal meaning of iconography, as 'imaging in writing,' a point others have implicitly made before; the similarity between the figural interpretations necessary for understanding both the art and the poetry of the Anglo Saxon period makes an analogy between the two modes themselves inevitable.[97] Furthermore, the development of hagiographic style may even resemble that of iconographic style in appropriating and modifying the features of an already-existent tradition. In Christian iconography symbols from pagan art are turned to specifically Christian uses. The image of a shepherd with a lamb, which signified *humanitas* in Roman art, became identified with Christ and the human soul;[98] a tunic draped over one shoulder, signifying the pagan philosopher, came to be Christ's costume in most Christian art.[99] In Old English poetic hagiography the best features of heroic discourse became stabilized as symbols for involvement in the body of Christ: formal, rhetorical, balanced, or symmetrical discourse comes to signify the essence of the saints' faith.

The term *iconographic style* appled to Old English poetry thus naturally arises in modern criticism of the period, [100] but no thorough attempt to explore the notion existed before James W. Earl's excellent article 'Typology and Iconographic Style in Early Medieval Hagiography.'[101] Earl argues that hagiography and iconography are related in the theological presuppositions underlying their methods, in their historical development, and in their subject matter. He perceives stylistic affinities as well:

> The stylistic qualities which the two forms share should be immediately apparent: the icon is primarily characterized as being 'frontal, laconic, and lacking of shadows.' Gerardus van der Leeuw sees as the icon's essential element its absolute stasis. To the modern casual observer the most outstanding features of the icon are its lack of realism and its conventionality. In fact, the icon is the epitome of those stylistic characteristics which are so basic to medieval art and so foreign to the modern bourgeois sensibility; it is the extreme form of

that art which reaches toward the other world by denying worldly realism, with its inevitable interest in the unique and the individualistic. [102]

Earl's admirable work gives the term iconographic style historical validity and does much to remove the stigma of impressionism from its use. Throughout this study his findings help to support a crucial analogy between iconography and hagiography: through syntactic and rhetorical analysis we will see that the Old English poets uniformly create stylistic norms or ideals – stylistic icons – in spiritually perfect characters, turning the language of the saints into sacred objects for contemplation, objects revealing Christian truths; the other characters' ability or inability to approximate the ideal in language reflects their various levels of sophistication and awareness, their various spiritual states. Close attention to this conventional feature and to the differences between the vernacular poems and the extant Latin sources will help us better to understand the artistry and better to define the major generic conventions of Old English poetic hagiography.

CHAPTER ONE

Old English Words as Deeds and the Struggle towards Light in *Guthlac A*

The first life we take up appropriately displays particular interest in verbal deeds, manifesting that interest at several points. The poet makes the words-deeds theme explicit six times (lines 60–1, 252b–4, 579–81, 618–19, 720–1a, 790–4a) and alludes twice to the efficacy of language: he states that Guthlac 'ne wond ... for worde' (did not turn before the words [294a]) of the railing demons, and the saint himself proclaims that the demons will never turn him 'of þissum wordum' (from these words [376a]).[1] In *Guthlac A* the necessity of matching imposing deeds to significant words becomes a dominant theme which ultimately helps to determine the poem's shape. Since every critic but one has virtually overlooked the words-deeds theme and its relationship to structure,[2] both structure and theme need to be discussed before we turn to the specific role of direct discourse in the poem.

Critical work on *Guthlac A* is meagre, and of the three scholars who deal with structure, two have done so without offering detailed explications of major thematic progressions and without fully and convincingly demonstrating the relationship between the poem's beginning and its end. Laurence K. Shook has delineated the four major threads binding the first twenty-nine lines of the poem to the final thirty-seven: the presence of a guiding angel, of a symbolic city, of a contrast between temporal and eternal joy, and of a mysterious, apocalyptic atmosphere 'springing from an acquaintance with apocryphal materials.'[3] Shook's observation has contributed greatly to an appreciation of the work and of the unified quality of its themes. But even though his theological discussion is important and thorough, as a justification of the poem's structure it does not go much beyond Rosemary Woolf's observation that the prologue has a 'general relevance'[4] to the poem because both emphasize angels.[5]

The other parts of the poem's ninety-two-line introductory section, with which Shook does not deal, raise even greater problems than the first part. Admitting both the validity and weakness of Shook's articles, Frances Lipp tries to resolve some of the poem's difficulties but finally does not perceive any logical, coherent links between the prologue and the poem proper. She writes that from line 93 on, the poem deals predominantly with the themes of God's love for man and the promise of eternal life as answers to despair. The poem's opening section, however, does not clearly relate to the rest of the poem and is incoherent even within itself, consisting of five separate sections. 'While there is nothing inherently illogical about the sequence,' she observes, 'the absence of transitions leaves the thematic intent in doubt.'[6]

One of the most recent commentators on the poem, Daniel G. Calder, has gone farthest in demonstrating the structural relevance of the prologue. He concedes that the five passages of the introduction may be separate, 'but they follow a necessary and clear progression'[7] that descends hierarchically from the 'generalized picture of the individual redeemed soul' in lines 1–29 to the many on earth capable of enjoying the same bliss (30–7a) and finally to Guthlac himself. The initial words of the three major sections between lines 1–29 and the introduction of Guthlac clearly indicate the intended structure: 'Monge,' 'Sume,' 'Sume.' The poem moves in five steps from a generalized perspective to Guthlac's specific temptations, as it emphasizes the world's hierarchical order, the necessity of obedience, and the saving power of God's love for all men.[8]

Calder's cogent argument has certainly helped to explain the prologue's raison d'être. But more remains to be said, for viewed in the context of the words-deeds theme and the didactic function of the saints' lives, the very separateness of the prologue's sections carries symbolic import. In her discussion of how an author can effect the 'mutation of themes' in a literary work, Pamela Gradon observes that medieval authors frequently use simple juxtaposition to create a meaningful pattern.[9] Although her argument concerns episodes with common characters and settings, such as the three hunting scenes in *Sir Gawain and the Green Knight*, it may also apply to the opening lines of *Guthlac A*, a poem with less apparent structural unity.

If we look at the prologue to *Guthlac A* afresh, a pair of configurations emerges. From the broadest perspective the introduction consists of four verse paragraphs dealing generally with heaven (lines 1–29), earth (30–59), common man (60–80), and the ascetic (81–92). Here we see the hierarchical narrowing of focus that Calder speaks of. Yet from a more constricted perspective only the first and fourth paragraphs appear unified, both dealing with single subjects (heaven and the ascetic) and displaying clear, logical development. The second and third paragraphs, by contrast, have dual subjects (a redeemed and a fallen world, redeemed and fallen men) and thus actually form four units instead of just two.[10] In addition, these two paragraphs show no clear development and are marred by weak or missing transitions between subjects (for example, line 37). The poet, it seems, deliberately envelops two weak and loosely organized verse paragraphs within two that are coherent and unified; because of the introduction's length we may assume that this procedure has significance.

The six sections of the prologue resemble scenes in a six-panelled tableau depicting an ideal scene (lines 1–29), two pairs of opposites totalling four sections (30–59 and 60–80), and a means for reconciling the antithetical entities (81–92). The poet first creates a picture of heaven, where the soul, accompanied by an angel, travels to the eternal city, devoid of decay, ruled by the highest king of all kings: 'Se bið gefeana fægrast' (It will be the fairest of joys [1]). The next paragraph contains two sections or panels, one (30–7a) depicting a redeemed world where men of all ranks can count themselves among the holy, the other (37b–59) showing earth 'onhrered' (shaken [37b]) and 'dalum gedæled' (separated into parts [54a]), where man's love for Christ 'colaþ' (cools [38a]) and the beauty of nature falls to ruin. In this second paragraph the poet develops a sense of incongruity by juxtaposing the redeemed or real world and the materialistic or false world, while he also establishes the cleavage between heaven and earth through the image of decay, an image theologically tied to the notion of man's falling from grace; it will form an important subsidiary theme throughout the poem.[11]

The poet also uses patterns of language to reinforce his point in these first two paragraphs, making the specific rhetorical strategy coincide with the broader strategy of meaning. The first paragraph (lines 1–29) depicts a unified heavenly realm – the connections between soul, angel, and God are firm – and the poet employs polysyndeton to highlight syntactically those spiritual connections. In the earthly realm, however, the poet sees little unity; he emphasizes that perception in the second paragraph by using asyndeton and hypozeuxis (lines 53b–9), where every clause has its own subject and verb. Both figures can represent disjunction.

The two panels in paragraph three (lines 60–80) depict two types of individuals within the spiritual community of man and thus advance the sense of incongruity begun in the second paragraph. The fourth panel (60–5) establishes the words-deeds theme by telling of those who wish to bear the honour of good men 'on wordum / 7 þa weorc ne doð' (in words and not perform the words [61]). They prize wealth and earthly prosperity over eternal life, and they despise those presented in the fifth panel (66–80), who reject earthly well-being and perform God's works. The latter live in obedient submission to God, and he in turn 'hyra dæde sceawað' (beholds their deeds [80b]). Two important points need to be made about this paragraph. First, although the poet articulates the words-deeds theme here, he does not link words positively to deeds. Line 61 sets them in opposition, and line 80 mentions deeds without mentioning words, though the implication that significant words lie behind the deeds certainly may be there. Second, the entire verse paragraph begins with a positive allusion to words (61a) and ends with a positive allusion to deeds (80b). In between come thirty full lines of verse dealing with the good deeds performed by the righteous. The separation of the two words becomes emblematic of the cleavage between these two groups – the talkers and the doers – and ultimately has rhetorical significance.[12] The sense of disjunction that the division promotes becomes symbolic of the disjunction evident in the entire prologue and of the problem suggested by it: how can we unite the heavenly realm with the earthly, true words with efficacious deeds?

The final panel, and final verse paragraph, describes those who dwell in deserts, waiting for their heavenly reward. These men are 'þa gecostan cempan / þa þam cyninge þeowað' (the choicest warriors who serve the king [line 91]), the ascetics who, as the poem will demonstrate, have the real power of bringing the theme together again, of yoking positive words with positive deeds. And one of their number will be the central subject of the poem. In one sense a very typical saint's life, *Guthlac A* outlines a plan for salvation, showing how heaven and earth can be joined, how we can thwart chaos and decay; and the abstract scheme of the introduction becomes that of the poem itself, for Guthlac's words and deeds ultimately come under one rubric ('dæde') when Bartholomew decides to inform God about the saint:

> Nu ic his geneahhe   neosan wille,
> 720 sceal ic his word 7 his weorc   in gewitnesse
> dryhtne lædon: he his dæde conn.

> Now I wish to seek him frequently, I must bring his words and his works to the knowledge of the Lord: he shall know his deeds.

Except for heaven and earth, the oppositions outlined above, of course, are not polar in any inherently logical way, nor are the opposing pairs mathematically equated. The diametrical opposition between heaven and earth does not coincide with the less rigid opposition between talkers and doers. But in terms of the controlling theme of the poem, the second opposition becomes symbolically as rigid as the first. Although on a spiritual continuum words minus deeds probably constitutes a worse condition than deeds minus words, in a cosmos where speech is action, the latter is as incomplete as the former.

Another device reinforces the impression that the poem deals with a disjointed world and that the prologue moves from wholeness to dissolution to wholeness. A cluster of key words or concepts – much like iconographic details signifying spiritual truths in a painting – congregates in three unified verse paragraphs: in the first panel (lines 1–29); in the sixth panel, combined with its correlate, the introduction of Guthlac (81–92; 93–107); and in the poem's conclusion (781–818). The cluster centres on heaven's attributes, and the poet diffuses it throughout the remainder of the prologue and then throughout the poem, gradually drawing it together as Guthlac gradually gains spiritual ascendancy over his tormentors. The principle of juxtaposition disappears as the poet reconciles opposites and reaffirms the possibility of man's regaining his blissful seat.

The cluster first appears in lines 1–29, where we see that the heavenly or ideal realm has five prominent elements attached to it – in the order of their introduction here, angel, soul, light,[13] the notion of home, and obedience. The poem begins with a joyous meeting between an angel and a blessed soul (2a), and the angel tells the soul that he will lead it wherever it wishes to go. The paths will be pleasant '7 wuldres leoht // torht ontyned' (and the light of glory brightly revealed [8b–9a]). The soul will be a 'tidfara // to þam halgan ham' (a traveller under summons to the holy home [8–10a]), where there is rejoicing after death for those who 'her Cristes æ // læraþ 7 læstaþ' (here teach and carry out Christ's law [23b–24a]).

Except for the concept of soul ('gæst' [line 36]), none of these five elements recurs in the prologue's next four panels, which, as we recall, concern the redeemed world (30–7a), the fallen world (37b–59), men without works (60–5), and men with works (66–80). The sixth panel, however, represents a return to the ideal offered in the first panel. It portrays angels (88–90) protecting desert dwellers who inhabit 'hamas in heolstrum' (homes in the retreats [83a]), and the description of Guthlac in lines 93–107 recapitulates the prominent elements of lines 1–29 but in precisely reverse order, putting the element essential for entry into heaven first: obedience, home, light, soul, angel. In alluding to Guthlac's obedience here, the poet uses a formula that has structural and thematic importance throughout the poem: Guthlac directs his mind 'in godes willan' (in God's will [95b]). The other four elements follow in close succession. The saint turns his thoughts to 'ham in heofonum' (home in the heavens [98a]), and light is shed upon him ('inlyhte' [99a]) by the One who guides souls ('gæstum gearwaþ' [100a]). God has given Guthlac 'engelcunde' (angelic [101a]) grace and sent a 'weard' (guardian [105b]) to watch over him. The poet has made the introduction into a coherent whole, the ending mirroring the beginning and the structure itself embodying an essential theological truth that Gregory stresses in his *Moralia* (PL 76, 775–6): because of the Fall, we cannot exactly reduplicate the original Paradise; what we can have in its place will contain the important attributes but will be a simulation reflecting the arduous labour required to produce it. What follows the introductory matter exemplifies an aspiring soul's struggle towards light and life, showing what Guthlac must overcome to achieve sainthood. The dispersal and gradual reunification of the five elements discussed above reflect the difficulty of that struggle.

Between lines 108 and 348 the poet employs only one of the key concepts – home. The first instance occurs when the saint's labours begin and God first reveals the secret spot to him:

> Wæs seo londes stow
> bimiþen fore monnum   oþþæt meotud onwrah
> beorg on bearwe   þa se bytla cwom
> se þær haligne   ham aræ;
> 150 nales þy he giemde   þurh gitsunga
> lænes lifwelan   ac þæt lond Gode
> fægre gefreoþode   siþþan feond oferwon
> Cristes cempa.

The spot of land was hidden from men until the Creator revealed the mound in the wood when the builder came, he who raised a holy home there; not because he cared in avarice for fleeting wealth, but that he might fairly protect that land for God once the warrior of Christ overcame his enemy.

The second instance concerns the demons' lacking homes – 'hy hleolease / hama þoliað' (comfortless, they lack homes [222]) – and the third occurs in the demons' first speech, when they mock Guthlac for his presumption: 'ðu þæt gehatest / þæt ðu ham on us // gegan wille: / eart ðe Godes yrming' (you vow that you will take our home from us: you are God's pauper [271–2]). All three instances arise before Guthlac has firmly established himself with his own discourse, before, in terms of the poem's controlling theme, he has gained the upper hand.

Guthlac remains firm in the face of the demons' onslaughts, and as the attacks become more intense and Guthlac's resolve stands unshaken, the poet brings more of the five key concepts into play, to indicate the saint's gradual victory over sin. Line 348b is a turning point in the poem. No matter what their plan of attack, the demons 'Symle ... Guðlac / in Godes willan // fromne fundon' (always found Guthlac strong in God's will [348–9a]). The repetition from line 95b of 'in Godes willan,' the crucial member of the cluster, signals that turn; the formula appears again at lines

538a and 805b, and with variation at lines 358b and 780a. After accomplishing the turn, the poet again uses the concept of home, again in reference to the demons' abode: 'in helle hus, // þær eow is ham sceapen' (in the house of hell, where a home is created for you [677]). Light then returns with increasing intensity ('leohtfruma,' source of light [593a]; 'leohtfruman' [609a]; 'leohtes lissum,' by the favour of light [613a]; 'leomum inlyhted,' lighted with rays of light [655a]; 'leohtes leoma,' beam of light [659a]); and Bartholomew's entrance in a ring of light physically manifests Guthlac's spiritual triumph: 'Ofermæcga spræc, // dyre dryhtnes þegn / dæghluttre scan' (The very illustrious being spoke; the thane dear to the Lord shone as the day [692b–3]). This influx of light imagery culminates in a statement that includes the concept of soul and a reiteration of the necessity for obedience:[14]

> Wile se waldend   þæt we wisdom a
> snyttrum swelgen   þæt his soð fore us
> 765 on his giefena gyld   genge weorðe
> ða he us to are   7 to ondgiete
> syleð 7 sendeð,   sawlum rymeð
> liþe lifwegas   leohte geræhte.
>   ...
> Wæs se fruma fæstlic   feondum on ondan
> geseted wið synnum;   þær he siþþan lyt
> 775 wære gewonade;   oft his word Gode
> þurh eaðmedu   up onsende,
> let his ben cuman   in þa beorhtan gesceaft.

The Ruler wills that we should always acquire wisdom, so that his truth, in payment for his gifts which he gives and sends to us in mercy and for our understanding, may become prevalent because of us. He manifests for souls gentle life-paths, brightly ordained ... The noble man was, to the rancour of the enemies, firmly set against sins; there afterwards he weakened little in the covenant; often he sent his words up to God in humility, let his prayer come into the bright creation.

The infusion of light, of course, also coincides with the development of the subsidiary theme of nature's decay established in the prologue. By the end of the poem nature is rejuvenated and subordinated to the glories of the saint, thus definitively indicating his holiness.[15] The world no longer wanes, and a new unity and sense of well-being permeate the remaining lines of the poem as the cluster of key concepts from the prologue emerges

in its entirety (soul, line 781; angels, 782; home, 796; light, 798). The poet
completes the cluster and binds the conclusion lexically to the prologue by
repeating line 22, 'Þider soðfæstra / sawla motun' (Thither the souls fast in
truth may), at line 790: 'Swa soðfæstra / sawla motun.' Within the envelope pattern, which mirrors the scheme of the prologue, the poet has constructed a complex, abstract poem.[16]

The progression of the cluster of concepts from wholeness to disunity to
wholeness again generally accounts for the prologue's and the poem's
movement. We now turn to the words-deeds theme as it is manifest in direct discourse, for the theme provides the specific means for resolving the
problem initially set forth in the first ninety-two lines: how to rejoin what
has been split asunder. Direct discourse, which is the most appropriate part
of the poem for bearing the major theme, causes the reunification of the
cluster and follows that reunification diagrammatically. The poem's seemingly repetitive structure, then, which prompts T.A. Shippey to remark
that the poet appears 'to be projecting effort and triumph when none is
clearly visible,'[17] becomes incremental. Progress, though slight, occurs
within it, predominantly through the dialogue.

The first consideration in approaching a life's use of direct discourse is
the rhetorical structure of whole speeches, from which we move gradually
down the stylistic hierarchy to the minutiae of style: syntax, rhetorical
tropes, diction. The salient features of the stylistic icon may emerge at any
point in the hierarchy or may embrace all of it, as they do in Cynewulf's
Elene. In *Guthlac A* the icon does not manifest itself in rhetorical structure
or in larger syntactic patterns but rather in more minute features. Since the
initial speeches in a saint's life have thematic ramifications for the entire
work, a look at the structure and syntax of the first speech in *Guthlac A*
will illustrate the point.

The saint addresses the threatening demons:

```
240                         Þeah þe ge me deað gehaten,
       mec wile wið þam niþum genergan    se þe eowrum nydum
                                                        wealdeð.
       An is ælmihtig God    se mec mæg eaðe gescyldan,
       he min feorg freoþað.    Ic eow fela wille
       soþa gesecgan:    mæg ic þis setl on eow
245    butan earfeðum    ana geðringan;
       ne eam ic swa fealog,    swa ic eow fore stonde,
       monna weorudes    ac me mara dæl
       in godcundum    gæstgerynum
       wunað 7 weaxeð    se me wraþe healdeð.
250    Ic me anum her    eaðe getimbre
```

hus 7 hleonað;   mec on heofonum sind
lare gelonge: mec þæs lyt tweoþ
þæt me engel to   ealle gelædeð
spowende sped   spreca 7 dæda.
255   Gewitað nu awyrgde,   werigmode,
from þissum earde   þe ge her on stondað,
fleoð on feorweg.   Ic me frið wille
æt Gode gegyrnan;   ne sceal min gæst mid eow
gedwolan dreogan   ac mec dryhtnes hond
260   mundað mid mægne.   Her sceal min wesan
eorðlic eþel,   nales eower leng.

Although you threatened me with death, the one who controls your
needs will save me from those attacks. Alone is almighty God, who
can easily shield me; he guards my life. I will tell you many truths:
I can gain this spot alone from you without troubles; nor am I so
destitute of men, as I stand before you, but in me a greater share of
divine spiritual mysteries dwells and grows, which gives me support.
Alone I may easily build house and shelter here; my teachings are
dependent on heaven. For me there is little doubt that an angel leads
me to thriving success in speeches and deeds. Depart now, accursed,
weary-hearted, from this ground on which you stand; flee on a distant path. I want to seek peace for myself from God; nor must my
soul suffer delusion with you, but the hand of the Lord mightily
protects me. Here my earthly home must be, not yours any longer.

Notice that despite the speech's firm message the poet provides no definite
markers to indicate its structure. When intent on doing so, Old English
scops often make good use of some kind of repetition at the beginning of a
half-line. The *Beowulf* poet, for example, binds up the passage relating
Grendel's approach to Heorot through the incremental repetition of 'com'
(lines 702b, 710a, 720a), and Cynewulf provides clear structural indicators
in both Juliana's and Elene's speeches: he gives Juliana's first utterance (46–
57) obvious bipartite structure by beginning it with the verb 'gesecgan' (say
[46a]) and placing a form of the verb at the midpoint of the speech ('secge'
[51a]),[18] and he gives Elene's first speech (288–319) unmistakable tripartite-
within-tripartite structure by repeating 'ge' (you) at lines 297b, 302b, and
310b.[19] In addition to the lack of structural indicators in Guthlac's first
speech, we also discover a random mix of complex and simple sentences,
indicating that neither has particular importance for measuring character.
    What we find in this first speech we also find in Guthlac's other four

speeches and in all three of the demons': they have no basic envelope, no bipartite or tripartite structure, and they show no preference for complex over simple sentences, as obtains, for instance, in the Beowulf-Unferth exchange. The poet's reason for not differentiating characters on these larger structural levels probably derives from the need to present the demons as formidable enemies of the equally formidable saint or figure of Christ. Giving the opponents in *Guthlac A* comparable linguistic capabilities while making the demons ludicrous and ineffectual in the narrative portions of the poem solves a complex problem. While on the one hand the devils are implacable, fearsome antagonists, on the other they exist in a universe controlled by God and have already met eternal defeat.

Though the saint and the demons are equals on the larger stylistic levels, certain dictional elements and minor syntactic constructions do aid the reader in measuring the relative strengths of the characters and in understanding precisely how Guthlac's words become his deeds. Two features of Guthlac's initial speech have significance. The first feature is used by the saint, by Bartholomew, and by the angel and forms the core of Guthlac's discourse. It is the only stylistic feature differentiating his dialogue from the demons' and symbolizes the steadfast quality of his faith. The auxiliary verb 'sculan' (lines 258b, 260b) appears eighteen times in the poem, only twice outside direct discourse, once when the poet injects some gnomic wisdom into the narrative ('Swa sceal oretta / a in his mode // Gode compian,' Thus must a warrior always fight for God in his heart [344–5a]) and again when he declares that Guthlac must suffer yet more torment ('sceolde he sares þa gen // dæl adreogan,' he had to endure yet a further share of pain [515–16]). Of the remaining sixteen instances ten belong to Guthlac, three to Bartholomew, one to the angel, and two to the demons. The most obvious importance of this word comes from the sense of obligation and moral resolve that it connotes. The two instances in Guthlac's opening speech establish the saint's fixity of purpose, a fixity that coincides with that of the angel and with that of Bartholomew. The angle says to the redeemed soul, 'ic þec lædan sceal' (I must lead you [7b]), and Bartholomew states that Guthlac 'sceal þy wonge wealdan' (must control the plain [702a]), then declares that 'ne sceal ic mine onsyn' (I must not [hide] my face, [707a]) before the host of demons: 'sceal ic [Guthlac's] word 7 his weorc' (I must [Guthlac's] words and his work [720a]) describe to the Lord. In *Guthlac A* the verb becomes what may be termed a theological modal, a verbal marker of spiritual power.

Guthlac regularly employs 'sculan' (lines 304b, 366b, 372b, 386b), but its grammatical function gradually shifts in accordance with other structural changes occurring in the poem, such as the reunification of the cluster of concepts. In the saint's fifth and last speech sculan appears four times: 'Ic

geþafian sceal' (I must accept, [600b]) God's judgment alone; 'ac ge deaðe
sceolon' (but in death you must [614b]) sing with lamentation; 'swa nu
awa sceal' (it must now as always [670b]) be that you will endure flames of
damnation; 'ge gnornende // dead sceolon dreogan' (mourning, you must
suffer death [679b–80a]) in hell. Whereas Guthlac previously used the
third-person singular form of sculan exclusively, each time referring to
himself (386b), an aspect of himself (258b, 366b–7a, 371–2), or the plain
where he lives (260b–1a, 304b), here he introduces the first-person singular
form once, thus implying a concentration of power within himself, and he
twice employs the second-person plural, focusing his comments and the
theological modal directly on the demons. One more indication of his spiritual victory, these alterations in the use of sculan show that as Guthlac
moves inevitably towards the light, he moves towards greater strength and
the perfect assurance of the demons' failure.

The demons' two uses of sculan do not undermine its theological status.
The first use, occurring in the first speech ('Bi hwon scealt þu lifgan?' What
shall you live by? [line 273a]), lacks power in a question and also seems to
be one of the rare instances in Old English poetry of the modal's connoting
the simple future tense.[20] And the intended force of the second, occurring
in the third speech ('nu þu in helle scealt // deope gedufan,' now you must
dive deep into hell [582b–3a]), gives way to the ironic context from which
it grows. This speech represents the demons' last frenetic attempt to intimidate the saint:

> Ne eart ðu gedefe   ne dryhtnes þeow
> 580   clæne gecostad   ne cempa god
> wordum 7 weorcum   wel gecyþed,
> halig in heortan: nu þu in helle scealt
> deope gedufan,   nales dryhtnes leoht
> habban in heofonum,   heahgetimbru,
> 585   seld on swegle,   forþon þu synna to fela
> facna gefremedes   in flæschoman.
> We þe nu willað   womma gehwylces
> lean forgieldan   þær þe laþast bið,
> in ðam grimmestan   gæstgewinne.

You are not a fitting nor a wholly tried servant of the Lord nor fully
shown a good warrior in words and in works, holy in heart: now
you must dive deep into hell, have not at all the light of the Lord in
heaven, the lofty mansions, a dwelling in the sky, because you have
performed too many sins, evils in the flesh. Now for each of sins we

will give you reward, where it will be most hateful to you, in the fiercest soul-torment.

Though the demons state that Guthlac is not a fitting servant of God (579–82a), that he must go to hell (582b–3a), and will have neither the light of God (583b–4a) nor the mansions of heaven (584b–5a), all else in the poem points to their error. Their most vitriolic attack becomes their least effective strategy and one sure sign of their irrevocable defeat.

The demons also share the second important feature evident in the saint's initial speech, but its eventual disappearance from the poem signals Guthlac's imminent spiritual victory. That feature is the use of 'þeah' (although), which initiates concessive clauses, usually in the subjunctive mood, indicating that a yielding occurs between the protagonist and antagonists. Despite the saint's resolve the opposition against him is strong, and he must concede that it affects him in some, though predominantly physical, way: 'Þeah þe ge me deað gehaten, // mec wille wið þam niþum generan / se þe eowrum nydum wealdeð' (Although you threatened me with death, the One who controls your needs will save me from those attacks [240b–1]).

Clauses of concession set up relatively balanced oppositions in a sentence. Protasis and apodosis, subordinate clause and conclusion, have equal validity, but they exist paradoxically, creating a tension essentially unresolved. The dynamics of such clauses can therefore become the syntactic analogues of a conflict such as that between Guthlac and the demons. And such use of balanced clauses can reinforce thematic concerns, helping to make clear that the struggle of the spiritual opponents is fierce and initially equal. The device adorns four of the saint's five speeches, appearing once in each of his first two, then, with ritualistic force, three times in his third speech and twice in his fourth. An analysis of the instances of þeah reveals a pattern coinciding with the other patterns we have discerned in the poem.

The concessive clause in Guthlac's second speech alludes to the demons' fruitless efforts to sway him. The saint states:

> þeah ge þa ealle   ut abonne
> 300 7 eow eac gewyrce   widor sæce
> ge her ateoð   in þa tornwræce
> sigeleasne sið.

Although you should summon out all of them and with you they should also work wider strife, here in your fierce vengeance you set out on a venture without victory.

A change in the use of þeah from the first speech, where Guthlac refers to his own death, occurs in these lines, for here he alludes to an ambiguous 'wider strife' inflicted by all the weapons the demons can wield. The focus of the dialogue expands as the saint's resistance intensifies with the increased magnitude of his afflictions.

In the third speech, that resistance receives further emphasis through the rhetorical use of anaphora,²¹ the piling up of the concessive clauses to underscore Guthlac's power to prevail and the demons' powerlessness to oppress:

> ðeah ge minne flæshoman   fyres wylme
> 375   forgripen gromhydge,   gifran lege,
> næfre ge mec of þissum wordum onwendað   þendan mec min
> gewit gelæsteð
> þeah þe ge hine sarum forsæcen: ne motan ge mine sawle gretan
> ac ge on betran gebringað.   Forðan ic gebidan wille
> þæs þe min dryhten demeð;   nis me þæs deaþes sorg.
> 380   ðeah min ban 7 blod   butu geweorþen
> eorþan to eacan,   min se eca dæl
> in gefean fareð   þær he fægran
> botles bruceð.

> Although fierce-minded you should assail my flesh with surging fire, with the greedy flame, you will never turn me from these words while my understanding lasts. Although you may afflict it with torments, you cannot touch my soul, but you will bring it to a better state. Therefore I will await what my Lord ordains; the sorrow of death is not upon me. Although both my bones and blood become an increase for the earth, my eternal part will travel to its reward, where it will enjoy a fairer dwelling.

By using three separate anaphoric clauses with individual emphases and following each with Guthlac's fixity of purpose ('you will never turn me'; 'you cannot touch my soul'; 'my eternal part will travel'), the poet diminishes the concessive status of the þeah clauses and provides yet another sign of progress in the saint's dialogue and spiritual development. The rhetorical flourish at once points to Guthlac's linguistic ability and to his spiritual resolve.

The final step in the thematic use of þeah clauses lessens their rhetorical impact before they disappear completely from the poem. So far, Guthlac has placed the concessive clauses in initial position in his sentences, thus giving them rhetorical prominence and alerting the reader to the opposing elements that follow. Guthlac's fourth speech contains two þeah clauses no longer initially placed in their sentences but rather following the principal constructions emphasizing the power of God. The syntactic shift reflects a shift in narrative focus: near his spiritual apotheosis Guthlac turns more unequivocally towards his Creator, who now takes pre-eminence in this aspect of the saint's dialogue. A closer look at the speech will put that shift and its relationship to other thematic concerns in the poem in clearer perspective:

> Ge sind forscadene!   On eow scyld siteð!
> Ne cunnon ge dryhten   duguþe biddan
> 480 ne mid eaðmedum   are secan
> þeah þe eow alyfde   lytle hwile
> þæt ge min onwald   agan mosten;
> ne ge þæt geþyldum   þicgan woldan
> ac me yrringa   up gelæddon
> 485 þæt ic of lyfte   londa getimbru
> geseon meahte.   Wæs me swegles leoht
> torht ontyned   þeah ic torn druge.

You are condemned! Guilt sits upon you! Nor do you know how to ask the Lord for salvation, nor with gentleness to seek mercy, although for a little while he allowed you to have power over me; nor would you receive that with patience, but you led me up angrily, so that I might see the buildings of the lands from the air. The light of the sky was brightly revealed to me, although I endured grief.

The cluster of themes starts coming together here. We have seen that, like much else in the poem, Guthlac's dialogue changes after the repetition of the phrase 'in Godes willan' (line 348b). In the saint's fourth speech the second major element of the cluster – light – returns to the poem as the progression in imagery coincides with the development in concessive-clause usage. As light returns, the previously equal tension between protasis and apodosis – and between saint and demons – decreases.

As in Guthlac's fourth speech, þeah clauses also appear at the ends of sentences in the demons' first and second speeches, with similar rhetorical effect. By placing the concessive clauses at the ends of sentences ('Bi hwon scealt þu lifgan / þeah þu lond age?' What shall you live by, although you possess the land? [273]), the demons minimize the importance of the saint's possessing the land they want and decrease the emphasis on something that

they know mitigates their argument: 'Fela ge fore monnum miþað / þæs
þe ge in mode gehycgað, // ne beoð eowre dæda dyrne / þeah þe ge hy
in dygle gefremme' (You hide much before men that you think in
your heart; your deeds are not hidden, although you do them in secret
[465–6]).[22]

The movement, then, in the cluster of concepts and in the use of sculan
and the concessive clause in direct discourse indicates that a progression,
albeit gradual and subtle, does occur within the poem. The clearest indication of that progression is yet to be discussed, however; it involves features
of the demons' first speech, when they are at the pinnacle of their power,
and the same features of Guthlac's last speech, when he reaches the pinnacle of his. The demons calculate their words to undermine the saint's faith,
using a rational strategy and their best rhetorical effects. After pointing out
that Guthlac will have trouble surviving in the land even though he pos-
sesses it, they state:

275   beoð þe hungor 7 þurst   hearde gewinnan
       gif þu gewitest   swa wilde deor
       ana from eþele.   Nis þæt onginn wiht.
       Geswic þisses setles.   Ne mæg þec sellan ræd
       mon gelæran   þonne þeos mengu eall.
280   We þe beoð holde   gif ðu us hyran wilt
       oþþe þec ungearo   eft gesecað
       maran mægne   þæt þe mon ne þearf
       hondum hrinan   ne þin hra feallan
       wæpna wundum;   we þas wic magun
285   fotum afyllan: folc inðriceð
       meara þreatum   7 monfarum.
       Beoð þa gebolgne   þa þec breodwiað,
       tredað þec 7 tergað   7 hyra torn wrecað,
       toberað þec blodgum lastum;   gif þu ure bidan þencest
290   we þec niþa genægað.   Ongin þe generes wilnian,
       far þær ðu freonda wene   gif ðu þines feores recce.

Hunger and thirst will be hard enemies to you if you depart like the
wild animals alone from your native land: that is no undertaking at
all. Relinquish this dwelling-place. No one can give you better counsel than all this troop. We will be kind to you if you will hear us or
again will seek you unprepared with a greater troop so that one will
not need to touch you with hands nor fell your body by the wounds
of weapons; we can demolish this dwelling with feet; people will
crush in with bands of horses and with moving hosts. They will be

angry then, will trample you then, tread on and tear you, and wreak their anger, will bear you off with bloody tracks; if you think to await us, we will assail you with torments. Try to ask for refuge for yourself; travel where you may expect friends, if you have a care for your life.

Aside from the use of the þeah clause, the effects of which we have seen, two other rhetorical devices set this speech apart as the best of three attempts to subvert Guthlac. The demons employ 'gif' (if) clauses only in this speech and do so four times in an effort to frighten and intimidate the saint through rational argument.[23] Hunger and thirst will oppress the saint if he goes alone from his native land like an animal (lines 276–7a); the demons will be kind to him if he will listen to them (280b); they will assail him if he plans to wait for them (289b); and Guthlac should seek protection if he cares for his life (291b). Tension between protasis and apodosis exists even here, but not in such equilibrium as in concessive clauses. Conditional constructions, which imply cause and effect, impetus and result, do not admit the possibility of paradoxical coexistence. The demons emphasize the unequivocal nature of their statement with a second rhetorical device, unique in the poem's discourse to their first and Guthlac's final speeches.[24] They rhyme the verb endings, employing what Isidore calls *homoioptoton* (*Etymologia* I, xxxvi, 15) in lines 287–9a. By binding the sounds together, they also bind and intensify the meanings: the hostile troop will trample, tread over, tear, wreak their anger on, and bear away poor Guthlac. Whatever the ultimate impact, when taken in concert these two features show a degree of rhetorical adornment absent from the demons' other speeches and from Guthlac's first four.

In his fifth and final speech, however, the saint does use both rhetorical devices and with telling effect. Guthlac uses the gif clause to highlight the dependence even of the demons on God's will. When the demons threaten that they will inflict cruel punishments upon him, he responds:

> Doð efne swa   gif eow dryhten Crist,
> lifes leohtfruma,   lyfan wylle,
> weoruda waldend,   þæt ge his wergengan
> 595 in þone laðan leg   lædan motan.

Do even so, if the Lord Christ, the Light-Source of life, the Ruler of hosts, will permit you to lead his follower into the hostile flame.

And by phonologically linking participles instead of finite verbs as the demons do, Guthlac underscores an achieved and continuing effect: the depraved, unchanging state of the damned:

> Sindon ge wærlogan: swa ge in wræcsiðe
> longe lifdon,   lege biscencte,
> 625   swearte beswicene,   swegle benumene,
> dreame bidrorene,   deaðe bifolene,
> firenum bifongne,   feores orwenan,
> þæt ge blindnesse   bote fundon.

You are troth-breakers: so long have you lived in exile, with flame for drink, being darkly deceived, deprived of the sky, bereft of joy, consigned to death, surrounded by sins, despairing of life, that you might [not] find cure for your blindness.

The rhetorical adornment of this final speech, reminiscent as it is of the demons' first and joined as it is with other thematic developments in the poem, points to the saint's supreme triumph.[25]

Direct discourse in *Guthlac A* forms an integral, essential part of the thematic structure. But although it is the medium through which the poet expresses his major theme, its great importance derives ultimately from its functioning in balanced, organic union with the schematic use of juxtaposition, the cluster of key concepts, and the development of the beorg (mound [line 148a]) as a symbol for spiritual strength. Stylistic analysis reveals that shifts in linguistic power do occur within the characters' dialogue as Guthlac definitely reunites words with deeds and eliminates the word's decay, putting together again through unshakeable faith the several parts of a defunct paradisal world. Beneath the ostensible simplicity of a saint's battling demons in *Guthlac A* lies an abstract treatment of sublime truth, a treatment which we may more clearly apprehend by carefully scrutinizing the structure and specific attributes of *sermo humilis* in the poem.

By the same method and through similar focus we may also better apprehend *Juliana*, a poem which has been labelled 'hack work'[26] and in which, according to its most recent editor, 'emotional overtones and stylistic variations are reduced to a minimum.'[27] As close scrutiny of *Juliana* will reveal, however, the level of abstraction and complexity beneath its simple façade is no less great than that in *Guthlac A*.

CHAPTER TWO

Saintly Discourse and the Distancing of Evil in Cynewulf's *Juliana*

The movement towards light and the development of the words-deeds theme, gradual and incremental in *Guthlac A*, occur quickly and dramatically in *Juliana*. Here an obvious structure, a simple theme, and a wealth of stylistic detail all conspire to make the didactic purpose intensely clear, so clear that there has never been any controversy over the precise meaning of the poem. Changed significantly over its Latin source to intensify the whiteness of the saint and the blackness of Affricanus, Eleusius, and the demon, *Juliana* illustrates the triumph of Christian virtue over satanic wrong. The characters in this spiritual combat polarize into representatives of heaven and hell, and the poem's major action consists of an undisguised battle between the two as the latter ritualistically tries to turn Juliana from her faith.[1]

In this battle the devil's craft and skill proceed from 'a terrible delusion' – an important addition to the Latin source.[2] The notion applies equally to Affricanus and Eleusius, less-adept purveyors of demonic untruth than the devil, for their action also proceeds from theological error. But not only are the antagonists possessed of a terrible delusion ('gedwola'); they consciously employ delusion to subvert Juliana's faith. The poet signals the thematic nature of gedwola by using the word four times (lines 138b, 202b, 301a, 368b), each instance an addition to the Latin source, and gives the theme dramatic structure in direct discourse, where attempts to delude increase in sophistication with the increased stature of the tempter. The gradual heightening of the persecutors' linguistic sophistication in the face of the saint's consistently sophisticated use of language largely accounts for our simultaneous perception of two states: Juliana's achieved sainthood and the process through which she must move to reach it.[3]

The virtues of Juliana's first utterance are those famous in Old English poetry generally: balanced and stately, her words manifest a control of syntax, verse form, and rhetoric for poetic effect. In response to Eleusius's eagerness for marriage she publicly declares her conditions and the stylistic icon emerges:[4]

> [A] Ic þe mæg gesecgan   þæt þu sylfne ne þearft
> swiþor swencan;   [B] gif þu soðne God
> lufast 7 gelyfest,   7 his lof rærest,
> ongietest gæsta Hleo,   ic beo gearo sona
> 50   unwaclice   willan þines.
> Swylce ic þe secge,   [B1] gif þu to sæmran gode
> þurh deofolgield   dæde biþencest,
> hætsð hæþenfeoh,   ne meaht þu habban mec,
> ne geþreatian   þe to sinhigan;
> 55   [A1] næfre þu þæs swiðlic   sar gegearwast
> þurh hæstne nið,   heardra wita,
> þæt þu mec onwende   worda þissa.[5]

I can tell you that you need not distress yourself further; if you love and believe in the true God and exalt his praise, recognize the Protector of souls, straightaway I will be resolutely prepared for your will. I also say to you, if through idolatry you entrust your acts to a worse god, vow a heathen sacrifice, you cannot have me nor force me to be a wife to you; never, through violent hatred, will you prepare such severe pain of hard torments that you might turn me from these words.

Distinctive formal features lend this statement its aura of grace and equanimity. The passage consists of an extended parison[6] with four sentences, each containing a subordinate clause answering to the subordinate clause in the sentence with which Cynewulf structurally pairs it. Sentence A parallels A1, B parallels B1, so that the first 'þæt' clause in line 46b is answered by the terminating þæt clause in line 57a. Similarly, the 'gif' clauses in lines 47b and 51b are matched, creating an impression of perfect syntactic balance. Furthermore, that impression of balance is solidified by the placement of the 'swylce ic þe secge' (I also say to you) clause, morphologically attracted to line 46a ('Ic þe mæg gesecgan'), in the structural and rhetorical turning-point of the speech.[7]

In addition to the syntactic expertise, we may also observe the rhetorical control manifested in Juliana's use of chiastic variation in lines 48b–9a and 52b–3a, reflecting the more general chiastic structure noted above: '7 his lof rærest, // ongietest gæsta Hleo' (and exalt his praise, recognize the Protector of souls); 'dæde biþincest, // hætsð hæþenfeoh' (entrust your acts, vow a heathen sacrifice).[8] This rhetorically simple figure, which is important as a *figura crucis*[9] in the Bible and in both Cynewulf's poetry and medieval vernacular and Latin poems on the Cross, naturally plays a significant role in the saints' lives. It appears here in a poetically apposite way. By placing one chiastic figure on each side of the swylce ic þe secge clause, Cynewulf creates a kind of isocolon, again promoting a balanced effect. The first use of chiasmus emphasizes the importance of worshipping the true God; the second underscores the gravity of bowing to meaningless idols. Finally, the use of homoioptoton in lines 48–9a ('lufast 7 gelyfest, / 7 his lof rærest, // ongietest gæsta Hleo') calls attention to the central importance of those verbs, and the initial stress on the finite verbs embedded in both instances of the chiasmus (48–9a, 53a) contributes to the sense of power and mastery that the speech conveys.[10] These are not the words of an hysterical woman facing death, but rather of a woman fully cognizant of her function in the ritualistic action of the poem. None of the stylistic features appears in the Latin source, where Juliana speaks simply and to a messenger, not to her father.[11]

Predictably, Juliana does not diminish our sense of her control of language in her other speeches, and the last line of her first speech takes on symbolic value: she will not turn from the meaning of the words, nor will she turn from their expressive form, a measure of their true worth, which in its uniformity defines her static, unswerving character. Her discourse with her father, Affricanus, after his attempts to persuade her to marry Eleusius, embodies a straightforward refusal of his request even in the Latin source: 'Si coluerit Patrem et Filium et Spiritum, nubam illi; quod si noluerit, non potest me accipere in conjugium' (Strunk, 34–5): 'If he will worship the Father, the Son and the Holy Spirit, I will marry him; if not, he cannot receive me in marriage' (Allen and Calder, 123). But the directness cannot conceal the devices giving the Old English version its simple strength. Moving from the abstract notion of marriage, or alliance, or kinship ('mæggræden' [line 109a]) to the comparatively concrete notion of sharing an abode ('bold' [114a]) and finally to that of sharing physical love ('brydlufu' [114b]), Juliana demonstrates in a logical progression of conceptual variants the total commitment of body and soul that the marriage vows imply, a commitment she reserves for Christ or one devoted to Christ:

> Næfre ic þæs þeodnes   þafian wille
> mæggrædenne,   nemne he mægna God
> 110   geornor bigonge   þonne he gen dyde,
> lufige mid lacum   þone þe leoht gescop,

heofon 7 eorðan   7 holma bigong,
eodera ymbhwyrft.   Ne mæg he elles mec
bringan to bolde.   He þa brydlufan
115   sceal to oþerre   æhtgestealdum
idese secan;   nafað he ænige her.

I will never consent to alliance with the prince unless he should
more eagerly worship the God of hosts than he has yet done, should
love with sacrifices the One who created light, heaven and earth and
the expanse of the seas, the circuit of the skies. Otherwise he cannot
bring me to his abode. With his possessions, he must seek bridal
love from another woman; he will not have any here.

The poet counterpoints the implication of total commitment in marriage
with an explicit affirmation of God's total power: he created light, the
heavens and the earth, and the circuit of the skies. The necessity of Eleusius's loving this God receives emphasis through chiasmus ('þonne he gen
dyde, // lufige mid lacum,' than he has yet done, should love with sacrifices
[110b–11a]) and through the stress placed on the finite form of the crucial
verb 'lufian' at the beginning of line 111a. Juliana's finely wrought, carefully reasoned language thus encases the immutability of the 'næfre ...
nemne' (never ... unless) mandate.

Her subsequent dialogue manifests many virtues of the first two
speeches. It is clearly and logically developed – for example, lines 132–9
rhetorically pair the 'næfre ... ne' of 134–5a with the 'ne næfre' of 138a,
while the saint asserts that she will not lie, will not fear Affricanus's judgment, and will not be turned from Christ.[12] Variational chiasmus (see
131b–2a, 421b–2a, 667–8a) and other figures appear in her speeches to emphasize meaning: the variation in lines 180b–2a, for instance, effectively
suspends the reader over the concept of God, and the asyndetic structure of
line 217 rhythmically stresses the uselessness of idols – they are 'idle, or-
feorme, / unbiþyrfe' (vain, worthless, unprofitable). Further, in a pun at
line 459, 'micelra manweorca / manna tudre' (great evil deeds to the children of men), Cynewulf exploits the homophonic attraction of 'man' (sin)
to 'mann' (man), to suggest man's innate capacity to work evil.[13] Juliana's
discourse also consistently displays balance and control: lines 149–59 have
their rhetorical fulcrum in the adversative conjunction 'ac' in line 153;[14]
similarly, lines 272–82 have theirs in line 278, where Juliana's prayer for
strength becomes a petition for God to reveal the true identity of the
messenger.

Less obtrusive aspects of the saint's dialogue are two syntactic patterns
that generate expectations that the other characters will fulfil or thwart.
The first, at work in many of Juliana's speeches and already indicated to be

present in lines 132–9, is simple parallelism. The second, an equally normal construct and seen in her initial speech, establishes an immediate cause-effect relationship between main and subordinate clauses ('Ic þe mæg gesec-gan / þæt þu sylfne ne þearft // swiþor swencan,' I can tell you that you need not distress yourself further [46–7a]); this same pattern occurs when-ever Juliana makes an assertion. For example, the subordinate clauses fol-low hard upon the main clause in lines 278–9a and 666–8a: 'Swa ic þe, bilwitne, / biddan wille // þæt þu me gecyðe' (So I will beseech you, gentle one, that you should make known to me); 'Biddað Bearn Godes / þæt me Brego engla, // Meotud moncynnes, / milde geweorþe, // sigora Sellend' (Ask the Son of God that the Prince of angels, the Creator of mankind, the Giver of victories, should be merciful to me). And in lines 272–7, although there is a delay between main and subordinate clause, it is caused by variation, not by modifiers qualifying and thus undermining what Juliana says:

> Nu ic þec, beorna Hleo,   biddan wille,
> ece ælmihtig,   þurh þæt æþele gesceap
> þe þu, Fæder engla,   æt fruman settest,
> 275   þæt þu me ne læte   of lofe hweorfan
> þinre eadgife,   swa me þes ar bodað
> frecne færspel,   þe me fore stondeð.

> I will now beseech you, Protector of men, eternal almighty, through that noble creation which you, Father of angels, established at the beginning, that you will not allow me to turn from praise of your grace according to the horrible, sudden message which the messen-ger who stands before me announces.

Both syntactic patterns lend support to Juliana's linguistic image and will have specific relevance to her father.

The saint's linguistic consistency, the fusing of her words and her deeds, indicates her spiritual stability; it also, at least in part, gives rise to Woolf's remark that the entire poem has 'a uniformity verging on monotony. The style – the word is being used in its broadest sense – is generally unre-lieved by any emotional or rhetorical emphasis or by any other gradations in tone.'[15] But this statement seems misguided, especially in regard to the poem's opening, where Juliana faces first her father and then Eleusius.

The initial appearance of the human persecutors occurs in a revealing dialogue between father and prefect. After hearing Eleusius's complaints against his daughter, Affricanus responds obsequiously to his lord, using the Praise of Rulers topos and exposing himself as Juliana's least impressive antagonist. The Latin source, direct and unencumbered, reads: 'Per misericordes et amatores hominum deos, quod si vera sunt haec verba, tradam eam tibi' (Strunk, 34): 'By men's merciful and loving gods, if these words are true, I will hand her over to you' (Allen and Calder, 123). But in the Old English a prolixity of pronouns, conjunctions, and prepositions (thirty-five, as opposed to twenty-eight in Juliana's first speech, which is three lines longer), as well as an overly complex sentence structure, impair the movement of his address as he vows to Eleusius:

80   Ic þæt geswerge   þurh soð godu,
        swa ic are æt him   æfre finde,
        oþþe, þeoden, æt þe   þine hyldu
        winburgum in,   gif þas word sind soþ,
        monna leofast,   þe þu me sagast,
85   þæt ic hy ne sparige, ac on spild giefe,
        þeoden mæra,   þe to gewealde.
        Dem þu hi to deaþe,   gif þe gedafen þince,
        swa to life læt,   swa þa leofre sy.

I swear through the true gods, so ever I may find favour with them, or, Prince, with you your grace in the joyous cities, if those words are true, dearest of men, which you speak to me, that I will not spare her, but will give her to destruction, great Prince, will give her into your power. Condemn her to death if it seems suitable to you, or allow her life, as that may be more pleasing.

Sentence structure, variation, and alliteration conspire here to reveal Affricanus as a man concerned more with offering his earthly lord deference than with seeking absolute truth and justice. As a result, he seems to have imperfect rhetorical control over his dialogue, and a number of stylistic facts contribute to that impression. He qualifies his first statement with a protracted adverbial clause (lines 81–4); in so doing he breaks up the major sentence constituents and thwarts our expectations conditioned by our knowledge of normal Old English usage[16] and by the saint's discourse, where we have never seen qualifiers delay an assertion. The tactic serves only to disperse the energy that Affricanus wishes to convey. Furthermore, even the meaning of the qualifying phrases helps to disperse energy, for each represents a perceptual shift: Affricanus's concern floats from the grace of the gods to the grace of Eleusius to the truth of the prefect's words. Nor do variation or alliteration help this speech. Merely repetitive, the former inhibits narrative flow: 'Monna leofast,' after all, can vary 'þeoden,' since the two epithets represent a perceptible shift in stress, but 'þeoden mæra' becomes redundant,[17] an instance of what Isidore calls 'tautologia.'[18] And the relatively frequent alliteration on insignificant words in the b-lines of this speech ('æfre,' 81; 'þine,' 82; 'me,' 84; 'þe,' 86) weakens the rhythmic and rhetorical impact of those lines. Finally, the speech's concluding line is an abortive attempt at syntactic and rhetorical balance, as a comparison with a similar construction in *Elene* will show. Elene announces to the recalcitrant Judas that two possibilities are prepared for him, 'swa lif swa deað / swa þe leofre bið // to geceosanne' (as well life as death as may be dearer to you for the choosing [606–7a]), and thus employs what E.E. Ericson terms a 'correlative pair in a modal sequence,'[19] relatively common in Old English. Affricanus, however, omits the first 'swa,' making the second act as a single co-ordinating conjunction. Because the modal has thus been 'forced to perform the accretive function,'[20] the clarity usually arising from swa ... swa constructions collapses.[21]

Cynewulf gives Affricanus more rhetorical control in Affricanus's first speech to Juliana, where the father's discourse rises towards the rhetorical standard that the daughter has already set. The patent, measurable changes in Affricanus's speech are perhaps the best evidence that Cynewulf allows his antagonists in this poem to use language as a weapon to delude. In what Woolf regards as one of the two speeches that 'echo a Latin warmth,'[22] but which is actually calculated flattery (lines 93–104), Affricanus assails his daughter, listing Eleusius's merits in acceptable discourse (except in 104b, 'ece eadlufan, / an ne forlæte,' he even alliterates effectively!). But his innate inferiority and his absolute frustration before his daughter's steadfastness reflect themselves in his reversion to his earlier linguistic instability and in his ultimate disappearance from the poem.

After Juliana's second speech (lines 108–16) Affricanus descends into almost total ineffectuality:

>   Ic þæt gefremme,   gif min feorh leofað,
> 120 gif þu unrædes   ær ne geswicest,
>   7 þu fremdu godu   forð bigongest,
>   7 þa forlætest   þe us leofran sind,
>   þe þissum folce   to freme stondað,
>   þæt þu ungeara   ealdre scyldig
> 125 þurh deora gripe   deaþe sweltest,
>   gif þu geþafian nelt   þingrædenne,
>   modges gemanan.   Micel is þæt ongin
>   7 þreaniedlic   þinre gelican,
>   þæt þu forhycge   hlaford urne.[23]

I will bring it about if I live, if you do not beforehand cease from the ill-advised course, and if you henceforth worship alien gods and reject those who are dearer to us, who stand as a help to this people, that you soon, being forfeit of life, through the grip of beasts will die the death, if you will not submit to the marriage proposal, union with the brave man. Great is that undertaking and calamitous for such as you, that you should disdain our lord.

The sense of this passage seems to struggle futilely against the syntax that bears it, but Cynewulf's syntactic strategy here appropriately bespeaks a debilitating inertia in Affricanus. The opening sentence consists of a main clause (119a) and a modifying 'gif' clause (119b), followed by an extremely complex subordinate-clause cluster with co-ordination within it (121a and 123a), all of which hinders progress to the recapitulating 'þæt' clause in line 124. The recapitulating clause in turn is limited by an additional gif clause, which, by paralleling line 120 structurally, places the marriage to Eleusius and acceptance of heathen gods on the same plane. The speaker's complex syntax, however, wholly obscures any resultant thematic clarity. The movement that does exist in the speech gravitates towards the medial þæt clause, which we must wait for in the first six lines and return to in the last four in order to grasp the father's meaning. This use of a recapitulating þæt in the middle of the speech creates an illusion of the balance or symmetry that characterizes Juliana's dialogue. But the symmetry in her speeches helps to make clear what she wishes to say; furthermore, as we have seen, she never delays a subordinate clause, as her father does here. Again suspended by Affricanus's convolutions and by synchisis, which Bede defines as 'a completely perplexing *hyperbaton* [a transposition of words],'[24] the reader must disentangle the layers of clauses and phrases to discover the message; we ultimately find that the information embedded in direct discourse 'is sometimes as difficult to extract as a chestnut from a green burr.'[25]

Further complication and a further indication of Affricanus's instability arise from his bewildering shift from negative to positive syntactic structure in his admonition. Whereas Juliana's speeches have conditioned the reader to expect a parallel series of negative or positive reasons for assertions, Affricanus thwarts that expectation. After the negative in line 120b the expected parallel negative in line 121 never appears. Momentary disorientation results, and his words accumulate an added dimension of obscurity. Affricanus cannot maintain the delusive strategy he adopts in lines 93–104; he is no match for the saint.

Nor is Eleusius, but his discourse and the physical torment he can bring to bear both befit a prefect. His first words to Affricanus in the poem, however, display his true character and deserve treatment now to show that when he does approach Juliana's stylistic ideal, he does so to delude her or

the public he addresses. Having been rejected by Juliana, Eleusius calls Affricanus to counsel, and, in contrast to the Latin, which states merely that
he 'dixit ei omnia verba quae ei mandaverat Juliana' ([Strunk, 34]: 'told
him word for word what Juliana had sent him' [Allen and Calder, 123]), he
speaks briefly, explaining the situation:

                    Me þin dohtor hafað
        geywed orwyrðu;   heo me on an sagað
70   þæt heo mæglufan   minre ne gyme,
        freondrædenne.   Me þa fraceðu sind
        on modsefan   mæste weorce,
        þæt heo mec swa torne   tæle gerahte
        fore þissum folce;   het me fremdne god,
75   ofer þa oþre   þe we ær cuþon,
        welum weorþian,   wordum lofian,
        on hyge hergan,   oþþe hi nabban.

To me your daughter has shown dishonour; to me she says outright
that she does not care for my love, my affection. To me those insults are most painful in mind, that she so grievously should attack
me with blasphemy before this people; she commands me to worship with riches, praise with words, exalt in mind a strange god over
the others which we knew before, or not have her.

These words pale in comparison to Juliana's first words (lines 46–57), in
which she shapes the various features of her dialogue into reasoned, un-
emotional discourse. Juliana's dual personal and religious insult against
Eleusius causes him, like Orgoglio in *The Faerie Queene*, to swell with uncontrollable wrath ('yrre gebolgen,' swollen with anger [58b]) and change
form, as his dialogue bursts syntactic and metrical boundaries. The speech
begins and ends with emotion-charged paratactic constructions, and in between comes a rising crescendo of rage made clear through the incantatory
effect of gradatio and through an excessive use of personal pronouns at the
beginnings of the b-lines: 'Me þin,' 'heo me,' 'minre,' 'me.' These two devices call as much attention to the wronged speaker as to his wrath, and the
deviation in rhythm concentrates the speech even more unequivocally on
Eleusius, since 'minre' in line 70b has metrical dominance but no rhetorical
significance. His self-centredness comes more fully to light. At the climax
of the short speech Eleusius, like Affricanus, injects an adverbial clause
mid-sentence (74b–6), cracking apart the sentence elements to show his 'ex-
uberance of emotion'[26] in a final burst of wrathful energy.
  His two remaining speeches contain some of the better features of the

saint's dialogue. After Affricanus's failure with Juliana, Eleusius tries the same initial strategy, using cajolery practically identical to that employed by the father earlier in lines 93–6a:

> Min se swetesta   sunnan scima,
> Iuliana!   Hwæt, þu glæm hafast,
> ginfæste giefe,   geoguðhades blæd!
> Gif þu godum ussum   gen gecwemest,
> 170   7 þe to swa mildum   mundbyrd secest,
> hyldo to halgum,   beoð þe ahylded fram
> wraþe geworhtra   wita unrim,
> grimra gyrna,   þe þe gegearwad sind,
> gif þu onsecgan nelt   soþum gieldum.[27]

> My sweetest splendour of the sun, Juliana! Lo, you have radiance, abundant grace, glory of youth! If you will yet propitiate our gods and seek their protection so mild, grace from the holy ones, from you will be averted a countless number of cruelly wrought torments, of horrible evils, which are prepared for you if you will not sacrifice to the true deities.

Eleusius couples the three-line salutation to a mild, nicely constructed six-line ultimatum, consisting of a single sentence. His statement begins and ends with a conditional 'gif' clause and contains two instances of variational chiasmus. The first example changes the *abba* pattern to *aba*,[29] and both examples are equidistant fom the beginning and end of the sentence respectively: 'to swa mildum / mundbyrd secest, // hyldo to halgum' (seek protection so mild, grace from the holy ones); 'wraþe geworhtra / wita unrim, // grimra gyrna, / þe þe gegearwd sind' (a countless number of cruelly wrought torments, of horrible evils, which are prepared for you). Eleusius also uses sound harmony in line 168 ('ginfæste giefe, / geoguð-hades blæd,' abundant grace, glory of youth), where 'all precedent sounds converge and produce what we have called the climax in intonation, breathing forth Heliseus's apotheosis of the girl's beauty.'[29] And the contrast between lines 166–8 and 172–3 'gives the suggestion that all her beauty and youthful splendour will not any way avail against the awful torments that are being prepared for her if she will not obey the heathen gods.'[30]

The rhetorical and syntactic balance in Eleusius's speech approximates that of Juliana's discourse. But whereas the extralinguistic world coincides with Juliana's linguistic world (that is, her words, which constitute the icon that expresses her, identify an absolute truth), Eleusius's linguistic world does not coincide with reality. The control he evidences in the manipulative attempt of lines 166–7a cannot extend through the whole speech, for irony, deriving from an adverse truth Eleusius does not perceive, undercuts the efficacy of his words. Laughter, not solemnity, results from the first use of chiasmus (170b–1a).[31] The only true protection and grace lie with Christ, a fact that Eleusius refuses to acknowledge. His stubbornness is self-deluding and renders his ostensible approximation of Juliana's linguistic ideal illusory in this and all his speeches; for in order to possess absolute linguistic control, one must be sensitive to both the linguistic surface of dialogue and the message it carries.

Unlike Affricanus, however, Eleusius does not entirely lose his control with the saint's next rejection. He has Juliana beaten, then delivers an unornamented speech of triumph: he will grant Juliana life (lines 191b–2a), despite her earlier blasphemies, if she makes peace with his gods (197b–200a). Admonishing her to set aside the battle, he states:

<blockquote>
Gif þu leng ofer þis

þurh þin dolwillen   gedwolan fylgest,
þonne ic nyde sceal,   niþa gebæded,
on þe þa grimmestan   godscyld wrecan,
205   torne teoncwide,   þe þu tælnissum
wiþ þa selestan   sacan ongunne,
7 þa mildestan   þara þe men witen,
þe þes leodscype   mid him longe bieode.[32]
</blockquote>

If concerning this through your foolishness you follow delusion longer, then by necessity, constrained by enmity, I must avenge on you the most horrible blasphemy, the grievous hurtful speech, with which you blasphemously set about to strive against the best and mildest whom men know, whom this people have long worshipped among themselves.

Again, the patent irony of his words vitiates their intended effect. Both Juliana and the reader realize that the delusion ('gedwola' [202b]) rests with Eleusius, not with the saint, and that the claim that his idols are 'þa selestan ... 7 þa mildestan' (the best and the mildest) that men know grotesquely inverts the true claims uttered by Juliana. The speech elicits derision from the reader and meets steadfast resistance from the saint. Eleusius cannot turn her from her faith.

In the demon, Juliana encounters her linguistic equal.[33] Unmarred by the syntactic convolutions that plague those of Affricanus, the demon's speeches are adorned by some expressive rhetorical devices, such as paronomasia, used as effectively as in the saint's discourse.[34] At lines 305 ('on rode aheng / rodera Waldend,' on the Cross hanged the Ruler of the heavens) and 447 ('Rodorcyninges giefe, / se þe on rode treo,' The grace of heaven's King, he who on the tree of the Cross) Cynewulf alliterates 'rod' with 'rodor,' thus employing a 'phonological coincidence to outline a basic Christian paradox: the lower thing (*rod*) juxtaposed with the highest (*rodera wealdend, rodorcyning* "lord of the heavens"), the mystery of Divinity's historical impact on mankind.'[35] This word-play occurs only in the demon's discourse. Further, Clæs Schaar lists four instances of variational chiasmus in his speeches.[36] The first, another variation of the *abba* structure, is aptly placed and underscores the torments Juliana will suffer if she does not sacrifice to the heathen idols: 'Ðe þes dema hafað // þa wyrrestan / witu gegearwad, // sar endeleas' (This judge has prepared for you the worst torments, endless pains [249b–51a]). The second (298b–301a) and the fourth (400–1a) emphasize the demon's delusive tactics by explaining the method of his assault on Simon, then by delimiting his plan before any attack – he determines 'hu gefæstnad sy / ferð innanweard, // wiþersteall geworht' (how the heart is established within, the defences worked [400–1a]). The third instance heightens both the demon's boldness and the gravity of his design in thinking he could so influence Juliana that she 'to sæmran gebuge, // onsægde synna fruman' (would bow to a worse god, sacrifice to the author of sins [361b–2a]). Each appearance of chiastic variation heightens our sense of the demon's verbal power.

Further indication of the demon's worthiness as a spiritual opponent arises from his skilful manipulation of more general structural aspects of discourse. Schaar notes the artistic felicity of the words in lines 382–97, where the demon explains his fate when he meets a Christian suitably armed against him:

> In these seemingly uncouth periods we have, it will be observed, a fairly skilful pattern of correspondences: the two *nele*-clauses are complementary, as are the first two *ac*-clauses. The second main clause *ac ic geormor sceal* (*oþerne ellenleasran*) etc. corresponds with *ic sceal feor þonan heanmod hweorfan*. Without this network of correlations the artistic value of the periods would of course be inferior, an accumulation of similar clauses being the only effect.[37]

Similarly controlled is the demon's catalogue of evil deeds in lines 472b–94a. His snares have broken the feet of some men; he has caused others to burn 'in liges locan' (in the embrace of the flame [474a]) and some 'blode spiowedan' (to spew blood [476b]) from their bodies. The Cross, the sea, and drunkenness have been his weapons (478b–90a), and with them and other devices he has slain many men. Such catalogues are common in Old

English poetry. They provide concrete detail for a particular doctrine and give that doctrine illustrative variety.[38] The demon gives this catalogue further rhetorical emphasis by putting the alliterative stress in the b-line on the particle 'minum' in two instances: some men drowned at sea 'minum cræftum' (by my skill [480]); some he has slain 'minum hondum' (by my hand [493]). This kind of facility typifies Juliana's major opponent, and more could certainly be said about the virtues of his discourse. But the point has been made that his linguistic skills equal the saint's. We must now turn to the differences between the demon's speeches and those of Eleusius and Affricanus.

We have seen Eleusius's linguistic capabilities, his control of language, compromised by the injection of irony into his speeches. Irony also permeates Affricanus's dialogue. The eternal affection ('ece eadlufan') he speaks of in lines 93–104 can only be found with Christ, not with Eleusius, and the chastisements levelled at Juliana in that speech turn ironically back upon the father. In contrast, once the demon has been unmasked, irony does not undermine the linguistic competency revealed in the surface of his dialogue, although an irony of situation underlies the scenes in which he speaks. An examination of two key words, 'gedwola' (delusion) and 'soð' (truth), both additions to the Latin source, will show that irony does not operate at the same level of intensity throughout the poem and that its relative absence indicates the stature of the antagonist and the difficulty of the challenge Juliana faces.

Words do not metamorphose in the mouth of Juliana as they do in the mouths of Affricanus and Eleusius. When she speaks of Affricanus's gedwola (line 138b), she gives an immutable condemnation of his error; when Eleusius talks of Juliana's gedwola (202b), his words roll back upon him. Similarly the word soð used by Juliana always represents the one transcendent reality (47b, 132a, 219a, 224b), while it sours on the lips of her human persecutors (80b, 83b, 174b, 194b). Both words when used by the demon, however, carry the same ineluctable force they do with the saint. He unambiguously tells how he compelled Simon to assail Christ's disciples:

> Eac ic gelærde
> Simon searoþoncum   þæt he sacan ongon
> wiþ þa gecorenan   Christes þegnas,
> 300   7 þa halgan weras   hospe gerahte
> þurh deopne gedwolan,   sægde hy drys wæron.

I also cunningly taught Simon so that he set about to strive against the chosen thanes of Christ, and he attacked with contumely the holy men through deep delusion, said they were sorcerers.

And at the insistence of Juliana, he reveals to her precisely how he subverts the righteous:

               Þus ic soðfæstum
þurh mislic bleo   mod oncyrre:
þær ic hine finde   ferð staþelian
365   to Godes willan,   ic beo gearo sona
þæt ic him monigfealde   modes gælsan
ongean bere   grimra geþonca,
dyrnra gedwilda,   þurh gedwolena rim.

Thus do I turn the mind of the righteous through my various forms: where I find him to fix his heart in the will of God, straightaway I am ready so that I bear the manifold lusts of the mind against him, horrible thoughts, secret errors, through countless delusions.

We do not dispute his use of gedwola nor his use of soð: we are quite sure that Juliana will 'soð gecnawan' (know the truth [342b]) when the demon reveals it to her; that what he says 'is soð, nales leas' (is true, not at all false [356b]); that he knows 'to soðe' (for a truth [547b]) that he has never before found Juliana's like among womankind.

What can we make of this situation? How do we explain the demon's linguistic expertise and his candour? As Banquo queries, 'Can the devil speak true?' Partial explanation resides in the dignity accorded the devil in the early Middle Ages; usually the chief opponent of martyrs, he had to be important and fearful, and in this poem his messenger does cause Juliana, 'seo þe forht ne wæs' (she who was not afraid [258b]), to become 'egsan geaclad' (terrified with dread [268a]). Or context may be responsible: one of the poem's great ironies is that its most overtly educative discourse comes from the demon. But the theme of delusion provides yet another explanation, for in a calculated strategy of duplicity, truth can be the most disengaging tactic of all.[39] Cynewulf's alterations of his Latin source indicate that he meant to heighten both the reader's potential sympathetic response to the demon and his admiration for Juliana, who remains inflexible in the face of the demon's compelling discourse. In a poem deliberately constructed on a pattern of extreme contrasts, any concession by one party to its polar opposite would be tantamount to defeat.

The demon's plan takes shape when Juliana seizes him and compels him to speak. In the Latin *Acta* he issues his catalogue, unmitigated by any note of regret or repentance:

Ego sum qui compunxi militem lancea sauciare latus Filii Dei; ego

sum qui feci ab Herode Joannem decapitari; ego sum qui per
Simonem locutus sum quia magi essent Petrus et Paulus; ego sum
qui ad Neronem imperatorem ingressus sum ut Petrum crucifigeret
et Paulum decapitaret; ego sum qui Andream feci tradi in regione
Patras; ego ista omnia et alia deteriora feci cum fratribus
meis.   (Strunk, 39)

It is I who goaded the soldier to pierce the side of God's Son with a
lance; I who had John beheaded by Herod; I who said, through Simon, that Peter and Paul were sorcerers; I who entered into the
Emperor Nero so that he crucified Peter and beheaded Paul; I who
had Andrew betrayed in the region of Patras. I and my brothers
have done all these things and worse.   (Allen and Calder, 126)

In Cynewulf's version the Christian diction and other additions create a
completely different tone. While the demon retains his boastful attitude, he
complicates it by employing details, absent from the Latin, which inject a
note of self-critical moral judgment on his own acts. Herod's 'unryhtre æ'
(unlawful marriage [297a]), for instance, is the root cause of his killing
John, 'se halga wer' (the holy man [295b]); and Simon assails 'Cristes þegn-
nas' (the thanes of Christ [299b]), 'þa halgan weras' (the holy men [300a]).
In the Old English, lines 307–15a reach an emotional pitch absent from the
Latin, adding the emotive concept of 'wuldres wlite' (the beauty of glory
[311a]) and an implied regret for the innumerable 'sweartra synna' (black
sins [313a]) that the demon has committed:

Swylce ic Egias   eac gelærde
þæt he unsnytrum   Andreas het
ahon haligne   on heanne beam,
310   þæt he of galgan his   gæst onsende
in wuldres wlite.   Þus ic wraðra fela
mid minum broþrum   bealwa gefremede,
sweartra synna,   þe ic asecgan ne mæg,
rume areccan,   ne gerim witan,
315   heardra hetaþonca.

Likewise I also taught Aegias so that he foolishly commanded the
holy Andrew hanged on a high tree so that from the cross he sent
his spirit into the beauty of glory. Thus with my brothers I committed many evils, black sins, which I cannot tell, relate in full, nor can
I know the number of hard thoughts of hate.

The demon in the Old English does not as clearly personify evil as does his counterpart in the Latin, who occasions immediate revulsion; the shift in focus represents a significant rhetorical strategy, one which does not, however, decrease the polarization of good and evil in the poem. It merely augments the subtle power of the instruments of darkness.

The principle of change seen in the passage above appears everywhere in the demon's dialogue. Lines 321–44, for example, contain similar amplifications of the Latin. The demon emphasizes the misery found in hell and uses his subordinate position to Satan to elicit compassion as well as fear.[40] The king of hell-dwellers is 'yfla gehwæs // in þam grornhofe / geornfulra' (more eager in the house of sorrow for every evil) than the demon (323b–4a), who is sad in heart (327b) when he must turn people from righteousness; but there is no hint of remorse in the Latin. And later in the *Acta*, after he suffers further torment from Juliana, the demon laments being sent to her and demands release. His words are abrasive:

> Sed quomodo nunc malo meo missus sum ad te! Utinam te non vidissem! Heu mihi misero quid perfero? Quomodo non intellexit pater meus quid mihi eveniret? Dimitte me, ut vel ad alterum mihi liceat transire locum. Nam accusabo te patri meo et non expediet tibi.   (Strunk, 41)

> But how miserable I am, now that I have been sent to you! If only I hadn't seen you! Alas, what I suffer in my misery! Why didn't my father see what would happen to me? Let me go, so I can cross over to the other place. For I will denounce you to my father and it will go badly with you.   (Allen and Calder, 127–8)

Such a threat does not seriously jeopardize a saint, so Cynewulf eliminates it, adding the concept of the Cross and making the Old English rendition of the Latin psychologically more compelling:

> Forþon ic þec halsige   þurh þæs Hystan meaht,
> Rodorcyninges giefe,   se þe on rode treo
> geþrowade,   þrymmes Ealdor,
> þæt þu miltsige   me þearfendum,
> 450 þæt unsælig   eall ne forweorþe,
> þeah ic þec gedyrstig   7 þus dolwillen
> siþe gesohte,   þær ic swiþe me
> þyslicre ær   þrage ne wende.

> Therefore I entreat you through the might of the Most High, by the grace of heaven's King, who suffered on the Cross, the Lord of

glory, that you have mercy on me in my needs, so that miserable I should not completely perish, although rash and thus foolish I sought you here in my journey, where I did not much expect such a time of distress.

Unaffected by the demon's rhetoric here and elsewhere, the saint commands him to speak still further of the damage he has done to men 'deorcum gedwildum' (through dark errors [460a]).

The demon consistently fails in his attempts to disarm Juliana through an emotive manipulation of truth and to earn a compassion he does not deserve. Like the delusive attempts of Affricanus and Eleusius before him, his are fruitless, and in a significant elaboration of the Latin he makes explicit the typological association of Juliana with Christ in his harrowing of hell, thus signalling the demon's and Satan's defeat and Juliana's and Christ's triumph:

	Ic þec halsige, hlæfdige min,
540	Iuliana, fore Godes sibbum,
	þæt þu furþur me fraceþu ne wyrce,
	edwit for eorlum, þonne þu ær dydest,
	þa þu oferswiþdest þone snotrestan
	under hlinscuan, helwarena cyning,
545	in feonda byrig; þæt is fæder user,
	morþres manfrea.[41]

I beseech you, my lady Juliana, by the peace of God, that you work not insults further on me, disgrace before men, more than you previously did, when you conquered in the darkness of the prison the wisest king of hell-dwellers in the city of fiends; that is our father, the evil prince of murder.

The saint has 'unscamge / æghwæs wurde // on ferþe frod' (become completely unconfounded, wise in mind [552–3a]).

The manipulation of dialogue in *Juliana* is a demonstrable aspect of Cynewulf's art. By means of it he establishes the saint's immutable character and makes clear his major thematic concerns, compelling the reader to react both to the stylistic icon defining Juliana and to her persecutors' abortive attempts to appropriate portions of that icon for their subversive ends. Rising above physical limitation, linking herself with the divine, the saint here and in all the lives stands firm at the linguistic and spiritual still point of the turning world.

CHAPTER THREE

Judas with a New Voice: Revelatory Dialogue in Cynewulf's *Elene*

In *Juliana* Cynewulf explores the fundamental antithesis between good and evil, Christian and pagan, as he records the struggle between two eternally opposed spiritual powers. The construction of the poem is ritualistic and ultimately rather simple, defining for us through a careful manipulation of discourse the invincibility of the one true faith. The poet faces a more complex problem in *Elene*, a poem that is essentially a double saint's life. Not dealing here with polar embodiments of pure good and pure evil, with the wholly saved and the unequivocally damned, Cynewulf must express Elene's realized and Judas's potential power without establishing the distinction he might have between their uses of discourse. We have seen the *Guthlac A* poet solve a distantly related but analogous problem – how to portray the demons as worthy, fearsome, but finally ludicrous opponents for the saint – by juxtaposing their well-wrought discourse, which symbolizes their power, to their laughable action, which symbolizes their ineffectuality. Cynewulf uses a similar technique, juxtaposing an iconographic and a personal style within Judas's dialogue to express Judas's human condition, his human capacity for both saintliness and wickedness.

The initial effect of this double focus, both on the two saints and within Judas's discourse, is unsettling for the reader, whose sympathies are now with Elene, the tormentor of an unrighteous one,[1] and now with Judas, whose punishment in the pit enables him to achieve sainthood as Cyriacus. But as the poetic message becomes increasingly clear, direct discourse attains a flatness and uniformity that permits us to see both the saints in the same light.[2] The iconographic pattern of direct discourse in *Elene* is not arbitrary but rather forms part of the poem's larger, coherent aesthetic, which the thematic use of paronomasia, centred around holiness, man, and sin, reflects. A brief look at the larger aesthetic will help us to understand the discussion that follows.

In a poem about the Invention of the Cross we would expect to find the kind of word-play already seen in *Juliana* (lines 305, 447): the play on 'rod' and 'rodora,' the lowest juxtaposed with the highest, a phonological coincidence outlining the basic Christian paradox of Christ's impact on mankind.[3] The figure as metaphor occurs twelve times in *Elene* (147, 206, 482, 624, 631, 855, 886, 918, 1022, 1066, 1074, 1234) and signals the transforming power of the Cross, which lifts the mean to the sublime and intensifies the vision of the central characters. Two other alliterative pairings, one a pun, show both the object and the result of that transformation. The first occurs when Elene outlines the conditions for going to heaven and having a longer life here on earth:

> Gif ðu in heofonrice   habban wille
> eard mid englum,   7 on eorðan lif,
> sigorlean in swegle,   saga ricene me
> hwær seo rod wunige   radorcyninges,
> 625   halig under hrusan   þe ge hwile nu
> þurh morðres man   mannum dyrndun.[4]

If you wish to have in heaven an abode with the angels, reward of victory in the sky, and life on earth, tell me quickly where the Cross of the King of heaven might dwell, holy under the earth, which you for a while now have concealed from men because of the sin of murder.

Here again, as in *Juliana* 459, the homophonic attraction of 'man' (sin) to 'mann' (man) in line 626 suggests man's innate capacity to work evil, just as the attraction of 'rod' to 'rador' in line 624 suggests that the convergence of the twain was predestined from the beginning.[5] Inextricably bound up with sins, unredeemed man cannot be free until the intermediary Cross liberates him, makes his capacity for good come to light. Once that liberation occurs, holiness supplants sin, a fact Cynewulf affirms through an alliterative coupling used three times after Judas's conversion and once before it: he alliteratively links 'hæleð' (man) with 'halig' (holy) in lines 679, 935, 1011, and 1203, intimating that man's belief in the Cross results in his absolute binding together with holiness and his consonant separation from sin. Cynewulf underscores the point at the poem's close by physically separating mann from man with four full verse lines:

swa bið þara manna ælc
ascyred 7 asceaden   scylda gehwylcre,
deopra firena,   þurh þæs domes fyr.
1315 Moton þonne siðþan   sybbe brucan,
eces eadwelan;   him bið engla weard
milde 7 bliðe   þæs ðe hie mana gehwylc
forsawon, synna weorc   7 to suna metudes
wordum cleopodon;   forðan hie nu on wlite scinaþ
1320 englum gelice,   yrfes brucaþ,
wuldorcyninges   to widan feore.

Thus each of men will be separated and held aloof from each of guilts, of deep sins, through the fire of judgment. Afterwards then they may enjoy peace, eternal well-being; to them the guardian of angels will be mild and blithe because they despised each of sins, the work of evil, and called in words to the son of the Creator; therefore they now shine in beauty, like unto the angels, enjoy the heritage of the King of glory forever.

As the poem progresses, as Judas and direct discourse progress, so does the meaning of the paronomastic and alliterative pattern. And our understanding of the conversion process advances as well.

The initial lack of focus in direct discourse, then, forms part of a larger pattern and becomes both one means of contrasting Elene's and Judas's words and a major didactic tool, as Cynewulf demonstrates his and our struggle to possess a full spiritual life. Stylistic and narrative ambiguities in *Elene* resolve themselves as the poem's theological premises are validated: man has within him capacities for both good and evil, and he moves towards embracing sanctification and light as he shuns sin, misunderstanding, and darkness.

The thematic movement of darkness towards light, or ignorance towards wisdom, or evil towards good in *Elene*[6] operates through a symbolic pattern based on what Earl R. Anderson has called the 'sapiential theme.' Anderson notes that movement 'from restriction or limitation to expansiveness' characterizes the poem. Cynewulf's symbolic use of time is one example of this pattern, 'seen in the movement from a preoccupation with the historical date of the *inventio crucis*, to its eternal presence in its liturgical celebration on May 3.'[7] Even the poem's setting expresses the sapiential theme, moving as it does from Constantine's defence of a small area against the barbarian hordes, to Elene's sea voyage, to Israel. Judas's confinement in the pit and his release likewise express the theme. Anderson concludes:

These incidents project, through setting, the objective correlatives of

changing mental states in Constantine, Judas, and Elene as their
spirits, under the intellectual and emotional force of the Cross in its
redemptive power, move, liberated, from spiritual darkness to sapiential light. In the epilogue Cynewulf applies the pattern of movement from confinement to expansiveness to his own religious
experience: the poet deliberated 'nihtes nearwe' (1239a) concerning
the Cross, until God disclosed to him 'rumran geþeaht' (1240b).[8]

The sapiential theme finds its stylistic embodiment in the direct discourse
of the poem basically through a progression from closure – a tendency of
the syntax and meaning to turn in on itself – to openness. Elene's discourse
(the iconographic norm to which Judas will eventually totally conform)
manifests that openness, and her first two speeches show the control that
creates the obtrusive stasis or uniformity that characterizes her. After sum-
moning all of the Hebrew wisemen to Jerusalem, she first addresses three
thousand of them:[9]

I   Ic þæt gearolice   ongiten hæbbe
          þurg witgena   wordgeryno
290   on Godes bocum   þæt ge geardagum
          wyrðe wæron   wuldorcyninge,
          dryhtne dyre   7 dædhwæte.
II   Hwæt ge þære snyttro   unwislice,
          wraðe wiðweorpon   þa ge wergdon þane
295   þe eow of wergðe   þurh his wuldre[s] miht,
          fram ligcwale,   lysan þohte,
          of hæftnede.   Ge mid horu speowdon
          on þæs andwlitan   þe eow eagena leoht
          fram blindnesse   bote gefremede,
300   edniowunga   þurh þæt æðele spald
          7 fram unclænum   oft generede
          deofla gastum.   Ge deaþe þone
          deman ongunnon   se ðe of deaðe sylf
          woruld awehte   on wera corþre
305   in þæt ærre lif   eowres cynnes.
          Swa ge modblinde   mengan ongunnon
          lige wið soðe,   leoht wið þystrum,
          æfst wið are,   inwitþancum
          wroht webbedan;   eow seo wergðu forðan
310   sceðþeð scyldfullum.   Ge þa sciran miht
          deman ongunnon,   on gedweolan lifdon
          þeostrum geþancum   oð þysne dæg.

III   Gangaþ nu snude,   snyttro geþencaþ
          weras wisfæste,   wordes cræftige,
315   þa ðe eowre æ,   æðelum cræftige,
          on ferhðsefan   fyrmest hæbben
          þa me soðlice   secgan cunnon,
          andsware cyðan   for eow[ic] forð
          tacna gehwylces   þe ic him to sece.

I have understood completely through the word-secrets of the
prophets in God's books that in former days you were precious to
the King of glory, dear to the Lord and bold. Lo, you foolishly,
fiercely cast away wisdom, when you cursed the one who thought to
loose you through his glorious might from damnation, from fiery
torment, from bondage. With filth you spat on the face of the one
who, with that noble spittle, worked remedy anew from blindness
for the light of your eyes and often saved you from the unclean
spirit of devils. You began to condemn to death the one who himself
from death had in that former life raised up the people of your race
in the company of men. Thus spiritually blind you began to confound lying with truth, light with darkness, malice with mercy, to
contrive slander with malice; therefore, damnation will harm you
sinful ones. You began to condemn the bright power, live in error
with dark thoughts until this day. Go now quickly, with wisdom
consider wise men, skilled in words those who, skilled in lineage,
most firmly have in their minds your law, those who can truly tell
me, reveal before you, the answer for every remarkable event I seek
from them.

The overall structure of this speech is triadic, with an introductory section
(I, 288–92), an analysis of the spiritual state of the Jews (II, 293–312), and a
concluding exhortation (III, 313–19). Additionally, Cynewulf binds the central and most important section together with anaphora, using three 'ge'
clauses in the b-lines (297b, 302b, 310b), thus giving the section a structure
not evident in the Latin source.[10] The repetition of 'deman ongunnon' (began to condemn [303a, 311a]) and the premise-conclusion kind of structure
in the central section ('hwæt ge' [293a]; 'swa ge' [306a]) give it further
rhetorical tightness while the repetition of 'snyttro' (wisdom [293a, 313b])
at equidistant points from the beginning and end of the speech, thus encas-
ing the analysis, contributes to its balance. The well-defined architecture of
the speech, however, does not diminish its power and sense of movement.
The first use of snyttro implicitly chastises the Jews' former folly; the sec-

ond calls them to re-embrace what they had lost. The speech moves to a definitive call for action, signalled in the use of the imperative mood, another salient feature of the stylistic icon. The active force of the speech becomes a measure of the woman uttering it.

Much more contributes to the speech's iconography. Chiasmus here, as in *Juliana*, marks linguistic expertise, becoming an essential part of the stylistic icon (as a *figura crucis*). The figure appears in five of Elene's seven major speeches,[11] beginning with the first: 'þæt ge geardagum // wyrðe wæron / wuldorcyning, // dryhtne dyre / 7 dædhwæte' (that in former days you were precious to the King of glory, dear to the Lord and bold [lines 290b–2]). In addition to using this figure Elene largely succeeds in creating a syntax that highlights the meaning it bears. From the outset of the first speech each half-line binds itself syntactically and rhythmically to its counterpart within the line or to the following a-line, creating enjambment, so that the natural caesural and end-of-line pauses are minimized. The strongest pause in the first five lines, for example, occurs before the subordinating conjunction 'þæt' in line 290b – 'on Godes bocum / þæt ge geardagum' (in God's books that in former days you) – and in the next thirteen (293–305) between the two adverbs 'unwislice' (foolishly [293b]) and 'wraðe' (fiercely [294a]). The pause emphasizes the adverbs' meanings and the enjambment following them intensifies pace and rhetorical effect. The rapid movement from line to line, from action to action, carries with it a sense of inevitability, of a movement towards a definite end. The end, of course, is damnation, or at least wretchedness, and when Elene mentions the spiritual blindness of the Jews, which has caused them to confound 'lige wið soðe / leoht wið þystrum, // æfst wið are' (lying with truth, light with darkness, malice with mercy [307–8a]), variation disrupts the characteristic syntactic flow from half-line to half-line, each variant depending on the clause 'swa ge modblinde / mengan ongunnon' (thus spiritually blind you began to confound [306]). The resultant intensified pauses, together with the antithesis of lines 307–8a, rhythmically underscore each failing in the Jews. In addition, the asyndetic structure of the lines conveys a sense of the isolation and disjunction that spiritual blindness implies.[12]

The rhythm also becomes emblematic of the two opposing forces in the poem. Outward directed, flowing from point to point, the enjambed lines connote action characteristic of Elene and of Constantine before her. Both seek to serve God by gaining new knowledge and eventually by unearthing the Cross, buried in a distant land. The Jews, on the other hand, do not seek new knowledge but cling tenaciously to the old, striving to keep the Cross hidden from all men. The asyndeton in lines 306–9a appropriately symbolizes the Jewish state. But the contrast between the two types of characters – and between their manifestations of what I term openness and closure – has even stronger and more easily defined structural and syntactic underpinnings.

One, discussed briefly in the introduction (see pages 11–12), is termed 'plurilinear alliteration' by Kemp Malone[13] and augments the rhythmic flow of the speech. David Hamilton demonstrates that Elene's first address to the Jews is more finely wrought in this respect than usual. Alliterating sounds, rather than confining themselves to single lines, extend through two or three 'as with *hwæt, unwislice, wraðe, wiðweorpon, wergdon, wergðe*, and *wuldres* in the opening three lines [293–5]; or *deofla, deaþe*, and *deman* interwoven with *gastum* and *ongunnon* in lines 302–3. *Wergdon, wergðe*, and *wergðu* (309b), moreover, repeat the same word base in order to emphasize one of the primary ideas of the passage.'[14] The plurilinear progression from sound to sound adds to the speech's sense of movement, its sense of openness, urging the reader forward and highlighting a tempo that forcefully punctuates Elene's message. Although the device appears throughout the poem, it has special significance here and in Elene's second speech, where it stands in definite contrast to Judas's use of it.

More important to the first speech's iconography and to the contrast between Elene and Judas is the use of a recapitulating *þæt* clause, which further intensifies the sense of openness. The '*þæt*' in line 288a anticipates the noun clause beginning in line 290b, thus conforming to a practice common in Old English when an author presents a fairly complex idea;[15] *þæt* appears here in order to prepare the reader for the exposition that follows. The recapitulating noun clause in turn elaborates – or 'opens' – the pronoun that anticipates it. Elene uses the device six times (four times in her long speeches, twice in her short speeches)[16] and always in the same way: to elucidate. Her usage will contrast markedly with that of Judas before his conversion.

The second of Elene's initial speeches (lines 333–76) shows the same scheme as the first. It too has triadic structure, which here centres around the use of indirect discourse ('be þam Moyses sang,' about him Moses sang [337b]; 'Be þam Dauid cyning,' About him King David [342a]; 'Swa hit eft be eow / Essaias, // witga for weorodum / wordum mælde,' Thus again with you Isaiah, the prophet before the multitudes, spoke in words [350–1]), and again it is encased by repetition ('hwæt' [334b, 364a]). The speech's power derives from the use of an introductory imperative ('gehyrað' [333a]) and from the frequent alliterative stress on finite verbs (333a, 335a, 353a, 355b, 356a, 358b, 360a, 364a, 373a), while three instances of variational chiasmus grace the lines: 'be þam Moyses sang // 7 þæt [word] gecwæð, / weard Israhela' (about him Moses sang and spoke these words, the guardian of Israel [337b–8]); 'Be þam Dauid cyning /

dryhtleoð agol, // frod fyrnweota, / fæder Salomones, // 7 þæt word
gecwæþ / wigona baldor' (About him King David chanted a heroic song, the
wise sage, the father of Solomon, and spoke these words, the leader of warriors [342–4]); '7 ge þam ryhte / wiðroten hæfdon, // onscunedon þone
sciran, / scippend, eallra dryhten' (and you have opposed the right,
shunned the bright creator, of all the Lord [369–70]).[17] Furthermore, the
rhetorical and spiritual gifts of both Elene and David are shown in lines
346b–7: 'he on gesyhðe wæs, // mægena wealdend, / min on þa swiþran'
(he was in my vision, the Lord of hosts, on my right hand). The alliterative
stress on 'min' emphasizes the pronoun, making clear that the vision is
David's alone. A full-line separation of the enclitic pronoun – normally
proclitic in Old English – from 'gesyhðe' ensures the effect: between noun
and modifier comes the object of the vision, 'mægena wealdend,' who
breaks through grammatical as well as physical and temporal barriers into
David's mind. A recapitulating þæt clause also appears in Elene's second
speech and, as elsewhere in her dialogue, illuminates what comes before:
'Hwæt we þæt gehyrdon / þurh halige bec // þæt eow Dryhten geaf / dom
unscyndne' (Lo, we have heard through holy books that the Lord gave you
stainless glory [364–5]).

Finally, the use of indirect discourse establishes one of the most significant features of the poem's stylistic iconography. All instances of it occur
in Elene's and Judas's speeches. Elene employs it in her second speech, and
Judas uses it in his first (lines 419b–535), in his sixth (725–801), and in his
last (1167–95). And all instances deal with some truth of Christianity or
prophecy. In Judas's speeches it emphasizes that Christ will ultimately
triumph (441–53); that his Crucifixion was unjust but that he rose from
the dead and made possible the conversion of saints such as Stephen (464–
527); that all heaven and earth proclaim God's glory (750–3); and that the
horse adorned with the nails from the Cross shall bear a warrior distin-
guished in war (1191–5). It is in Elene's second speech, however, that
Cynewulf fixes the norm for the use of indirect discourse.

The second speech basically elaborates her first,[18] tying specific prophetic
words to a general evaluation of the Jews' spiritual state. Her words narrow, and the pressure she exerts on the Jews intensifies as their numbers
simultaneously decrease. The first speech concentrates on the Jews' blindness; the second, on their inability to hear the word of God. Three of their
greatest leaders, who talked of Christ's coming, support Elene's argument
in an integrated, logical way: Moses foretold his birth (lines 339–41);
David pledged never to turn his eyes from him (348b–9); and Isaiah told of
God's bringing forth a child who would be rejected by his own people (361–
3). The Latin source differs significantly from the Old English poem at this
point:

Helena autem dixit ad eos, Audite mea verba, auribus percipite meos sermones. Non enim intellexerunt patres vestri neque vos in ser- monibus Prophetarum, quemadmodum de adventu Christi prophe- taverunt, quia prius dictum est, 'Puer nascetur et mater ejus virum non agnoscet:' et Isaias vobis dixit, 'Filios genui et exaltavi, ipsi au- tem spreverunt me: cognovit bos possessorem suum et asinus prae- sepe Domini sui, Israel autem me non cognovit, et populus meus me non intellexit:' et omnis Scriptura de ipso locuta est. Qui sciebatis legem errastis. (Kent, 31–2)

Helene said to them, 'Listen to my words; give an ear to my speech. For neither you nor your fathers have understood how the prophets' sayings foretold Christ's coming. It was prophesied before, 'A child will be born and his mother will not know man.' And Isaiah told you, 'I have begotten and raised children, but they have spurned me. The ox knew his owner and the ass his master's stable, but Is- rael did not know me nor my people understand me' (Isaiah 1.3). All Scripture has spoken about Him. You, who knew the law, have erred.' (Allen and Calder, 62)

The patent triadic structure and the progression of the Old English from foreknowledge to revelation to rejection does not appear in the Latin, where no clearly discernible structure exists. Elene's use of indirect discourse forms part of a rhetorical strategy that Cynewulf designs to isolate the source of the Jews' sins while, by reproducing a basic structure, it combines with and reinforces the stylistic icon he aligns with the saint. One further device, plurilinear alliteration, reinforces the strategy while it makes indi- rect discourse an integral part of the icon. We have seen that cross-alliteration from line to line urges the reader forward and binds a passage together, emphasizing its rhetorical unity. Notice the effect in the following lines:

> Gehyrð higegleawe   halige rune,
> word 7 wisdom;   hwæt ge witgena
> 335   lare onfengon   he se liffruma
> in cildes had   cenned wurde,
> mihta wealdend   be þam Moyses sang
> 7 þæt [word] gecwæð,   weard Israhela,
> 'Eow acenned bið   cniht on degle
> 340   mihtum mære   swa þæs modor ne bið
> wæstmum geeacnod   þurh weres frige.'
> Be þam Dauid cyning   dryhtleoð agol,

frod fyrnweota,   fæder Salomones,
7 þæt word gecwæþ   wigona baldor,
345 'Ic frumþa God   fore sceawode,
sigora dryhten;   he on gesyhðe wæs,
mægena wealdend,   min on þa swiðran,
þrymmes hyrde;   þanon ic ne wen[d]o
æfre to aldre   onsion mine.'

Listen, wise men, to the holy secret, to my words and wisdom; lo,
you have received the teaching of the prophets, how the Lord of life
was born in the form of a child, the Ruler of might about whom
Moses sang and spoke these words, the guardian of the Israelites, 'A
boy will be born to you in secret, glorious in might, whose mother
will not be increased with child through the love of a man.' About
him King David chanted a heroic song, the wise sage, the father of
Solomon, and spoke these words, the leader of warriors, 'I have
foreseen the God of creation, the Lord of victories; he was in my
sight, on my right hand, the Ruler of hosts, the Guardian of glory. I
thought never to turn my face from there.'

Cynewulf interweaves at least five complementary alliterating strands in
this passage. The first begins with the consonant *w*: 'word' and 'wisdom'
(line 334), 'witgena' (334), 'wealdend' (337), 'word' and 'weard' (338),
'wæstmum' and 'weres' (341), 'word' and 'wigona' (344), 'wæs' (346),
'wealdend' (347), and 'wendo' (348). At the start of the *w* strand a second
begins, alliterating on *c* ('cildes' and 'cenned' [336], 'gecwæð' [338],
'acenned' and 'cniht' [339], 'cyning' [342], and 'gecwæð' [344]), while a
third, alliterating on *s*, begins immediately after the second: 'sang' (337),
'Salomones' (343), 'sceawode' (345), 'sigora' and 'gesyhðe' (346), and 'swiðran' (347). Next comes an *m* strand, beginning in line 340, followed by an
f strand, beginning with line 341. The interlace of these strands makes direct and indirect discourse alliteratively undifferentiated and for a very important reason: the structural and rhetorical yoking of one to the other
indicates a character's ability to respond to the truths of indirect discourse,
and becomes another index of spiritual perfection.

Elene's remaining speeches display the linguistic expertise of the first
two, although the saint will eventually assume a role subordinate to that of
her newly converted counterpart. The triadic structure of her initial
speeches aligns itself with a pattern of threes very common in the poem as
a whole but not necessarily in its Latin source. There are, for example,
three baptisms (Constantine, line 192, Stephen, 490, and Judas, 1033), three
references to the date when the action takes place (1–4a, 632–5, 1226b–8a),

and three conversions (Constantine, Judas, the poet), together with three
styles (literal narrative, psychological dialogue, poetic monologue) corre-
sponding to the three conversions in the poem.¹⁹ In relation to Elene and
the Jews there are three uses of the imperative 'gangaþ' (313a, 372b, 406b)
before the attention shifts to Judas. Elene uses the structure again in her
third, fifth, seventh, and tenth speeches. In the third speech (386–96) she
once more delineates the extent of the Jews' sin: they scorned Scripture,
denied Christ's birth, and would not heed the law, though they knew it.
Each accusation forms part of the triadic structure signalled by the use of
'ge': 'oft ge' (386a), '7 ge' (390a), and 'þeah ge' (393b). The same pronoun
marks the separate sections of her fifth speech in lines 643–54 ('þæt ge'
[644a]; 'ge þæt' [648b]; 'ge þa' [652b]), but the triadic structures of her
seventh and tenth speeches depend on devices more subtle than repetition
of a word or phrase.

Again pronouns mark the structural divisions of the seventh speech (lines
1073–92). The first ('þu me, eorla hleo' [1073a]) obviously begins that part
of the speech directed to God, giving thanks for the discovery of the Cross;
the second ('mec þæra nægla gen' [1077b]), still directed to God, displays
Elene's wish also to find the nails; and the third ('ne þu hrædlice' [1086b])
directs the speech's force towards Cyriacus. The tenth speech, quoted at the
beginning of the chapter, has a less obvious arrangement and, because
short, can be repeated in full. Elene advises Judas:

>   Gif ðu in heofonrice   habban wille
>   eard mid englum   7 on eorðan lif,
>   sigorlean in swegle,   saga ricene me
>   hwær seo rod wunige   radorcyninges,
> 625   halig under hrusan   þe ge hwile nu
>   þurh morðres man   mannum dyrndun.

If you wish to have in heaven an abode with the angels, reward of
victory in the sky, and life on earth, tell me quickly where the Cross
of the King of heaven might dwell, holy under the earth, which you
for a while now have concealed from men because of the sin of murder.

The structure here derives from a progression of alliterative pairings expressing spiritual truths. By simultaneously offering life on earth and in
heaven, Elene implicitly yokes body and soul in line 622; she connects the
Cross ('rod') with God ('radorcyning') in line 624; and she links man
('mannum') to sin ('man') in line 626, thus outlining the universal condi-

tion of the unredeemed. In between the possibility of simultaneous life for body and soul and the reality of death for sinful humanity comes the only agent who can set man free: the heavenly king.

After their appearance in Elene's first speech, chiasmus and recapitulating þæt clauses also continue to play their iconographic roles. Elene ends her threat in lines 574–84a to the recalcitrant Jews with an emphatic instance of chiasmus:[20] 'ne magon ge þa wyrd bemiðan, // bedyrnan þa deopan mihte' (nor can you conceal those words, hide the deep powers [583b–4a]). And in lines 670–82a and 1073–92 she employs chiasmus to evoke the sublimity of the Creator: 'þæt me halig God // gefylle, frea mihtig' (so that for me holy God, the mighty Lord, might fulfil [679b–80a]); 'Godes agen bearn, // nerigend fira' (God's own child, the Saviour of men [1076b–7a]). The recapitulating þæt clauses in lines 643–54, 670–82a, 686–90, and 852–8 all conform to Elene's earlier usage: in lines 643–54 she asks how it happened that the Jews knew the details of the Trojan War and then reveals specific knowledge of their background, while she twice states that through holy books she has obtained various information about Christ's death on the Cross (670–82, 852–8). And she gives substance to the anticipatory 'þæt' in her oath, lines 686–90, through the recapitulating þæt clause beginning in line 687b: death by starvation faces Judas if he does not reveal the truth about the Cross.

The foregoing discussion of Elene's dialogue provides a fairly accurate outline of the poem's stylistic icon: it depends on a basic triadic kind of structure that integrates and subordinates the various elements of discourse so that each speech is unified and moves unmistakably forward or outward. Elene seeks the truth, and the syntax, rhythm, grammatical mood, and rhetorical structure – the economy – of her dialogue reflect her search. In Judas's dialogue we find many of the same features, but Cynewulf initially juxtaposes them to elements of a personal, and thus antithetical, style.

The poet describes Judas twice as 'wordes cræftig' (skilled in words), first though a proleptic reference by Elene in line 314b, and then in line 419a. As Thomas D. Hill, Jackson J. Campbell, and Varda Fish point out, Cynewulf seems to insist through this and other epithets that in his unredeemed state Judas merely manipulates words and the letter of the law, without having access to their spiritual depths.[21] With his conversion, however, his craft turns to wisdom as his knowledge of the letter and the spirit merge. In his unsanctified discourse the cleavage between skill in words and true wisdom gains expression through a double style that contributes to the poem's ambiguity. Its iconographic portions show Judas's innate capacity to achieve the ideal established by Elene and link him with the body of saints, while the vagaries of the personal section connect him with the body of the unredeemed.[22]

A comparison of the Latin source for the initial lines of Judas's first speech with the Old English rendition of them will help to clarify these points. He responds to the Jews' bewilderment over Elene's zeal in this way:

> Ego scio, quia quaestionem vult facere ligni, in quod Christum sus-
> penderunt patres nostri: videte ergo nemo ei confiteatur: nam
> vere destruentur paternae traditiones, et lex ad nihilum redigetur.
> (Kent, 34)

> I know. She wants to question us about the wood on which our
> fathers hanged Christ. Therefore, see that no one confesses to her.
> For truly our ancestral traditions will be destroyed and the law re-
> duced to nothing.   (Allen and Calder, 63)

Cynewulf's version represents a considerable elaboration of his source:

<blockquote>

               Ic wat geare
420   þæt hio wile secan   be ðam sigebeame
       on ðam þrowode   þeoda waldend
       eallra gnyrna leas,   Godes agen bearn
       þone [or]scyld[ne]   eofota gehwylces
       þurh hete hengon   on heanne beam
425   in fyrndagum   fæderas usse.
       Þæt wæs þrealic geþoht!   Nu is þearf mycel
       þæt we fæstlice   ferhð staðelien,
       þæt we ðæs morðres   meldan ne weorðen
       hwær þæt halige trio   beheled wurde
430   æfter wigþræce   þylæs toworpen sien
       frod fyrngewritu   7 þa fæderlican
       lare forlet[e]n.

</blockquote>

> I know well that she wants to ask about the tree of victory on which
> the Lord of men, free of all sins, God's own child, suffered, whom,
> guiltless of each of sins, our fathers in former days hanged on the
> high tree in hate. That was a terrible thought! Now is the need
> great that we set our hearts firmly so that we do not become in-
> formers about the murder nor where that holy tree was hidden after
> the strife, lest the wise old writings should be destroyed and the
> teachings of our fathers renounced.

An obvious tonal change from the Latin occurs in the Old English. Cynewulf alters the material of lines 419b–25 in much the same way that he alters the demon's speeches in *Juliana* by infusing the straightforward Latin ('ego scio, quia quaestionem vult facere ligni, in quod Christum suspenderunt patres nostri') with Christian diction and a litany of truths central to Christian doctrine.[23] The unadorned 'ligni' becomes the compound 'sigebeame' (tree of victory) and the 'heanne beam' (high tree); the simple naming of Christ turns into a tendentious delineation of his might and sinless state; and the Jewish fathers, given no motive for their actions in the Latin, are moved by hate in the Old English.

Some critics have questioned the artistic appropriateness of these changes, and at least one feels that the Christian vocabulary of the passage violates verisimilitude.[24] But one justification for it bears on the argument here. The Cross is an icon, a symbol of Christ's power and grace that man cannot modify. As an image it has special status, as James Earl explains:

> The image is not an idol, precisely because it is not considered to have been made by human hands at all. Because the image conforms rigorously to ancient conventions, and thus displays no human imaginative artistry, it is considered *non manufacta*; it is only the end product of what is thought of as a self-reproducing original prototype, which is sanctified by its age and its spontaneous miraculous origins.[25]

The description of the Cross can also be considered iconographic, and as an example of the *imago non manufacta* it must be accompanied by the traditional doctrine attendant upon it. In the mouth of a future saint the description is particularly appropriate, explicitly showing what Judas must eventually subordinate himself to. Furthermore, in juxtaposition to his own style it functions much as indirect discourse does and helps to isolate his personal style as the barrier he must overcome before reaching his destiny. The technique creates an ambiguity important in the Old English version but not evident in the Latin source.

The clause 'þæt wæs þrealic geþoht' (that was a terrible thought [line 426a]) marks the transition between the iconographic and the personal styles, and fittingly is one of the most ambiguous half-lines in the entire poem. We simply cannot know whether the terrible thought refers to the Jews' crucifying Christ or to Judas's implicit condemnation of the deed. In addition, the demonstrative 'þæt' is important here for two other reasons: it differs from the unambiguous use of such pronouns in Elene's dialogue, and it introduces a þæt cluster which functions in contrast to the expository nature of the subordinating conjunction 'þæt' in the second line of Judas's speech (420a). For in lines 426–30a Judas displays his 'word-craft' by em-

ploying ploce, the repetition of a word that has a different meaning the second time it appears. He shifts the function of þæt from a demonstrative
pronoun to a subordinating conjunction in two successive purpose clauses
and then shifts it back to a demonstrative pronoun, thus embedding his in-
tention to deceive in a carefully wrought grammatical-envelope pattern.
The tendency of Judas's dialogue to turn in upon itself, to resist yielding up
information, begins with these words.

Indirect discourse in Judas's first speech creates further ambiguity and a
more well-defined impression of the iconographic mode he tries to reject.
We have seen that Elene carefully integrates indirect discourse into her dialogue, using it to illustrate her points and to add support to the overall
sense of power and control that her words convey. In contrast, Judas displays a lack of profound spiritual understanding by using indirect discourse
as mere ornament.[26] He does not integrate it well into his discourse. The
cleavage between the two features of Judas's dialogue again derives partially
from the clashing of two styles, personal and iconographic, first made apparent in the lack of sustained plurilinear alliteration. The three transitions
from direct to indirect discourse illustrate the point:

eaferan;

440   wend hine of worulde   7 þæt word gecwæð,
    'Gif þe þæt gelimpe   on lifdagum
    þæt ðu gehyre   ymb þæt halige treo
    frode frignan ...'

the child; he turned from the world and spoke these words, 'If it
should happen to you in the days of your life that you should hear
wise men ask about the holy tree ...'

    Þa ic fromlice   fæder minum,
455   ealdum æwitan   ageaf andsware,
    'Hu wolde þæt geweorðan   on woruldrice
    þæt on þone halgan   handa sendan ...'

Then boldly I gave answer to my father, to the old man versed in
the law, 'How would that happen in the worldly kingdom that
[they] should lay hands on the holy one ...'

    Ða me yldra min   ageaf andsware,
    frod on fyrhðe   fæder reordode,
    'Ongit guma ginga   Godes heahmægen,
465   nergendes naman   se is niða gehwam ...'

Then my parent gave answer to me, wise in heart my father spoke, 'Understand young man God's great power, the Saviour's name, which is to each of men ...'

Binding cross-alliteration does not appear in these lines, as it does in Elene's, and its absence prohibits Judas from integrating his words with those he relates. Furthermore, the style of Sachius's discourse contrasts with his own. The father admonishes the son:

441   Gif þe þæt gelimpe   on lifdagum
        þæt ðu gehyre   ymb þæt halige treo
        frode frignan   7 geflitu ræran
        be ðam sigebeame   on þam soðcyning
445   ahangen wæs,   heofonrices weard,
        eallre sybbe bearn,   þonne þu snude gecyð,
        min swæs sunu,   ær þec swylt nime.
        Ne mæg æfre ofer þæt   Ebrea þeod,
        rædþeahtende   rice healdan,
450   duguðm wealdan   ac þara dom leofað
        7 hira dryhtscipe
        in woruld weorulda   willum gefylled
        ðe þone ahangnan cyning   heriaþ 7 lofiað.

If it should happen to you in the days of your life that you should hear wise men ask and raise dispute about the holy tree, about the tree of victory on which the true King was hanged, the Lord of heaven, the Child of all peace, then, my dear son, speak quickly before death should take you. Thereafter the deliberating people of the Hebrews can never hold the kingdom, rule men, but their fame and authority will live for ever and ever for those who, filled with joy, honour and praise the hanged King.

These lines are rife with Christian diction and employ a recapitulating þæt clause in a manner typical of Elene, not of Judas. The style of the passage implies the speaker's acceptance of the doctrine it contains. Similarly, Sachius's response (lines 464–527) to Judas's next question (why did the Jews crucify Christ if they knew he was the son of God?) is a further elaboration of Christian doctrine and a further display of many of the iconographic features that characterize Elene's dialogue. The structure resembles that of Elene's first speech: basically triadic ('næfre ic' [468a]; 'ne meahton' [477a]; 'þonne broðor þin' [489b]), it begins with praise of God (464–7) and closes with an exhortation to Judas (511–27). Sachius claims that he opposed the Crucifixion, and he testifies to the power of Christ in overcoming death and in converting Saul, the persecutor of Christians such as Judas's brother, Stephen. The speech moves chronologically through the events preceding and following the Crucifixion, as well as through the Crucifixion itself. The use of the imperative mood ('ongit guma ginga,' understand young man [464a]), also characteristic of the iconographic portions of the poem,[27] augments the sense of movement, while variational chiasmus and paronomasia enhance the sense of rhetorical control. The first occurs in lines 486–8: 'ealles leohtes leoht / lifgende aras, // ðeoden engla / 7 his þegnum, // soð sigora frea / seolfne geywde' (the Light of all light living arose, the Prince of angels and his thanes; the true Lord of victories revealed himself). The second occurs in line 482: 'of rode ahæfen / rodera wealdend' (the Ruler of the heavens was taken down from the Cross). Sachius's concluding exhortation to Judas forms a logical and fitting extension of his speech:

```
511   Nu ðu meaht gehyran,     hæleð min se leofa,
      hu arfæst is     ealles wealdend
      þeah we æbylgð wið hine     oft gewyrcen,
      synna wunde     gif we sona eft
515   þara bealudæda     bote gefremmaþ
      7 þæs unrihtes     eft geswicaþ.
      Forðan ic soðlice     7 min swæs fæder
      syðþan gelyfdon
      þæt geþrowade     eallra þrymma God,
520   lifes lattiow     laðlic wite
      for oferþearfe     ilda cynnes.
      Forðan ic þe lære     þurh leoðorune,
      hyse leofesta,     þæt ðu hospcwide,
      æfst ne eofulsæc     æfre ne fremme,
525   grimne geagncwide     wið Godes bearne;
      þonne ðu geearnast     þæt bið ece lif,
      selust sigeleana     seald in heofonum.
```

Now you may hear, my loved man, how gracious is the Lord of all, although we often commit transgression against him, wound him with sins, if we will immediately afterwards work remedy for the evil deeds and desist from wrong. Therefore truly I and my dear father after believed that the God of all glories, the Leader of life, had suffered hateful torment because of the great need of the race of men. Therefore, I instruct you through wise counsel, dearest youth, that you should never express blasphemy, envy or slander, grim answer, against God's Child; then you will earn that eternal life, the best of victory rewards given in heaven.

The fidelity of Sachius's words to the Latin source[28] does not undermine the conclusions reached here, for that fidelity fits the pattern of change we have already seen Cynewulf effect. The alterations necessary elsewhere, especially in Elene's second speech, where Cynewulf imposes a triadic structure, apparently are not necessary here. After the close of Judas's speech, however, Cynewulf does alter the original version, which tends to obscure the schematic structure he seeks to outline. When Judas asks the Jews what he should do if questioned about the Cross, they advise him unequivocally in the Latin source:

> Nos talia numquam audivimus, qualia a te hodie dicta sunt. Si ergo inquisitio facta fuerit de hoc, vide ne ostendas. Manifeste autem qui haec dicis et locum nosti.   (Kent, 39)

> We have never heard such things as you have told us today. So if there is an inquiry about this, make sure you reveal nothing. Since you tell us this, you obviously know the place.   (Allen and Calder, 64)

The Old English version reads:

Næfre we hydron   hæleð ænigne
on þysse þeode   butan þec nuða,
540   þegn oðerne   þyslic cyðan
ymb swa dygle wyrd;   do swa þe þynce,
fyrngidda frod,   gif ðu frugnen sie
on wera corðre.   Wisdomes beðearf,
worda wærlicra   7 witan snyttro
545   se ðære æðelan sceal   andwyrde agifan
for þyslicne   þreat on meþle.

We have never heard any man from this nation except you just now, any other thane, thus speak about so secret an event; do what seems best to you, wise in ancient lore, if you should be questioned in the company of men. He has need of wisdom, of cunning words and of the wisdom of a sage, who must give answer to the noble woman in council before this troop.

In these lines Cynewulf shifts all responsibility to Judas so that he will be as much a free agent as a representative of the Jews in his discussions with Elene. The poet thus insures a focus on individual conversion.

The tendency towards closure in Judas's dialogue, evident in lines 426–30a, is likewise manifest in the overall structure of his first speech (419b–535). Anderson points out that the entire speech is circular and based on a kind of chiastic arrangement of parts beginning with 'Ic wat geare,' (I know well [419b]), ending with 'Nu ge geare cunnon' (Now you know well [531b]), and having the Crucifixion in between (454–521). Judas rhetorically and figuratively conceals the Cross through the speech's 'asymmetrical dislocation.'[29] Circularity and closure become even more pronounced in Judas's confrontations with Elene, where his personal style dominates. His first response to Elene's interrogation has occasioned numerous comments from numerous critics, who mainly point to the irony of Judas's referring to the parable of the bread and stone. Jackson J. Campbell observes that because of the Eucharistic associations of the bread, Judas's speech 'loses most of its power to inspire pity,'[30] while Gordon Whatley demonstrates that perhaps the greatest irony of the speech comes from Judas's actually choosing the hard instead of the soft.[31] In either case, the rhetorical device functions as it does in *Juliana*: by making the speaker's words turn back upon him, it undermines his strategy and his control of language.

Judas takes his stand as follows:

> Hu mæg þæm geweorðan   þe on westenne
> meðe 7 meteleas   morland trydeð,
> hungre gehæfted   7 him hlaf 7 stan
> on gesihðe bu geweorðað
> 615   stea[r]c 7 hnesce,   þæt he þone stan nime
> wið hungres hleo,   hlafes ne gime,
> gewende to wædle   7 þa wiste wiðsæce,
> beteran wiðhyccge   þonne he bega beneah.

How may that happen for the one who in the wilderness, weary and without food, treads the moorland oppressed with hunger and to him bread and stone both appear to his vision, the hard and the soft, that he should take the stone for refuge against hunger, heed not the bread, turn to want and refuse the food, scorn the better when he might have both at his disposal.

Two additional and central points need to be made here about this passage. First, the irony is part of the complex web of language that creates the double focus or ambiguity of the poem's first half. Judas may deserve ridicule in his role as an adversary of Christianity, but as a future saint, one about to become part of Christ's body or the communion of saints, he understandably uses proleptic language.[32] Judas's reference to the parable of the bread and stone is the first of a number of increasingly specific associations of the Jew with the Saviour. Second, the structure of the speech reflects its evasive strategy. The Latin source is direct: 'Et quis in solitudine constitutus, panibus sibi appositis, lapides manducat?'[33] The Old English account, however, becomes a complex syntactic knot, consisting of a single sentence. The recapitulating þæt clause (line 615b) occurs midway through the speech, four lines distant from the anticipatory 'þæm,' which it must clarify. The syntactic hiatus delays the meaning and forces us to concentrate as much on the surface of the language as on the message borne. Similar to the delay caused by Affricanus's use of a suspended recapitulating þæt clause in *Juliana* (119–29),[34] the one here becomes one more indication of the speaker's diminished rhetorical cunning.

Even more inwardly directed than the first, Judas's second response to Elene turns on a circular argument:

> Hu mæg ic þæt findan   þæt swa fyrn gewearð
> wintra gangum?   Is nu worn sceacen
> tu hund oððe ma   geteled rime;
> 635   ic ne mæg areccan   nu ic þæt rim ne can;
> is nu feal[a] siðþan   forð gewitenra
> frodra 7 godra   þe us fore wæron
> gleawra gumena;   ic on geogoðe wearð
> on siðdagum   syððan acenned
> 640   cnihtgeong hæleð;   ic ne can þæt ic nat
> findan on fyrhðe   þæt swa fyrn gewearð.

How can I find that which happened so long ago in the course of winters? A great many have now passed away, two hundred or more reckoned in numbers; I cannot declare now since I do not know the number; now afterwards many of wise and good and sagacious men who were before us have departed; I in youth was born afterwards a young man in later times; I cannot find in my heart what I do not know, what happened so long ago.

The circularity begins and ends with the clause 'þæt swa fyrn gewearð' (what happened so long ago), which creates antistrophe;[35] and it is compounded by the lack of logical development between the two instances of the formula. The recapitulating þæt clause in line 632b represents a dead end. Rather than opening a new area of knowledge to the reader, as such clauses do in Elene's discourse, it closes an area of knowledge to which Judas patently has access. Two other features intensify the sense of closure. First, the anaphoric first-person singular pronoun – the first-person plural appears in the Latin source – concentrates the speech on the individual, Judas.[36] Second, the speech's inward direction is emphasized by its centripetal movement, beginning with the external world of history and ending in Judas's internal world: 'Ic ne can þæt ic nat // findan on fyrhðe / þæt swa fyrn gewearð' (I cannot find in my heart what I do not know, what happened so long ago). The ineffectuality of his words, underscored finally in the tautologia of lines 638b ('on geogoðe,' in youth) and 640a ('cnihtgeong hæleð,' young man), reflects Judas's stubborn retreat into self.

The retreat culminates in a disintegration of personal style. The Judas of lines 656–61 is a dejected and trapped character,[37] as the two speeches which remain before his conversion illustrate. Both show a certain loss of rhetorical control as the weight of truth builds against Elene's opponent. Judas responds impotently to the saint's relentless logic:

> We þæs hereweorces,   hlæfdige min,
> for nydþearfe   nean myndgiaþ
> 7 þa wiggþræce   on gewritu setton,
> þeoda gebæru   7 þis næfre
> 660   þurh æniges mannes   muð gehyrdon,
> hæleðu[m] cyðan   butan her nuða.

> We remember that warfare close at hand by necessity, my lady, and in writing set down the strife, the behaviour of nations, and have never heard this through the mouth of any man revealed to men except here just now.

A pair of deficiencies mars Judas's lines. Loss of power results from a careless manipulation of alliterative stress, for in three of the six lines, particles ('nean' [657b]; 'þis' [659b]; 'her' [661b]) determine alliteration for no apparent rhetorical reason. In all of Judas's previous 134 lines of dialogue particles take alliterative stress only three times (434b, 507b, 639b). Finally, although he does not employ chiasmus in the speech preceding this one, the other structural and rhetorical weaknesses in these lines make its absence particularly noticeable. Judas ultimately descends into a self-centred plea for mercy, beginning with a clause associated with the tormented demon in *Juliana* (446a, 539a) and with the unsanctified Beccel in *Guthlac B* (1203a):

Ic eow healsie   þurh heofona God
700 þæt ge me of ðyssum earfeðum   up forlæten,
heanne fram hungres geniðlan;   ic þæt halige treo
lustum cyðe   nu ic hit leng ne mæg
helan for hungre;   is þes hæft to ðan strang,
þreanyd þæs þearl   7 þes þroht to ðæs heard
705 dogorrimum;   ic adreogan ne mæg
ne leng helan   be ðam lifes treo
þeah ic ær mid dysige   þurhdrifen wære
7 þæt soð to late   seolf gecneowe.

I beseech you by the God of the heavens that you should loose me,
wretched from the torment of hunger, from these tortures; I will
gladly make known that holy tree, now that I can no longer conceal
it because of hunger; this captivity is so strong, the cruel necessity
so severe, and this affliction so hard in daily number; I cannot endure, nor longer conceal the tree of life, although earlier I was per-
meated with folly and too late knew that truth for myself.[38]

Judas's cry from the pit, of course, marks the turning point in his spiritual
development, and the shifting perspective in the poem stops here, as Cynewulf now links Judas to the body of saints. Judas's subsequent invocation to
God (725–801; 807–26) takes on the static rhetorical qualities of the stylistic icon.

The invocation conforms structurally to Elene's first and second speeches
and to Sachius's speech embedded in Judas's first: Judas offers an introductory section, praising God the Creator (lines 725–34a), follows the introduction with a tripartite discussion of good angels (734b–59), fallen angels
(759b–71), and Christ's imminent rule on earth, contingent upon the discovery of the Cross (772–92a), and concludes with a petition: 'Forlæt nu,
lifes Fruma, // of ðam wangstede / wynsumne up, // under radores ryne, /
rec astigan // lyftlacende' (Now, Author of life, let a joyful smoke, moving
about in the air under the orbit of the heavens, rise up from that place
[792–5a]). The sense of movement and openness, dominant in Elene's dialogue, also characterizes this speech. We have seen, for example, that the
overall structure of Judas's first speech is circular, reflecting his desire to
conceal his knowledge about the location of the Cross. The structure of his
invocation, on the other hand, is linear, chronologically relating the events
of salvation history from Creation to Doomsday.[39] The logical development
of the speech therefore augments the sense of openness it creates, and both
the imperative mood and the alliterative stress, which here tends to fall on

substantives or finite verbs, intensify that sense. Furthermore, in lines 735b ('up'), 738b ('þinre'), 766b ('þinum'), 769b ('þin'), and 776b ('þin') alliteration reinforces a rhetorical point: no longer inward directed, Judas emphasizes forces outside himself and ceases to focus on the individual *I*. In his seventy-six-line invocation Judas uses the pronoun 'ic' only twice (788a, 795b), a significant change over his earlier practice.

Judas has rejected the personal style and embraced the iconographic, as his use of chiasmus and indirect discourse show. The former device appears here once again, initially in what Schaar terms a 'studied triple nominal chiasmus':[40]

> 7 þu geworhtest   þurh þines wuldres miht
> heofon 7 eorðan   7 holmþræce,
> sæs sidne fæðm   samod ealle gesceaft,
> 7 þu amæte   mundum þinum
> 730 ealne ymbhwyrft   7 uprador ...

and you make through the might of your glory the heaven and the earth and the stormy sea, the wide bosom of the deep together with all creation, and you measure with your hands all the orb and firmament ...

Judas uses the device again in lines 757b–9a: 'Heardecg cwacaþ, // beofað brogdenmæl' (The hard edge quakes, quivers the patterned sword). And he employs a chiastic arrangement in lines 776b–82:

> gif he þin nære,
> sunu synna leas   næfre he soðra swa feala,
> in woruldrice,   wundra gefremede
> dogorgerimum   no ðu of deaðe hine
> 780 swa þrymlice,   þeoda wealdend,
> aweahte for weorodum   gif he in wuldre þin
> þurh ðe beorhtan   bearn ne wære –

if he were not your Son without sins, he never would have performed in the earthly kingdom so many of true wonders in his number of days, nor would you, Ruler of nations, so mightily have raised him from death, awakened him before the troops, if he were not your Son in glory through the bright Virgin.[41]

The use of indirect discourse in Judas's invocation represents an important departure from his former usage and shows him to have the immediate

spiritual awareness of an Elene or a Juliana. Lines 750–3a coincide perfectly
with the purpose of Judas's initial exclamation – to praise God and his lim-
itless power. Judas describes part of the race of angels, then quotes the
Seraphim:

> singaþ in wuldre
> hædrum stefnum   heofoncyninges lof,
> woða wlitegast   7 þas word cweðaþ,
> clænum stefnum –   þam is Ceruphin nama –
> 750 'Halig is se halga   heahengla God,
> weoroda wealdend;   is ðæs wuldres ful
> heofun 7 eorðe   7 eall heahmægen
> tire getacnod.

[They] sing in glory with clear voices the praise of the heavenly
King, the most beautiful of songs, and utter these words with pure
voices – they are named the Seraphim – 'Holy is the holy God of
the high angels, the Ruler of hosts; heaven and earth are full of his
glory, and all his sublime power is shown forth in honour.'

Note also here the binding force of plurilinear alliteration. An *s* strand begins in line 746b ('singaþ,' 'stefnum,' 'stefnum'), followed by *h* ('hædrum,'
'heofoncyninges,' 'halig,' 'halga,' 'heahengla,' 'heofun,' and 'heahmægen')
and *w* strands ('woða,' 'wlitegast,' 'word,' 'weoroda,' 'wealdend,' and
'wuldres') that extend into the quoted passage. The repetition of 'wuldor'
(746b and 751b) further ensures the alliterative – and rhetorical –
tightness.[42]
 In his invocation Judas demonstrates that his new-found faith causes him
to assimilate, not merely articulate, the principal truths of Christianity. He
has been purged, and his dialogue and spiritual state become Elene's. Here-
after, his new, unified voice appears in his remaining speeches in a consistent and effective use of iconographic features. Each speech, for example, is
characterized by the imperative mood. And each returns to stressing substantives and finite verbs, except when disruption of the pattern would be
rhetorically meaningful, as in line 816, where 'minra' takes alliterative
stress to emphasize Judas's individual culpability ('þæt þu ma ne sie /
minra gylta,' that you should not be mindful any more of my guilts).
Chiasmus also appears in two of the speeches (813–14a and 1181b–3a), and
the open use of the recapitulating þæt clause appears once (1167). In addition, two of the speeches have triadic structures, that of lines 807–26 being
signalled by 'nu ic' (807a), 'nu ic' (813a), and 'læt mec' (818b) while 'þæt'
(1167a), 'þæt' (1175b), and 'þis' (1186b) mark the structural and rhetorical

ELENE

Speech	Triad	Imperative	Chiasmus	Recapitulation
288–319	yes	yes	yes	yes
333–76	yes	yes	yes (3)	yes
386–96	yes			
574–84			yes	
643–54	yes			yes
670–82			yes	yes
1073–92	yes	yes	yes	
Short speeches				
406–10		yes		
605–8		yes		
621–6	yes	yes		
663–6				
686–90				yes
852–8		yes		yes

JUDAS (Cyriacus)

Speech	Triad	Imperative	Chiasmus	Recapitulation
419–535			yes (4)	yes
611–18			yes	yes
632–41				yes
656–61				
699–708				
725–801	yes	yes	yes (2)	yes
807–26	yes	yes	yes	
939–52		yes		
1167–95	yes	yes	yes	yes

sections of lines 1167–95. The chart above summarizes the major iconographic features appearing in the discourse of both saints.

Having dealt with the saints' discourse, we have yet not dealt with all of the major speeches in the poem. As in the other four saints' lives, the devil must make an appearance in this one, and at the instant when he seems most likely to lose part of his human treasure. But the devil's role is simpler in *Elene* than in a poem such as *Juliana* or even *Guthlac A*; he exists primarily to validate Judas's new voice by offering a contrast to it much like the contrast provided by Judas's now-discarded personal style. The devil's single speech contains material stylistically antithetical to the poem's iconography, and Judas's resistance to the devil's rhetoric implies a permanent attachment to the holy life.

In the first part of his speech the devil depicts himself as a victim:

>   Hwæt is þis, la, manna   þe minne eft
>   þurh fyrngeflit   folgaþ wyrdeð,
>   iceð ealdne nið,   æhta strudeð?
> 905 Þis is singal sacu;   sawla ne moton,
>   manfremmende   in minum leng
>   æhtum wunigan;   nu cwom elþeodig
>   þone ic ær on firenum   fæstne talde,
>   hafað mec bereafod   rihta gehwylces,
> 910 feohgestreona;   nis ðæt fæger sið.
>   Feala me se hælend   hearma gefremede,
>   niða nearolicra,   se ðe in Nazareð
>   afeded wæs;   syððan furþum weox
>   of cildhade   symle cirde to him
> 915 æhte mine;   ne mot ænige nu
>   rihte spowan;   is his rice brad
>   ofer middangeard,   min is geswiðrod,
>   ræd under roderum;   ic þa rode ne þearf
>   hleahtre herigean;   hwæt, se hælend me
> 920 in þam engan ham   oft getynde
>   geomrum to sorge.

Lo, what man is this who again through ancient strife destroys my retinue, increases the old enmity, robs my possessions? This is perpetual strife; sinful souls can no longer dwell in my possession; now a stranger has come, one whom I earlier supposed bound fast in sins, has bereft me of each of rights, of treasures; that is not a fair experience. The Lord to me has done many harms, grievous enmities, he who was reared in Nazareth; as soon as he grew from childhood, he always turned my possessions to himself; now I cannot succeed in any right; his kingdom is broad throughout the earth; mine is diminished, my counsel under the heavens; I have no need to praise the Cross with exultation; lo, the Lord often enclosed me in that narrow home as a sorrow to the sorrowful.

The sense of closure that marks Judas's initial dialogue also marks these words. An excessive use of first-person pronouns (lines 902b, 906b, 908a, 911a, 915a, 917b, 918b, 919b) makes clear that the devil views himself as victim, but it also shows that the focus of the speech is inward. Alliterative stress intensifies the effect: in lines 902b, 906b, 915a, 917b (and 929b – '7 manþeawum / minum folgaþ,' and will follow my sinful custom) the possessive pronoun becomes metrically dominant, governing the alliterative pattern of the lines in all cases except line 915a. Our attention moves to the recipient of the action, not to the action itself, and the speech's power decreases. Other alliterative pairings in the first part of the speech detract from its potential for movement. Finite verbs take major stress only twice (904a and 914b), and both times the devil's opponent, not the devil, performs the action.

The devil's shift from object to subject in the second part of the speech represents a grammatical change but not a change in the speech's impact. The imperative mood does not appear, and the focus remains fixed on the devil, since three instances of the pronoun 'ic' occur in five lines (921b–6a), a rather high concentration for this poem. Only Judas, in lines 632–41 and 699–708, uses the pronoun more frequently. The controlled power the devil wishes to convey diminishes further because of a piling of paratactic constructions. He simply protests too much, employing a succession of parallel clauses whose rhetorical and emotional impact must substitute for real strength:[43]

	ic awecce wið ðe	
	oðerne cyning	se ehteð þin
	7 he forlæteð	lare þine
	7 manþeawum	minum folgaþ
930	ond þec þonne sendeð	in þa sweartestan
	7 þa wyrrestan	witebrogan
	þæt ðu sarum forsoht	wiðsæcest fæste
	þone ahangnan cyning	þam ðu hyrdest ær.

I will raise another king against you, one who will persecute your [followers?] and will despise your teaching and will follow my sinful custom and will send you then into the blackest and the worst of terrible punishments, so that you, afflicted with pains, will firmly renounce the hanged King, whom you obeyed before.

The devil's discourse closely resembles Judas's personal style and thus becomes emblematic of the capacity for evil that Judas had within him before his conversion, before his giving himself over to his innate capacity for good.

Direct discourse in *Elene* has not received much praise, since it sometimes seems too expository and, in Elene's case, always too static. She consistently employs a stylistic ideal which places her in the company of the Old English saints and which, to many, makes her speeches tedious clichés, embodiments of an intense didacticism, having 'virtually no dramatic or narrative function.'[44] But the static structure of her dialogue does not conceal its unmistakable power, which functions significantly in Judas's conversion. She melds the static form with the powerful message of her faith, which, because absolute, is uniform, resilient, unmoveable. Judas's early discourse interests us more than hers because it displays more fluctuation. And that is the theological point. He vacillates, so his words do also. The form of his dialogue before he speaks in a new voice is kinetic, but its substance is static; it goes nowhere, and its syntax and meaning turn in upon themselves in an ever-constricting ring of darkness and futility. Judas's liberation, then, is a liberation to the stasis of his mentor's dialogue, distasteful though that stasis may be to a modern sensibility. Cynewulf gives direct discourse thematic prominence and links it to paronomasia and other rhetorical and poetic elements to make his message clear: the opening up of Judas's dialogue, the ultimate separation of 'man' from 'mann' in the poem's concluding lines, and the unearthing of the Cross finally become related aspects of a single redeeming act.[45]

CHAPTER FOUR

The Artist of the Beautiful: Immutable Discourse in *Guthlac B*

In the Old English saints' lives thus far discussed we have seen the poets use direct discourse and its syntactic and rhetorical features consistently, subordinating them to larger thematic matters and to the total poetic vision of their works. Despite the complex execution in the first two poems, both always focus unequivocally on the saints themselves and serve clear didactic purposes. *Elene*, however, more complex, more subtle, yet still unmistakably didactic, tends to shift focus from Elene to her antagonist (or victim), as Cynewulf manifests his theme by elaborating the character of the human, vacillating Judas, who becomes the poem's real subject. The pain and spiritual struggle of the developing Cyriacus ultimately gains thematic and structural prominence.

The narrative in *Guthlac B* has similar focus, and our attention shifts even more strongly towards a human character, so that while we perceive the saint's spiritual victory, we simultaneously fix our attention on Beccel's very real agony. Guthlac's relationship with his servant is a major concern and functions as an integral part of the overriding theme, compelling us to consider Beccel's relationship to and understanding of death. We never grieve for the 'dying' Guthlac, after all, for his joy is consummate and eternal, his belief inflexible; we do grieve for the 'living' Beccel, who in his lack of a perfect faith paradoxically suffers the pangs of a more significant weakness – his humanity and attendant mutability. Much of the poem's meaning derives from this shift in focus. The life becomes not so much a description of a saint's physical demise as an exemplum on how to overcome death; and the already victorious Guthlac, who provides the example of steadfast faith, becomes less the object of interest for the reader than does his fallible servant, who serves as a painful reflection of ourselves. A study of direct discourse illuminates how the poet creates his exemplum, but before we turn to it, we must first review the death theme itself and its relationship both to a second theme, beauty, and to the poem's typology.

If the general concept of death forms the central subject matter of *Guthlac B*, the precise nature of death is the poem's primary concern. The poem, says James L. Rosier, might as easily be termed one 'on the subject of death, or the coming of Death, as a poetic account of the last days of a particular saint.'[1] Rosier, of all commentators on the poem, has done the most thorough explication of the death theme, showing that the poet conceives of death as a separation of soul from body; and further, that he structures his imagery and the development of his poem accordingly, expanding a mere hint from his Latin source, Felix's *Vita Sancti Guthlaci*. Thus, in 'varied lexical compositions'[2] such as 'bancofa,' 'lichord,' 'banfæt,' 'banhus,' 'banloca,' and 'sawelhus' the interest in the death-as-separation motif can be seen playing, while the predominating terms for death give it yet more weight:[3] 'gæstgedal,' 'deaðgedal,' 'sawelgedal,' 'lifgedal,' 'nydgedal,' 'feorggedal,' and 'þeodengedal.'

Though Rosier makes an invaluable contribution to the study of the poem, he fails to establish precisely what thematic function the stylistic features serve. He does not consider the larger vision, which incorporates a concept of the beautiful and the loss of beauty through sin as a correlate of the death theme.[4] The two themes of death and beauty, however, are interdependent. Each reflects the division or separation – of soul from body and beauty from life – that man must endure because of sin. The entrance of death causes the loss of beauty, and in *Guthlac B* the poet has altered the Latin source so that the themes become part of a complex typological structure. As the poem advances, the poet clearly shows how the saint's deeds reverse the destructive process that sin has initiated.[5] Becoming an obvious type of Christ, Guthlac ultimately re-enacts the redeeming, revivifying ritual of Christ's death and resurrection.

The poet makes the identification of Christ and Guthlac manifest by variously developing the nascent typology of the Latin life. In the opening fourteen lines, for instance, the poet takes what is in Felix's account a simple allusion to Adam's bringing death into the world and turns it into an extended discussion of the first man's creation, thus elaborating the typological associations among Adam, Christ, and Guthlac.[6] At another point in Felix's treatment of Guthlac's life we find an intimation of alignment between the saint and Christ, but the two figures remain distinct: 'Interea, decursis quaternarum dierum articulis, dies Paschae pervenit; in qua vir Dei contra vires exsurgens, immolato dominici corporis sacrificio et gustato sanguinis Christi libamine, praefato fratri verbum Dei evangelizare coepit' (Meanwhile four days had passed away hour by hour, and Easter Day arrived. On it the man of God rose in spite of his weakness and, having of-

fered the sacrifice of the Lord's body and tasted the outpoured blood of
Christ, he began to preach the word of God to this same brother [154 and
155]).[7] The Old English, however, establishes that Guthlac and Christ –
two conquerors of death – are one:

> Ða se wuldormaga   worda gestilde,
> 1095 rof runwita: wæs him ræste neod
> reonigmodum.   Rodor swamode
> ofer niðða bearn,   nihtrim scridon
> deorc ofer dugeðum.   Þa se dæg bicwom
> on þam se lifgenda   in lichoman
> 1100 ece ælmihtig   ærist gefremede,
> dryhten mid dreame,   ða he of deaðe aras,
> onwald of eorðan   in þa eastortid,
> ealra þrymma þrym   – ðreata mæstne
> to heofonum ahof,   ða he from helle astag.
> 1105 Swa se eadga wer   in þa æþelan tid
> on þone beorhtan dæg,   blissum hremig,
> milde 7 gemetfæst   mægen unsofte
> elne geæfnde.[8]

Then the glorious man stilled his words, the brave sage: rest was a
necessity to him, weary in spirit. The skies grew dark over the sons
of men; a number of nights glided by, dark over the troops. Then
the day came on which the Living, the Eternal, Almighty brought
about a resurrection in the body, the Lord with a host, when he rose
from death powerful from the earth in the Easter time, glory of all
glories, raised to the heavens the greatest of hosts, when he as-
cended from hell. So the blessed man in that noble time on that
bright day rejoicing in bliss, mild and modest, with courage severely
performed a feat of strength.

The typology of the liturgical week further aligns Guthlac with Christ;
both ascend on the eighth day.[9] By developing his two major themes
(beauty and death) and by carefully structuring direct discourse in the
poem, the poet elaborates the Christ-Guthlac identification still more.
Guthlac transcends death with Christ and speaks the message of that tran-
scendence to Beccel and the reader. He is the eþelboda – the homeland (of
heaven) announcer[10] – who places the immutable joy of glory before himself and Beccel as a goal and offers the model of his unswerving fortitude,
made palpable in his unchanging discourse, as the means for attaining that
goal. The salient features of his dialogue tie it to the descriptive portions of

the poem dealing with the beauty of heaven and solidify his identification with the Conqueror of death.

We may begin the discussion of direct discourse with Rosier's treatment of narrative style in the poem, since Guthlac's has close, typologically purposeful affinities with it. Rosier states that 'the patterns of repetition, recomposition, and balance, which occur in the configurations based on *lic ond sawel*, are typical of the style of *Guthlac B*,'[11] adding that they typify Old English poetic style generally but do not occur elsewhere in such profusion. So, for example, with the figure of death-as-trespasser seeking to plunder the body's (door's, house's, hoard's) treasure, the poet begins with a general description of the action,[12] then employs 'many lexical and phrasal recombinations' to develop the metaphor: death approaches, and the door 'sona ontyneð, // ingong geopenað' (immediately uncloses itself, the entrance opens [992b–3a]). Disease oppressed Guthlac's bone-coffer, and his body-hoard was unlocked ('lichord onlocen' [956a]); suffering entered, unlocked the body-hoard ('lichord onleac' [1029a]); death unlocked the life-hoard ('feorhhord onleac' [1144b]) and sought it with cunning keys ('searocægum gesoht' [1145a]). The 'grit-hoard' (body) mourns ('greothord gnornað' [1266a]).[13]

The same principle applies throughout the poem, as Rosier demonstrates in an analysis of lines 894–910, which show the poet's preference for 'parallel phrases with lexical repetition (duguþa *by*scyrede ... hiwes *bi*notene, / dreamum *bi*drorene; *Hwilum* wendende ... *hwilum* cyrdon *eft* ... *hwilum* brugdon *eft*, 907–10),' in contrast with Felix's 'prolix culling of synonyms and odd words in series (bestiarum hinnitus, grunnitus, crocitusque, pp. 114–15).'[14] Similarly, in lines 1278–95 the poet develops the motif of light overcoming darkness by employing a number of rhetorical devices. He uses balanced antithetical words, such as 'under' and 'ofer,' as well as 'multiple lexical generation (e.g. æþela ... æþele ymb æþelne, halig ... halge hus, heofonum ... heofonlic, etc.)' and 'ablaut pairs (glæm ... glæm ... æfenglome, ende-dogor ... dægred-woma).'[15]

Rosier's stylistic analysis suggests symmetry as a basic aesthetic principle in the poem: one sound balances another; one pattern of imagery echoes and develops a previous pattern until the principle culminates in Guthlac's transfiguration through death. The *Guthlac B* poet thus obeys one of the rules of iconography, a rule based on 'a kind of sacred mathematics' that emphasizes the importance of symmetry, number, and harmony,[16] all of which lie behind the poem's ideal of beauty.

The exploitation of the harmonious and the symmetrical, of course, has theological import. In its more sophisticated forms Christian art suggested those numbers that govern all creation, and thus it ultimately suggested the supreme Creator, or God.[17] Poetry and music likewise functioned as *specula*

reflecting the universal order, as Augustine in book 6 of *De musica* and
Boethius in *De institutione musica* both attest.[18] The patterns of repetition,
parallelism, and balance in *Guthlac B*, then, coincide with the ultimate harmonious ideal; and the saint's dialogue here, as in all the Old English lives,
attaches itself to that ideal.

Like the speeches of Juliana and Elene, Guthlac's first contains the iconographic features tying him to the body of saints, and it offers an abstract
scheme that would allow Beccel – or the reader – to cleave to the unchanging realm of heaven. Responding to Beccel's insistent questioning, he
states:

> Ic wille secgan   þæt me sar gehran,
> wærc in gewod   in ðisse wonnan niht,
> lichord onleac;   leomu hefegiað,
> 1030 sarum gesohte.   Sceal þis sawelhus,
> fæge flæschoma   foldærne biþeaht,
> leomu, lames geþacan,   legerbedde fæst
> wunian wælræste.   Wiga nealæceð
> unlæt laces: ne bið þæs lengra swice
> 1035 sawelgedales   þonne seofon niht
> fyrstgemearces   þæt min feorh heonan
> on þisse eahteþan   ende geseceð,
> dæg scriþende.   Þonne dogor beoð
> on moldwege   min forð scriþen,
> 1040 sorg gesweðrad,   7 ic siþþan mot
> fore meotudes cneowum   meorda hleotan,
> gingra geafena,   7 Godes lomber
> in sindreamum   siþþan awo
> forð folgian.   Is nu fus ðider
> 1045 gæst siþes georn,   nu þu gearwe const
> leoma lifgedal: long is þis onbid
> worulde lifes.

I will say that pain seized me, suffering entered in during this dark
night, unlocked the body-hoard; my limbs grow heavy, seized with
pains. This soul-house, the fated fleshly home, the covered earth-
house, the limbs, the clay wrappings, fast in the sickbed must dwell
in death-rest. The warrior approaches, ready for the struggle. The
delay until soul parts from body will not be longer than seven
nights in the measurement of time, so that my heart hence on this
eighth will seek its end, the day passing. Then my days on the
earth-way will be past, sorrow stilled, and then before the knees of

the Creator I can share in rewards, in new gifts, and always follow the Lamb of God in eternal joys. Now the spirit, eager for the journey, is ready thither; now you clearly know the life-parting of the limbs: long is this waiting in the life of the world.

Five rhetorical features are important here, beginning with a basic structural one. The principle of balancing equal phonemic, syntactic, or structural units so that they reflect each other is important in the poem generally and operates in this speech's larger rhetorical structure. The speech is relatively equally divided between the concepts of physical death (lines 1027–38a) and eternal life (1038b–47), as Guthlac logically explains his situation, beginning with his earthly plight, moving to his death and imminent joy in heaven, and returning with different emphasis to the undesirable state of earthly existence: 'long is þis onbid // worulde lifes' (long is this waiting in the life of the world [1046b–7a]). A change of tone in the saint's words, from melancholy to happiness, accompanies a change in perspective. In the first half of the speech variation emphasizes the unpleasant notion of physical decay after death (1031b–3a), and a form of the word 'long' focuses attention on the regrettably short time left to Guthlac on earth ('ne bið þæs lengra swice // sawelgedales þonne seofon niht,' the delay until soul parts from body will not be longer than seven nights [1034b–5]); the second half rhetorically balances both the variation (1038b–44a) and the use of the word 'long' (1046b), concentrating on the more important, spiritual aspects of death. The movement of the speech shows Beccel how he should regard Guthlac's and his own demise.

In addition to the repetition of 'long' in the speech, lines 1029a and 1030a ('lichord onleac'; 'sarum gesoht': unlocked the body-hoard; seized with pains) repeat lines 956a and 957a from the narrative ('lichord onlocen'; 'sarum gesohte'), and line 1046b echoes 904b, also from the narrative ('long is þis onbid'; 'ne þæt onbid long': long is this waiting; nor that waiting long). The repetition here and elsewhere in Guthlac's dialogue has two complementary functions which are absent from Beccel's dialogue. Guthlac's using repetition links him positively with the harmonious ideal of the poem, represented in this major stylistic feature; and his nearly verbatim echoing of lines from the narrative functions much as plurilinear alliteration does with indirect discourse in *Elene*: by crossing from one section of the poem into another, it binds those sections together, making them practically undifferentiated. Guthlac's words interact closely with those of the omniscient narrator.

The three remaining features to note in this speech also contrast with those of Beccel's speeches. Least imposing, but still significant, is the use of hypotaxis in lines 1027 and following, and 1034 and following. As we have

seen elsewhere, especially in *Beowulf* and *Juliana*, the rational control manifested through subordination of sentence elements becomes a measure of
the speaker and of his ordered world; in *Guthlac B* the saint displays that
control in his words, but his servant does not. Neither does he show the
fourth rhetorical feature of Guthlac's first utterance. The use of vocalic consonance – a kind of rhyme – in line 1041 ('fore meotudes cneowum /
meorda hleotan,' share in the rewards before the knees of the Creator) further links Guthlac's words to the harmonies of the poet's. This device
should not be underestimated in *Guthlac B*; though rhyme 'cannot be
termed more than occasional'[19] in the poem, its few appearances do enhance
the ideal of the beautiful that is central to the poem's meaning.

Sound harmony, or paromoeosis, forms a direct connection with musical
analogies, from which, as we saw earlier in this chapter, medieval concepts
of beauty derive, analogies again based on number and rhythm.[20] Thus, in
Guthlac B rhyme appears most noticeably in the opening description of
Paradise ('þær him nænges wæs // willan onsyn / ne welan brosnung // ne
lifes lyre / ne lices hryre // ne dreames dryre,' there for him was no lack of
desired things nor decay of happiness nor loss of life nor crumbling of body
nor decline of joy [827b–30a]), reinforcing through sound the description of
the perfect harmony there. The poet employs some form of sound harmony (such as word-repetition or consonance) in several other sections of
the narrative:[21] 'sume ær, sume sið, / sume in urra' (some early, some late,
some in our [876]); 'wide 7 side' (far and wide [882b]); 'eard weardade'
(guarded the abode [897b]); 'ealra þrymma þrym' (glory of all glories
[1103a]); 'leof mon leofum' (the man loved to the beloved [1164a]); 'æþele
ymb æþelne' (noble around the noble one [1287a]); 'breahtem æfter
breahtme. / Beofode þæt ealond, // foldwong onsprong' (resonance after
resonance. The island quaked, the earth burst forth [1325–6a]); 'æfter
sundplegan / sondlond gespearn, // grond wið greote' (after the wave-play
trod the land, ground against the sand [1334–5a]). In addition to these
eight, we may add two more: 'geongum geocor sefa, / geomrende hyge'
(the youth's sad heart, mourning mind [1048]) and 'þrong niht ofer tiht'
(the night thronged over the world [1281b]). Significantly, the poet restricts
the use of sound harmony to the poem's descriptive portions and to the
saint's dialogue.

The fifth and final rhetorical feature of Guthlac's first speech augments
our sense of his linguistic control and occurs in lines 1030b–3a:

> Sceal þis sawelhus,
> 1030 fæge flæschoma   foldærne biþeaht,
> leomu, lames geþacan,   legerbedde fæst
> wunian wælræste.

This soul-house, the fated fleshly home, the covered earth-house, the limbs, the clay wrappings, fast in the sick-bed must dwell in death rest.

In the introduction (page 14) we saw that syntactic disjunction is a fairly common feature of Old English verse but can have aesthetic effect when it disrupts expectations established in the context of a specific poem. So in *The Wanderer*, lines 19–29a, the separation of the modal auxiliary 'sceolde' from the infinitive 'sælan' both reflects the speaker's separation from his homeland and creates a syntactic analogue to his oppressed, 'enclosed' state of mind. In the above lines from *Guthlac B* disjunction appears once more, and again as a deviation from a norm set up in the poetic context.[22] The separation of the auxiliary 'sceal' from the infinitive 'wunian' is an atypical feature of the poem except in direct discourse, where it highlights the linguistic and spiritual differences between the two speakers.

Both saint and servant use disjunction, and it always has aesthetic justification, implying control, in Guthlac's speeches. Beccel, however, shows poor control of the device, never subordinating it to an aesthetic end. In his speeches the words master him, not he the words. The use of disjunction in Guthlac's speech is apt because it disrupts a syntactic expectation, thus calling attention to itself in order to underscore the poem's major theme. The lines deal with death, and the division of the verb's components reveals death's dominant characteristic. Furthermore, the positioning of the auxiliary verb at the beginning and the infinitive at the end of the sentence has much the same effect that such placement does in *The Wanderer*, creating here a syntactic analogue to the embedding, enclosing action of burial.

Guthlac's control of the device has one more purpose: to link his words even more positively with those of the omniscient narrator, who manifests the same control in the only narrative instance where more than one line separates auxiliary and infinitive or linking verb and complement:

>   eal þæt beacen wæs
> 1310 ymb þæt halge hus,   heofonlic leoma
>   from foldan up   swylce fyren tor
>   ryht aræred ...

That beacon was completely around that holy house, the heavenly light, up from the earth like a fiery tower rightly raised.

Again syntax underscores meaning, for between 'wæs' and 'aræred' comes the sentence's substance, which concerns the divine light engulfing the house in which Guthlac's lifeless body lies.[23]

As Guthlac moves towards death, his dialogue remains unweakened, though his physical life wanes. In his second speech he responds to his servant's intense grief:[24]

      Ne beo þu unrot;   ðeah þeos adl me
1065   innan æle,   nis me earfeðe
      to geþolianne   þeodnes willan,
      dryhtnes mines,   ne ic þæs deaðes hafu
      on þas seocan tid   sorge on mode,
      ne ic me herehloðe   helleþegna
1070   swiðe onsitte,   ne mæg synne on me
      facnes frumbearn   fyrene gestælan,
      lices leahtor;   ac in lige sceolon
      sorgwylmum soden   sar wanian,
      wræcsið wepan,   wilna biscirede
1075   in þam deaðsele,   duguða gehwylcre,
      lufena 7 lissa.   Min þæt leofe bearn,
      ne beo þu on sefan to seoc.   Ic eom siþes fus
      upeard niman,   edleana georn
      in þam ecan gefean   ærgewyrhtum,
1080   geseon sigora frean.   Min þæt swæse bearn,
      nis me wracu ne gewin   þæt ic wuldres God
      sece, swegelcyning.   Þær is sib 7 blis,
      domfæstra dream,   dryhten ondweard,
      þam ic georne   gæstgerynum
1085   in þas dreorgan tid,   dædum cwemde,
      mode 7 mægne.   Ic þa meorde wat
      leahtorlease,   lean unhwilen,
      halig on heahþu   þær min hyht myneð
      to gesecenne;   sawul fundað
1090   of licfate   to þam longan gefean
      in eadwelan.   Nis þes eþel me
      ne sar ne sorg.   Ic me sylfum wat
      æfter lices hryre   lean unhwilen.

Do not be sad; although this disease should burn within me, it is no hardship for me to endure the will of the Prince, of my Lord, nor do I have sorrow in mind because of death in this time of illness, nor do I greatly fear the hostile troop of thanes from hell, nor may the first-born child of evil accuse me of sin, of wickedness, crime of the body, but in the flame, afflicted with whelmings of sorrow, they must bewail their pain, lament the exile-journey, stripped of desires in the death-hall of each glory, of hopes and mercies. My dear child, be not sick at heart. I am prepared for the journey, eager to grasp the dwelling of rewards on high in that eternal joy, for former works to see the Lord of victories. My dear child, it is not enmity or strife for me that I seek the God of glory, the heavenly King -- there peace and bliss is, the joy of the faithful -- the present Lord whom with spiritual mysteries, in this dreary time, I pleased with deeds in heart and strength. I knew that flawless reward, eternal requital, holy in the heights. There my hope directs itself; the soul struggles from the body to that long joy in blessedness. This abode is neither pain nor sorrow to me. I know that for me eternal reward awaits after the fall of the body.

Basic to this as to the first speech is the principle of balance. The two references to time here ('on þas seocnan tid' [line 1068a]; 'in þas dreorgan tid' [1085a]) represent complementary, though opposed points of view and a shift in focus similar to that seen in the uses of the word 'long' in lines 1034b and 1046b. The first reference – 'in this time of sickness' – concentrates our attention on the immediate moment of Guthlac's disease and impending death; the second – 'in this sorrowful time' – broadens our perspective, putting Guthlac at once in the realm of all history and above it through the saving power of his saintly deeds. The poet augments the sense of progress in the speech by concentrating a number of negatives in the first eight lines (1064a, 1065b, 1067b, 1069a, 1070b), then counteracting them after the adversative conjunction 'ac' in line 1072b. As Schaar observes, ac constructions tend to be 'restricted to the beginning of the poem and to contrasts between worldly and heavenly life, the saint and the devils, the illness and Guthlac's boldness.'[25] The balanced use of the narrow and broader references to time and the consonant perceptual shift here again imply that the longed-for release from the weakened body has already taken place. Guthlac can disengage himself from the world and its pains and direct his thoughts to the heavenly realms.

Guthlac's second speech exploits other stylistic principles developed in the first. Calder points out that the echo of line 987a ('þurh ærgewyrht,' by former works) in line 1079b ('ærgewyrhtum') sets up a contrast between the works of Adam's descendants, which occasion punishment, and those of the saint, which occasion reward,[26] and thus functions in the poem's typology. Similarly, the close repetition of line 1076b ('min þæt leofe bearn,' my dear child) in line 1080b ('min þæt swæse bearn'), the partial repetition of line 1086b ('ic þa meorde wat,' I knew that reward) in line 1092b ('ic me sylfum wat,' I knew for myself), and the full repetition of line 1087b ('lean unhwilen,' eternal reward) in line 1093b reinforce the stylistic affinities of the saint's dialogue with the poet's narrative,[27] while highlighting Guthlac's consolatory function and his certainty about eternal reward. Rhyme also appears in this speech, with the same effect – of creating a link with the ideal of beauty – that it had previously: lines 1079a and 1080a rhyme together in 'gefean' and 'frean.'[28]

All of the iconographic points discussed thus far appear in Guthlac's third speech (lines 1166–96). Both partial repetition within the speech itself and repetition from other parts of the poem occur here: line 1186b echoes 1181a; 1188a echoes 1184a; 1192b echoes 1182b; and 1166a ('min þæt swæse bearn,' my dear child) is a verbatim repetition of line 1080b in Guthlac's second speech. Though not as prominent in this speech as elsewhere in the poem, paromoeosis nevertheless does appear in lines 1193b–4a ('beorge *bi*fæste, // lame *bi*luce,' should fasten in the mound, should enclose with clay), in 1189 and 1190, where both a-verses begin with 'þær,' and in 1195 and 1196, where both a-verses begin with 'in.' Subordination also appears, and indeed is the dominant syntactic feature (1168b, 1179a, 1183b, 1186a, 1193a); finally, the separation of the auxiliary 'scealt' (1168b) from the infinitive 'gehyran' (1170b) highlights the importance of Guthlac's words and of his approaching death:

> Min þæt swæse bearn,   nis nu swiþe feor
> þam ytemestan   endedogor
> nydgedales   þæt ðu þa nyhstan scealt
> in woruldlife   worda minra
> 1170 næfre leana biloren   lare gehyran
> noht longe ofer þis.

> My dear child, it is not now very far to the outermost final day of death, so that not long after this you must next hear the teaching in this worldly life of the last of my words, never bereft of rewards.[29]

The saint's fourth (lines 1227–69a) and fifth (1295b–99) speeches provide the last instances of the stylistic icon. A balanced, architectonic structure in the fourth speech makes Guthlac's consummate skill and control apparent, his words and deeds one, while it again calls attention to the temporal and to the eternal. The first two and last two sections of the speech (marked respectively by the introductory words 'hwæt' [1227a], 'huru' [1234b], 'nu' [1263b], and 'nu' [1268b]) deal with the temporal aspects of Guthlac's situation: during his last moments, the saint will speak for the first time about his diurnal angelic visitor, and he is now ready for his physical death. Between the references to earthly time come three sections (marked by the introductory words 'symle' [1238a], 'a' [1255a], and 'a' [1262b]) dealing with the healing, edifying power of the visiting angel and Guthlac's lasting love for Beccel.[30]

Repetition also occurs at two points in the fourth speech and has an importance that will later become apparent: 'Hwæt, þu me, wine min, / wordum nægest' (Lo, you, my friend, accost me with words [line 1227]) echoes Beccel's 'ær þu me, frea min, / furþor cyðe' (before you, my lord, should make further known to me [1222]); '7 on morgne eft' (and in the morning again [1243b]) echoes Beccel's '7 on morgne swa' (and in the morning also [1219b]). Likewise, minor instances of sound harmony appear in two places (1235b and 1236b both end in 'mines'; 1267a and 1268a both begin with 'on'), while subordination graces this speech as it does all his others (1228b, 1232a, 1239b, 1251a, 1254a, 1258b).

In his very last speech Guthlac brings the fifth iconographic feature into play:

1295   Tid is þæt þu fere
    7 þa ærendu   eal biþence,
    ofestum læde,   swa ic þe ær bibead,
    lac to leofre.   Nu of lice is,
    goddreama georn,   gæst swiðe fus.

It is time that you should go and consider all the errands, guide the gift hastily, as I earlier bade you, to the beloved. Now from the body, eager for the joys of God, is the spirit greatly ready to depart.

Again, the separation of verb ('is' [line 1298b]) from complement ('fus' [1299b]) symbolically reflects the separation from the body that the soul must experience. This stylistic feature in the Old English takes the place of explicit statement in the Latin source:

Fili mi, praepara te in iter tuum pergere, nam me nunc tempus cogit ab his membris dissolvi, et decursis huius vitae terminis ad infinita gaudia spiritus transtolli malit.   (158)

My son, get ready for your journey, for now the time has arrived for me to be loosed from the body; the end of my life has come and my spirit is eager to be carried away to joys without end.   (159)

Guthlac's dialogue, then, has many features characterizing the saints in the other Old English lives: it too is static and symmetrical, allowing the saint to take on the generalized, immutable essence of the communion of saints. Turning to his servant's three speeches, we find the stylistic icon absent and the words mercurial. In contrast to Guthlac's balanced, reasoned discourse, Beccel's first speech, a considerable amplification of the emotionless Latin, lacks intellectual control. The Latin reads:

Domine mi, quid novi tibi accidit? an forte nocte hac ulla te infirmitatis molestia tetigit? ... Scisne, pater mi, tuae infirmitatis causam,
aut quem finem huius molestae egritudinis esse putas?   (152)

My lord, what new thing has happened to you? Perhaps some illness
has touched you during the night? ... Father, do you know the
cause of your illness, or do you know what the end of this trouble
and sickness will be?   (153)

The Old English poet changes the speech in this way:

```
       Hu gewearð þe þus,    winedryhten min,
       fæder, freonda hleo,    ferð gebysgad,
       nearwe geneged.    Ic næfre þe,
       þeoden leofesta,    þyslicne ær
1015   gemette þus meðne.    Meaht þu meðelcwidum
       worda gewealdan?    Is me on wene geþuht
       þæt þe untrymnes    adle gongum
       on þisse nyhstan    niht bysgade,
       sarbennum gesoht;    þæt me sorgna is
1020   hatost on hreþre    ær þu hyge minne,
       ferð, afrefre.    Wast þu, freodryhten,
       hu þeos adle scyle    ende gesettan?
```

How are you thus, my friendly lord, father, protector of friends, afflicted at heart, closely subdued? I have never, dearest prince, thus
before found you so weary. Can you wield words in speech?
It seems to my mind that the course of the disease afflicted you last
night, beset you with painful wounds; that for me is the hottest of
sorrows in my heart, until you might comfort my mind, my spirit.
Do you know, noble lord, how this disease shall make an end?

If we search for a key to the logic of this speech, we will not find one.
Beccel's reaction is emotional and human; syntactic features of his discourse reflect that condition. Like the Latin, the speech in Old English consists of three questions. But whereas the Latin questions progress
somewhat logically, becoming gradually longer and mutually dependent,
the questions in the Old English are not of graduated length and do not
seem logically connected because of the interspersed observations relevant
to the grieving servant, not to the dying saint. Beccel cannot focus his attention on the objective truth of Guthlac's disease, for that truth has tre-
mendous subjective ramifications. Guthlac is a saint, not an ordinary man,
but the shock of seeing him struck down by sickness makes Beccel aware of

his physical likeness to other men; the servant remarks that 'ic næfre þe ... þyslicne ær // gemette þus meðne' (I have never thus before found you so weary [lines 1013b–15a]). The terrifying realization of Guthlac's approaching death engenders in Beccel doubt that will continue to grow. This first speech is a plea for comfort which he does not receive in the poem as we have it: for me, he laments, Guthlac's sickness is 'hatost on hreþre, / ær þu hyge minne, // ferð, afrefre' (hottest in my heart, until you [Guthlac] might comfort my mind, my spirit [1019b–21a]).

Variation in Beccel's opening question also contributes to the speech's instability.[31] The conceptual variation in the Praise of Ruler topos, the deferential attitude and implication of the saint's superiority running throughout the passage, clashes with the obvious uncertainty of the speaker's real feelings: despite Guthlac's spiritual status, Beccel must recognize that the saint will ultimately die. The poet emphasizes Beccel's unstable emotional state by having Guthlac comfort the distraught servant four times in the poem, while Felix has him do so only once. The variation in Beccel's speech has a definite syntactic impact as well, since it breaks up the major sentence constituents of lines 1011–13a. The disrupted flow causes the rhythm of the sentence to reflect the speaker's faltering emotional condition, as does the predominantly paratactic mode of the entire speech. Taken in contrast to the saint's dialogue, Beccel's first speech seems inept, unadorned by repetition, rhyme, symmetry, or any discernible structure. It is totally removed from the realm of sanctified beauty in which Guthlac moves.

The poet deepens our impression of Beccel in the servant's second speech, as Beccel pleads to the dying saint:

```
       Ic þec halsige,    hæleþa leofost
       gumena cynnes,    þurh gæsta weard
1205   þæt þu hygesorge    heortan minre
       geeþe, eorla wyn.    Nis þe ende feor
       þæs þe ic on galdrum    ongieten hæbbe.
       Oft mec geomor sefa    gehþa gemanode
       hat æt heortan    hyge gnornende
1210   nihtes nearwe    7 ic næfre þe,
       fæder, frofor min,    frignan dorste.
       Symle ic gehyrde    þonne heofones gim,
       wyncondel wera,    west onhylde,
       sweglbeorht sunne,    setlgonges fus
1215   on æfentid    oþerne mid þec
       þegn æt geþeahte.    Ic þæs þeodnes word,
       ares uncuþes    oft neosendes
       dægwoman bitweon    7 þære deorcan niht,
       meþelcwide mæcges    7 on morgne swa
```

1220   ongeat geomormod   gæstes spræce
      gleawes in geardum.   Huru ic giet ne wat
      ær þu me, frea min,   furþor cyðe
      þurh cwide þinne   hwonan his cyme sindon.

I beseech you, dearest of heroes of the race of men, by the Guardian
of spirits that you might alleviate the sorrow of my heart, joy of
men. The end is not far, as I have understood by your divinations.
Often my sad heart of cares admonished me, hot at heart, my mind
mourning closely at night, and I never, father, my consolation,
dared to ask you. Always I heard, when the gem of heaven, the joy
candle of men, reclined in the west, the heaven-bright sun eager for
setting in the evening time, another with you, a thane at council.
The words of the prince, of the unknown messenger visiting often
between dawn and the dark night, the discourse of the man, and in
the morning also, I understood sad at heart, the speech of the spirit,
of the wise one in the yards. Lo, I still do not know until you, my
lord, further make known to me through your speech whence his
comings are.

The speech opens with a phrase we have seen used by the demon in *Juliana*
(lines 446a, 539a) and by Judas in *Elene* (699a) and which is used elsewhere
in Old English poetry by spiritually weak or debased creatures, as in *Christ
and Satan*, line 420; *Descent into Hell*, lines 107 and 118; and *A Prayer*,
line 67. The narrative requirements in *Guthlac B*, of course, are far different from those in the other poems, where the poets basically oppose good
to evil. In this poem the central opposition arises between a sanctified human and an ordinary mortal, who is also a Christian. Only a few stylistic
options, however, were available to poets creating visions of perfect and imperfect or good and evil worlds, and so some devices used to define the
realm of evil were also used to define the realm of mortals. Beccel's use of
'Ic þec halsige,' then, does not equate him with the devil; it merely helps
put him more unequivocally in the company of unsanctified men. Because
his deeds are not perfect, neither can his words be.
    The rest of Beccel's second speech intensifies our feelings of his imperfec-
tion. Again the variation in lines 1203–6a and in 1208–11 reflects an obsequious attitude and adds nothing to the argument or to the coherence of
the speech. Again major sentence constituents are broken up for no apparent purpose in lines 1212–15, where the object of 'gehyrde' (heard) does
not appear until three lines later: 'oþerne mid þec' (another with you). And
again the speech is predominantly paratactic in accordance with its emotional, not rational, content. Beccel moves closer and closer to despair, ex-

hibits less and less control, much as Judas does in *Elene* before his conversion; the poet ensures that impression in lines 1216b–21a. There he rearranges chronology in order to reflect the disorder in Beccel's mind: '7 on morgne swa' (and in the morning also) seems injected as an afterthought, since the preceding line ('dæghwoman bitweon / 7 þære deorcan niht,' between dawn and the dark night) sufficiently reproduces the sense of the Latin original ('Nam ab eo tempore, quo tecum, domine, habitare coeperam, te loquentem vespere et mane audiebam, nescio cum quo,' From the time I first began to live with you, my lord, I have heard you talking, evening and morning, with someone, I know not whom [156 and 157]). Beccel's faltering logic and syntax come more fully to light in Guthlac's response, where he repeats the reference to the morning, deliberately echoing his servant's words, and rearranges the tangled sentence structure to reproduce more accurately the straightforward Latin:[32] God sent him a holy spirit 'se mec efna gehwam, // meahtig meotudes þegn, / 7 on morgne eft / / sigor fæst gesohte' (who each of evenings, the mighty thane of God, and again in the morning, sought me fast in victory [1242b–44a]).

In the last speech, we have a clear picture of Beccel overcome with grief:

```
        Ellen biþ selast    þam þe oftost sceal
        dreogan dryhtenbealu,    deope behycgan
1350    þroht, þeodengedal,    þonne seo þrag cymeð
        wefen wyrdstafun.    Þæt wat se þe sceal
        aswæman sarigferð,    wat his sincgiefan
        holdne biheledne;    he sceal hean þonan
        geomor hweorfan    þam bið gomenes wana
1355    ðe þa earfeða    oftost dreogeð
        on sargum sefan.    Huru ic swiðe ne þearf
        hinsiþ behlehhan.    Is hlaford min,
        beorna bealdor    7 broþor þin,
        se selesta    bi sæm tweonum
1360    þara þe we on Engle    æfre gefrunen
        acennedne    þurh cildes had
        gumena cynnes    to Godes dome,
        werigra wraþu,    worulddreamum of,
        winemæga wyn,    in wuldres þrym,
1365    gewiten, winiga hleo,    wica neosan,
        eardes on upweg.    Ne se eorðan dæl,
        banhus abrocen,    burgum in innan
        wunað wælræste,    7 se wuldres dæl
        of licfæte    in leoht Godes
1370    sigorlean sohte;    7 þe secgan het
```

þæt git a mosten   in þam ecan gefean
mid þa sibgedryht   somud eard niman,
weorca wuldorlean,   willum neotan
blædes 7 blissa.   Eac þe abeodan het
1375   sigedryhten min   þa he wæs siþes fus
þæt þu his lichoman,   leofast mægða,
eorðan biðeahte.   Nu þu ædre const
siðfæt minne.   Ic sceal sarigferð
heanmod hweorfan   hyge drusendne.

Courage is best for the one who most often must endure great mis-
fortune, consider deeply the dire separation from his lord, when the
time comes, woven by the decrees of fate. He knows that who must
grieve sad at heart, knows his dear treasure-giver is buried;
wretched, he must turn sorrowful from thence. There will be want
of gladness for him who most often endures hardships in his sor-
rowing heart. Truly, I need not greatly exult over his departure. My
lord, master of men, and your brother, the best between the seas of
those whom we in England ever heard born in the form of a child of
the race of men, the support of the weary, dearest of kinsmen, at
the judgment of God, has gone from worldly joys into the majesty
of glory – the protector of friends – to seek an abode in the land on
high. Now the earthly portion, the broken body, waits in its death-
rest inside the dwelling, and the glorious part from the body has
sought the reward of victory in the light of God; and he bade me
say that you two might always in that eternal joy with the peaceful
host have a common home, a glorious reward for works, enjoy according to your desires prosperity and bliss. He also bade me order
you, my victory-lord, when he was ready for the journey, that you,
dearest maiden, should cover his body in the earth. Now you fully
know my mission. I must sad at heart, downcast, turn away with
drooping spirit.

This speech represents a mixture of modes, a definite alteration over Beccel's previous technique. The first nine lines (1348–56a) impress us as more
measured and melancholic, less frenetic than what came before. The use of
subordination and of a generalized third person that universalizes the advice
and objectifies the situation while it consoles Beccel helps to create that
impression. But even though a calmness has settled over the servant's
words, that change does not represent an advance for him, since the mode
of the discourse is gnomic or native Germanic, not positively Christian.[33]
The phrase 'ellen biþ selast' (courage is best [line 1348]) perfectly conforms

to a pattern characterizing gnomic poetry in Old English, as in *Maxims* I, line 80b ('dom biþ selast,' fame is best), *Maxims* II, 16a ('ellen sceal on eorle,' courage must be with an earl), and *Resignation*, 117–18 ('Giet biþ þæt selast ... þæt he þonne [wyrd] wel þolige,' yet it is best that he should endure fate well). The gnomic quality of Beccel's words thus becomes another index of the servant's separation from the poem's harmonious ideal, since neither the saint nor the narrator couches his words in gnomic terms and so never furnishes Beccel with a model for his third speech. The servant draws on material outside that provided by his master and by the poem's narrator.

The gnomic passage failing to ameliorate his state, Beccel continues to separate himself from the ideal of beauty in lines 1356b and following, where he reverts to his earlier syntactic patterns. The variation once again has a retarding effect, breaking up the major constituents of the sentence, while the variants themselves become random, having no progressive logic. Guthlac is 'hlaford min, // beorna bealdor / 7 broþor þin, // se selesta / bi sæm tweonum // þara þe we on Engle / æfre gefrunen // acennedne / þurh cildes had // gumena cynnes' (my lord, master of men, and your brother, the best between the seas of those whom we in England ever heard born in the form of a child of the race of men [1357b–62a]). Through the single instance of rhyme 'min' [1357b] and 'þin' [1358b]) in Beccel's speeches we can surmise the reasons for the disruptive use of variation. Despite his attempts to be objective and view Guthlac as belonging to God and all humanity, Beccel finally must feel the loss of the saint in an intensely personal, emotional way, so he binds himself through rhyme to the saint's grieving sister; the variation, though intellectually directed away from himself, ultimately turns back on him and on Pega, who he believes will react as he does. The other attributes of the saint, which the servant dutifully lists, are superfluous to his central personal importance for his two followers.

The disrupting effect of variation produces another link with Beccel's earlier speeches. The separation of 'is' (line 1357b) from its complement 'gewiten' (1369a) is protracted, causing a syntactic delay similar to that seen in his first speech. But in neither instance does the separation justify itself aesthetically. Because both occur in otherwise uncontrolled contexts, their suggestion of the poem's major theme (death as separation) becomes accidental, an ironic commentary on the speaker's immature view of life and death.

Two other points are important to note here, both concerning dictional echoes. We saw earlier that the phrase 'ic þec halsige' (line 1203a) is unique to the emotionally wretched Beccel and to spiritually wretched characters in Old English poetry. In his last speech he uses phrases unique to him and to the devil. Beccel's comment that he 'swiðe ne þearf // hinsiþ behlehhan' (does not need to exult greatly over his departure [1357b–8a]) strongly recalls the devil's remark in *Elene* that he 'þa rode ne þearf // hleatre herigean' (has no need to praise the Cross with exultation [918b–19a]), and the last two lines of the speech (1378–9a) come very close to the demon's words in *Juliana* ('ic sceal feor þonan // heanmod hweorfan,' I must far from thence downcast turn [389–90a]). Again we must emphasize the narrative requirements in *Guthlac B* and deny any equation between Beccel and Satan. Guthlac's servant, 'gleawmod' (wise-minded [1002a]) and 'leofast monna' (dearest of men [1173a]), is decidedly not a member of the dryht of hell. But the literary echoes in the poem[34] do remind us that Beccel inhabits an area between the two absolute realms of heaven and hell and shows the influence of both. Like the Middle English *Pearl* poet, he may accept death intellectually but cannot emotionally. He cannot emulate Guthlac's perfect peace.

The other dictional echo occurs at line 1379b ('hyge drusendne,' with drooping spirit), which strongly recalls line 1061a ('drusendne hyge'). This repetition shows that Guthlac's words have had no effect on Beccel, who remains inconsolable. Though this last speech does have some triumphs (Beccel creates a nice balance, for example, between 'se eorðan dæl,' the earthly portion [1366b], and 'se wuldres dæl,' the glorious part [1368b]), the defects push him farther away from the perfect company of saints, farther into the mutable world.[35]

Guthlac, then, is demonstrably attached to the beautiful, immutable Other through his saintly essence and the iconography of his discourse, while Beccel falls somewhat short of being a member of the saintly community. The one transcends the body and death with Christ; the other remains subject to both. And the features we have noticed in the dialogue underscore the major themes, structure, and purpose of this particular life.

A simple equation and a simple moral emerge from all this. Changeableness is a kind of death, as Gregory says in his commentary on Job,[36] and in *Guthlac B* mutability appears at every turn. Flux characterizes Beccel's fallible, changeable discourse and thus ties the servant to all humanity, to all those who, not being saints and immediate expressions of Christ, must live under the terrible truth of Gregory's dictum. Flux characterizes the references to time, which appears in various forms: it is simply 'ælda tid' (time of men [line 835a]), or, more poignantly, 'lænan tid' (fleeting time [967a, 1120a]) and 'geocran tid' (sad time [976b]); and it becomes 'sliðan tid' (cruel time [992a]) as Guthlac's illness progresses. And flux, of course, characterizes the several references to Guthlac's body: 942b, 954b, 980a, 1193a, 1265b, 1266a. The only points where mutability has no effect are in the saint's discourse, tied to the harmonious ideal of beauty, and in unchanging references to the eternal joy of heaven, also linked indubitably to that ideal ('in þam ecan gefean,' in that eternal joy [1079a, 1186b, 1371b]; 'to þam longan gefean,' to that long joy [1090b, 1307a]; 'to þam fægran gefean,' to that fair joy [1181a]; and 'to þam soðan gefean,' to that true joy [1264a]). Although Beccel – human, weak, and mutable – departs in a state of uncontrollable grief, a grief that has caused critics to conclude that he would remain so even in the lost ending to the poem,[37] we should not be forlorn. Despair can still give way to joy; changeableness can paradoxically move us ever closer to the perfect, static faith that sustains Guthlac. The secular spirit animating Beccel in his concluding words perhaps makes us forget too quickly that *The Wanderer*, a poem with tonal affinities with the servant's dialogue, also begins in despair but ends with an eschatalogical vision that bespeaks an absolute hope. We should expect no less a development in this thoroughly Christian, thoroughly didactic, thoroughly Anglo-Saxon example of hagiography.

CHAPTER FIVE

Typology and the Structure of Repetition in *Andreas*

This book begins with a study of the words-deeds theme in Old English, showing its particular importance to hagiography. In every instance of saintly discourse in the poems, we have seen the theme at work. The saints' words become their acts, and the poets create immutable icono- graphic ideals to express the doctrine of the Logos. The theme continues to play a crucial role even in *Andreas*, a poem difficult to categorize. The poet states the theme explicitly – 'Nu ðu miht gehyran, / hyse leofesta, // hu us wuldres weard / wordum ond dædum // lufode in life,' Now you can hear, dearest youth, how the Guardian of Glory loved us in life through words and through deeds (lines 595–7a) – while also suggesting the ancillary theme of heavenly symmetry and perfection; he twice refers to God's har- monious words (93b and 708b). In addition, we see both Christ and An- dreas bearing treasures of words (316b, 601b), and Christ's power over mutability and death manifests itself through his utterances. Andreas tells the ship's pilot that Christ 'on grundwæge / gumena cynnes // manige missenlice / men of deaðe // worde awehte' (on the earth raised from death with a word many various men of the race of men [582–4a]). These lines prefigure Andreas's later acts, since he too will use words to raise men from the dead.[1]

The words-deeds theme, thus at work in all five of the Old English lives, links saints to Christ and forms a vital part of the typological matrix of hagiography. And typology itself, a central aspect of what Jean Daniélou terms the 'theology of recapitulation,'[2] operates vitally, of course, in all the lives. *Guthlac A* and *Guthlac B* are shaped by the stories of Christ's Temp- tation, Passion, Resurrection, and Ascension,[3] while *Juliana* concentrates on his harrowing of hell (see lines 539–46a) and *Elene* on a generalized identi- fication of Christ and Cyriacus (see 905–21a). The *Andreas* poet centres his attention on the figural connection between Andreas's trials and Christ's Passion. Typology, however, paradoxically binds the lives together but also sets *Andreas* apart, for there it is a blatant and central feature of the narrative that is developed purposefully 'in an essentially schematic way'[4] and deliberately given a prominence it does not have either in the Latin version of the life or in the other four Old English verse lives.

Several critics have dealt with the poem's typology, all affirming its centrality and most attending to the sacramental branch of the mode. Thomas D. Hill and Marie M. Walsh[5] both discuss the typology of baptism in the poem, thus explaining in figural terms what appears to be nonsense to some, part of the generally 'tasteless,'[6] 'sensational,'[7] and 'bizarre'[8] fabric of *Andreas*. Hill counts the calling forth of water from the pillars, the resultant flood and fire, the parting of the water, and the raising of the youth killed by the flood as important narrative details underlying a simple pattern that reflects various aspects of the baptismal rite. The individual or priest performing the baptism becomes a figure of both Noah and Moses as saviours of mankind.[9] Lending incidental support to Hill's thesis, Penn R. Szittya deals with Christ's commandment to a different kind of stone earlier in the poem. He shows that descriptive changes and additions in the text connect the living stone with the temple of Solomon and the Celestial Church, which descends with or as an embodiment of Christ to supplant the Old Law.[10] Finally, John Casteen approaches the cannibalism in the poem from a broadly figural standpoint, demonstrating that even such a grotesque detail can have specific religious and scriptural underpinnings: medieval explicators stressed that God punishes a nation that eschews him by making it cannibalistic.[11]

While these critics acknowledge the 'larger' typological framework of the poem – the Christ-saint figural connection – they do not deal with it. Hill states that the connection is a simple and obvious one, one that serves a moral more than it does a typological purpose.[12] But an actual appearance by Christ in the Old English saints' lives is unique to *Andreas* and should not be dismissed so lightly. Constance B. Hieatt recognizes that importance and demonstrates that the poem is primarily concerned with the Andreas-Christ connection, so that even the naming of Moses, Joshua, and Tobias, all saviour figures, strengthens the typological association.[13] The Christological aspect of the poem, then, is a rich area for further study, and direct discourse, a sizable portion of which Christ himself utters, provides ample material for such a study.

As I argued in chapter 1, a saint's life may establish its iconographic ideal on any level of the stylistic hierarchy. So in *Juliana* and *Elene* the larger structures of speeches, as well as syntax, rhetorical tropes, and diction, comprise the stylistic icons, while in *Guthlac A* only the more minute features of dialogue, such as the theological modal and concessive and conditional clauses, manifest them.[14] The *Andreas* poet, on the other hand, may entirely lose sight of the hierarchy and seems more often concerned with spectacular effect, with making 'the big bow-wow,'[15] than with constructing a poem precise in every detail. Throughout the poem, he tends to use a broad stroke, to depend on an established convention to make a grand gesture. Stylistic details thus play a much less important role here than in the other lives. There are few structural differences, for instance, from the dialogue of one character to that of the next; each speech, with the major exception of Andreas's first, is as symmetrical as any other, and no particular character employs a structure – bipartite or otherwise – unique to him. The practice of placing the initial stress on a finite verb in the b-line, which operates significantly in at least the two Cynewulfian lives, likewise belongs to each character except Matthew and the devil,[16] and so do the sporadically appearing rhetorical figures, such as chiasmus,[17] hypozeuxis,[18] polyptoton,[19] asyndeton,[20] and anaphora,[21] as well as homoioptoton[22] and other kinds of rhyme or sound harmony.[23] Even word-order variation in phrases introducing the speeches, which two critics believe has meaning,[24] proves to be inconclusive evidence on closer inspection. Although the *verba dicendi* tend to remain the same with God ('ondswarode,' answered) and vary with Andreas, Bartlett's contention that the name of Andreas always precedes and the name of the Lord always follows the verb simply is not true, even within the limited scope of the saint's conversation with Christ.[25]

Thus again I must emphasize that *Andreas* seems to fit only uneasily into any genre, heroic or hagiographic. And, in comparison with that of the other vernacular lives, its use of direct discourse to convey meaning seems lifeless and inexact. But despite the lack of stylistic or iconographic fixed points in the minutiae of its speeches, the poem does invest meaning in direct discourse and uses it, if only in a general, rudimentary way, as the other lives do. The poet disregards the smaller syntactic and rhetorical features of the stylistic pattern, so essential to the controlled universe of the other saints, while seeming to have retained some notion of the fundamental idea behind the use of discourse. The stylistic icon, for example – the *imago non manufacta* linked directly to Christ – still appears in the poem, chiefly in the person of Christ himself.[26] And Andreas's increasing recognition of and identification with the Saviour signals his gradual induction into the communion of saints.

Since Christological typology – the broad stroke – forms such an important aspect of *Andreas*, we may begin our examination with the disguised Christ's confronting an ardent but unsuspecting Andreas. David Hamilton has dealt admirably with Andreas's situation and has shown that the poem's allegorical meaning, created by the repetition of key concrete terms referring to food or diet,[27] is reinforced by irony. He states first that 'repetitious imagery of food and drink is ... a major factor of the poem's design,' then continues:

> but, although this diction is obviously suggestive when lifted from its narrative context, it would be much less forceful were it not for the carefully structured and extended dramatic irony that highlights its figurative use. When, for example, Andreas negotiates for passage and the pilot rebukes his poverty, Andreas becomes angry and accuses the pilot of pride:
>
> > Ne gedafenað þe,   nu þe dryhten geaf
> > welan ond wiste   ond wuldorspede,
> > ðæt ðu ondsware   mid oferhygdum,
> > sece sarcwide. (317–20a)
>
> Dramatic irony tightens this speech, for by calling attention to Andreas's ignorance it urges our consideration of the theme of spiritual refreshment. This theme, conveyed chiefly by the figurative language – 'welan ond wiste' – becomes the kernel of the poem to which the irony repeatedly draws our attention. If food be the stuff of this allegory, dramatic irony is its alimentary canal.[28]

Irony functions in concert with other features of the poem as well, serving an iconographic purpose and relating directly to typological structure. Andreas's failure to recognize his Lord and the irony resulting from that lack of perception, an irony manifested in his situation and in the didactic tone or supercilious attitude he sometimes assumes towards the pilot, become the barriers he must surmount in his *rîte de passage* to sainthood. Dramatic irony in *Andreas*, like the irony in *Juliana* or Judas's personal style in *Elene*, comes to signify a separation from God; its breakdown signifies an increased typological identification with him.[29]

While dramatic irony and its implication of spiritual deficiency inform the entire Christ-Andreas dialogue, Andreas is still God's chosen messenger, and the potential alignment of the figure of Christ and the figure of Andreas can be seen even here, under the quasi-comic layers of discourse. In his second utterance in the poem Christ warns Andreas of the dangers awaiting him in Mermedonia:

> Ne magon þær gewunian   widferende,
> 280   ne þær elþeodige   eardes brucað,

ah in þære ceastre   cwealm þrowiað
þa ðe feorran þyder   feorh gelædaþ;
ond þu wilnast nu   ofer widne mere,
þæt ðu on þa fægðe   þine feore spilde?[30]

Wide travellers may not dwell there, nor may there foreigners enjoy the land, but in that city they suffer death who bear their lives there from afar; and you want now to cross over the wide sea, so that you should lose your life in strife?

The formulaic expression of risking life in Mermedonia, which does not appear in the Latin source, occurs four times in the poem, twice prior to and once after lines 281–2. God first uses the formula in telling Andreas of his mission ('Ðu scealt feran / ond frið lædan,' You must travel and venture safety [174]), then repeats it when Andreas hesitates ('Ðu scealt þa fore geferan / ond þin feorh beran,' You must go on a journey and venture your life [216]). Christ's use of the phrase follows in lines 281–2, and finally Andreas employs it, telling his followers 'ge on fara folc / feorh gelæddon' (you would bear your lives among the hostile people [430]). Hamilton discusses the importance of this pattern in relation to a similar one in *Beowulf*, where weapons are the objects being ventured or borne.[31] But the significance goes beyond the poet's supplanting traditional weapons of battle with weapons of spirit. The major significance lies more in the fact of repetition itself than in the particular theme the technique highlights, for repetition allows us to see past surface differences, made particularly strong by irony, to a coming unity, a coming truth.[32] Repetition becomes, in a way, a deliverer from the mundane and from history, as it abolishes profane time and projects man and Andreas into mythical time.[33] The device can be a highly effective one in a typological mode, in the 'theology of recapitulation,' and the *Andreas* poet uses it much as the *Guthlac B* poet does, to connect the saint with the ideal of beauty, and as Cynewulf employs plurilinear alliteration in *Elene*, to bind the truths of indirect discourse to the saint's words. In *Andreas* the use of common formulas and diction verbally link God, Christ, and Andreas, and typologically connect the last two.

The poet gives us further indications of that increasing connection at several other specific points in the Christ-Andreas exchange. Once Andreas has gained passage to Mermedonia and the ship has set sail, Christ asks him for an exposition of his faith:

Gif ðu þegn sie   þrymsittendes,
wuldorcyninges,   swa ðu worde becwist,

rece þa gerynu,   hu he reordberend
420 lærde under lyfte.   Lang is þes siðfæt
ofer fealuwne flod;   frefra þine
mæcgas on mode.   Mycel is nu gena
lad ofer lagustream,   land swiðe feorr
to gesecanne;   sund is geblonden,
425 grund wið greote.   God eaðe mæg
heaðoliðendum   helpe gefremman.

If you are a thane of the One sitting in majesty, of the King of
glory, as you declare in words, relate the secrets, how he taught the
speech-bearers under the air. This journey is long over the fallow
flood; comfort your men in mind. Great yet is the way over the
ocean current, the land very far to seek; the flood is stirred up, the
ocean with the bottom. God can easily provide help for warlike voy-
agers.

Two typological markers occur here, first in the formula 'swa ðu worde
becwist' (as you declare in words [line 418b]), used twice before by Andreas
alone (193b, 304b); again this formulaic pattern has no source in the Latin.
The second marker occurs in the concluding sentence of the Old English,
which has dictional similarities to Christ's later assertion in lines 932b–4:
'wast nu þe gearwor, // þæt ic eaðe mæg / anra gehwylcne // fremman ond
fyrþran / freonda minra' (now you more clearly know that I can easily aid
and support any of my friends). The ironic context of lines 425b–6a complicates the allusion to the ease with which God offers succour to man, and
implies that the link signalled by the repeated formula is nascent, not ful-
filled. The pilot, ostensibly a human being subservient to Andreas in spiritual matters, allows his passenger to count himself the mediator between
God and man. The later allusion in lines 932b–4, not complicated by irony,
issues from the revealed Christ, who offers assurance of immediate aid to a
humbled Andreas.

Three other instances of repetition in the Christ-Andreas exchange, incremental in import, deserve attention. The first two are phrases that only
Christ and Andreas use. In praising Andreas's faith, Christ states that because of it 'is gesyne, / soð orgete, // cuð oncnawen, / þæt ðu cyninges
eart // þegen geþungen' (the truth is manifest, clear, known, and recognized, that you are a virtuous servant of the King [lines 526–8a]). Andreas
also employs the phrase 'soð orgete' in line 851b. And both characters –
Andreas inadvertently – apply the formula 'word ond wisdom' to Christ
(569a and 650a). Most important, however, is a phrase which Christ uses in
describing his own purpose on earth and the men who did not recognize it:

'synnige ne mihton // oncnawan þæt cynebearn, / se ðe acenned wearð //
to hleo ond to hroðre / hæleða cynne, // eallum eorðwarum' (sinners could
not recognize that royal child, who was born *as a protection and as a consolation* for the race of men, for all earth-dwellers [565b–8a, my emphasis]).

These lines form part of a passage revealing the typological focal point of
the poem: Christ's Passion. Moving from mild censure to overt praise of
the pilot, Andreas exclaims, 'ic æt efenealdum / æfre ne mette // on mod-
sefan / maran snyttro' (I have never met greater wisdom of mind in one of
equal age [lines 553–4]), thus expressing the *puer senex* topos[34] and thus
also expressing his faith and his potential understanding of the man accom-
panying him. From this point on the poet develops the notion of Christ's
Passion more explicitly while both diminishing the poem's ironic sense and
intensifying Andreas's association with the Passion. This process continues
unabated throughout but reaches one high point in lines 973–4, when
Christ tells Andreas that his sufferings in Mermedonia will turn many to
the heavenly light; he then links Andreas's acts to his own, making them
part of the redemptive process. Significantly, at the start of this development Christ uses the phrase 'to hleo ond to hroðre' (567a) to describe himself, for the phrase represents, not part of a common diction linking Christ
and Andreas, but a point of view common to Christ and to God, who uses
the same words earlier in the poem to describe Andreas's purpose to Matthew: 'Ic þe Andreas / ædre onsende // to hleo ond to hroðre / in þas
hæðenan burg' (I will send Andreas to you at once as a protection and as a
consolation in this heathen city [110–11]). The Latin source here reads simply 'micto ad te andream apostolum fratrem tuum ut eruam te simul cum
omnibus qui tecum sunt'[35] (I will send you the apostle Andrew, your
brother, to rescue you and all those with you [Allen and Calder, 16]). As
Andreas moves towards the light and a clearer perception of it, the Old
English poetic signposts indicating his close association with Christ become
more prominent.

We have seen, then, that in Christ's appearances in this poem he employs phrases tying him both to God and to Andreas, and that as Andreas's
faith grows more firm, manifest, and sure, the irony dividing the truth
from the saint collapses. The dictional similarities could be dismissed as
happy coincidence if they graced this exchange alone. Christ should speak
like God, after all, and the likenesses between his phraseology and
Andreas's are highly probable in a formulaic system of poetry such as
Old English.[36] Still more evidence rises from the poem, however, to show
that its author probably worked consciously with situational and phrasal
repetition to bring the typological structure to the surface. Returning to the
poem's first few speeches, we can see the tendency develop.

Matthew has the first word, and his speech, otherwise unstriking and a rather close rendering of the Latin source,[37] shows elements in retrospect important to the poem's structure. Captive and eyeless in Mermedonia, he addresses God:

> Hu me elþeodige   inwitwrasne,
> searonet seowað!   A ic symles wæs
> 65   on wega gehwam   willan þines
> georn on mode;   nu ðurh geohða sceal
> dæde fremman   swa þa dumban neat!
> Þu ana canst   ealra gehygdo,
> meotud mancynnes,   mod in hreðre;
> 70   gif þin willa sie,   wuldres aldor,
> þæt me wærlogan   wæpna ecgum,
> sweordum aswebban,   ic beo sona gearu
> to adreoganne   þæt ðu, drihten min,
> engla eadgifa,   eðelleasum,
> 75   dugeða dædfruma,   deman wille.
> Forgif me to are,   ælmihtig God,
> leoht on þissum life,   þy læs ic lungre scyle,
> ablended in burgum   æfter billhete,
> þurh hearmcwide   heorugrædigra,
> 80   laðra leodsceaðena,   leng þrowian
> edwitspræce.   Ic to anum þe,
> middangeardes weard,   mod staþolige,
> fæste fyrðlufan;   ond þe, fæder engla,
> beorht blædgifa,   biddan wille
> 85   ðæt ðu me ne gescyrige   mid scyldhetum,
> werigum wrohtsmiðum,   on þone wyrrestan,
> dugoða demend,   dead ofer eorðan.

How foreigners link an evil chain, a web of guile for me! Always at all times I was in every way eager in mind to do your will; now through griefs I must perform deeds as the dumb cattle do! You alone, Lord of mankind, know the thoughts of all, the mind in the breast; if it should be your will, Prince of glory, that troth-breakers should destroy me with the edges of weapons, with swords, I am straightway prepared to endure what you, my Lord, the angels' Giver of prosperity, Deed-Lord of the troop, will deem for me, bereft of a homeland. In mercy grant me light in this life, Almighty God, lest I must immediately, blinded in the city because of sword-hate, through the blasphemy of the blood-thirsty, of the hateful public enemies, long endure scornful speech. In you alone, Guardian

of the earth, I fix my heart in firm heartfelt love; and to you, Father
of angels, Bright Giver of prosperity, Judge of the troop, I pray that
you do not allot to me among the enemies, the cursed workers of
evil, the worst death on earth.

Most important here is the initial instance of what I term situational repetition, which helps to create the poem's typological focus. Matthew, a perse-
cuted man, enduring torture for the sake of God and man, is an established
saint (the poet refers to him as 'se halga,' the saint [line 48a])[38] and in that
role becomes an image of Christ, the prototype of all saints. The first five
lines of his speech reflect the weary, nearly doubting words of a tormented
man, but they also reflect the same kind of weariness and doubt that afflicted Christ on the Cross when he cried out, 'Deus meus, Deus meus, ut
quid dereliquisti me?' (Matthew 27:46). The connection between Christ and
Matthew has important ramifications for Andreas, for as he moves closer to
his goal, he too takes on this particular aspect of Christ's image. After
lengthy torment by the Mermedonians he finally cries out to God in a
manner reminiscent of Christ and of Matthew; he also echoes Matthew's
words in lines 68–9 – 'Þu ana canst / ealra gehygdo, // meotud mancynnes,
mod in hreðre' – in lines 1282–3:

              Geseoh nu, dryhten God,   drohtað minne,
              weoruda willgeofa!   Þu wast ond const
              anre gehwylces   earfeðsiðas.
              Ic gelyfe to ðe,   min liffruma,
1285   þæt ðu mildheort me   for þinum mægenspedum,
              nerigend fira,   næfre wille,
              ece ælmihtig,   anforlætan,
              swa ic þæt gefremme,   þenden feorh leofað
              min on moldan,   þæt ic, meotud, þinum
1290   larum leofwendum   lyt geswice.
              Þu eart gescyldend   wið sceaðan wæpnum,
              ece eadfruma,   eallum þinum;
              ne læt nu bysmrian   banan manncynnes,
              facnes frumbearn   þurh feondes cræft
1295   leahtrum belecgan   þa þin lof berað!

Look now, Lord God, Gracious Lord of hosts, at my lot. You know
and understand the hardships of all. I trust in you, my Creator, that
you mild-hearted because of your power, Saviour of men, eternal
Almighty, never will abandon me, inasmuch as I shall work, while
my life lasts on the earth, that I, Creator, will forsake little your

pleasant teachings. You are the Protection against the weapons of
the enemy, eternal Author of blessedness, for all your people; do
not let the murderer of mankind, the first born of wickedness, insult
through the craft of the fiend, afflict with malice those who bear
your praise.

The end of the situational repetition begun by Matthew occurs in lines
1400 and following, where Andreas makes typological meaning explicit by
imaginatively identifying himself with the crucified Christ, then quoting his
words. Andreas can no longer bear the excruciating torment inflicted upon
him and prays for release through death:

> Hwæt, ðu sigora weard,
> dryhten hælend,   on dæges tide
> mid Iudeum   geomor wurde,
> ða ðu of gealgan,   God lifigende,
> 1410   fyrnweorca frea,   to fæder cleopodest,
> cininga wuldor,   ond cwæde ðus:
> 'Ic ðe, fæder engla,   frignan wille,
> lifes leohtfruma;   hwæt forlætest ðu me?'
> Ond ic nu þry dagas   þolian sceolde
> 1415   wælgrim witu!   Bidde ic, weoroda God,
> þæt ic gast minne   agifan mote,
> sawla symbelgifa,   on þines sylfes hand.

Lo, you, Guardian of victories, Lord Saviour, in the time of a day
grew sad among the Jews, when you from the Cross, living God,
Lord of ancient works, to the Father, the Glory of kings, called and
thus spoke: 'I wish to ask you, Father of angels, Light-Creator of
life; why do you forsake me?' And I now for three days have had to
endure cruel torments! I pray you, God of hosts, that I may give
my spirit, Feast-Giver of souls, into your own hand.

Apart from situational repetition, three other features of Matthew's
speech are relevant, for they augment the poem's ironic development. First,
the formula 'ic beo sona gearu' (I am straightway prepared [line 72b]),
shows an immediate willingness to perform God's will, despite the hardships involved. This readiness becomes an important aspect of saintly living
and will be noticeably absent from Andreas's first speech and ironically
present in the speeches and actions of the devil, especially in lines 1347 and
1368b–9. Second, the structure of the speech also reflects Matthew's alac-

rity in obeying God, and its major features will likewise be missing from
Andreas's first speech. Though clearly oppressed by the burden of God's
work, Matthew does not shirk his responsibility, a fact underscored by syntax and variation: the speech displays a balanced use of personal pronouns
in both subject and object form ('ic,' 64b, 72b, 77b, 81b; 'me,' 71a, 76a,
85a), implying a balanced view of himself as both agent and recipient, and
employs variation in lines 73–5a to amplify the concept of God, not to
change subtly the direction of the speech. Matthew is immediately prepared
to endure what 'drihten min, engla eadgifa, dugeða dædfruma' judges best,
even if it should be death. A consideration of Andreas's first speech makes
the import of these points clearer.

Matthew's typological association with Christ does not conflict with his
only appearance in the poem, as the previous discussion shows. That is, the
saint fully realizes his role, and no aspect of his discourse, such as irony,
divides his words from the narrative surrounding them or undermines the
speaker's status as a figure of Christ. The poet also introduces Andreas in
typological terms in lines 161–9, where we are told that God did not forget
the suffering that he himself endured 'in ellþeodigum' (among strange people [163a]); he then appears to Andreas. But a gap exists between the typological introduction of Andreas – which seems to refer as much to
Matthew as to Andreas – and Andreas's response to God's call, a gap reminiscent of that between Judas's direct and indirect discourse in *Elene*. The
excess and the shifting subject of Andreas's speech make clear the doubt
and emotional turmoil he experiences because of God's command, and the
speech as a whole does not seem appropriate for an obedient saint:

190   Hu mæg ic, dryhten min,   ofer deop gelad
       fore gefremman   on feorne weg
       swa hrædlice,   heofona scyppend,
       wuldres waldend,   swa ðu worde becwist?
       Ðæt mæg engel þin   eað geferan,
195   halig of heofenum;   con him holma begang
       sealte sæstreamas   ond swanrade,
       waroðfaruða gewinn   ond wæterbrogan,
       wegas ofer widland.   Ne synt me winas cuðe,
       eorlas elþeodige,   ne þær æniges wat
200   hæleða gehygdo,   ne me herestræta
       ofer cald wæter   cuðe sindon.

How can I, my Lord, over the deep sea, make a journey on the distant path as quickly, Creator of the heavens, Ruler of glory, as you
command by your word? Your angel can perform that easily, holy
from the heavens; he knows the expanse of the oceans, the salt sea-

streams and the swan-road, the strife of the eddying surf and the terrible water, the paths over the wide land. Nor are friends known to me, the foreign warriors, nor do I know anything of the thoughts of men there, nor are the highways known to me over the cold water.

The separation of 'heofona scyppend, // wuldres waldend' from the opening 'dryhten min' disrupts the flow of the first sentence, expressing Andreas's hesitation, even reluctance, to do as asked. In contrast to Matthew, who uses three variants for God in three lines (73–5a) without a break in rhythm, Andreas uses two variants separated by two full lines. The second term in line 192b is somewhat jarring since we expect a continuation of both thought and rhythm from the preceding adverb 'hrædlice' (quickly) but get instead a variant of dryhten, forcing us back to the speech's first half-line for its logical referent. Andreas reacts humanly to an overwhelming task and tries to shift the reader's and God's attention away from himself, away from the subject 'ic' in line 190a to the angel in line 194a. The poet puts Andreas in the position of indirect object in line 198b, the farthest syntactic remove from God's command.[39] Andreas's obsequious use of variation further removes him from the centre of attention.[40] Failing the first test and revealing the chasm between ultimate goal and immediate reality, Andreas is prepared for his ironic journey with Christ.

One of Andreas's other speeches, portions of the narrative, and the theologically climactic encounter with the devil further corroborate the centrality of the typological mode to the poem. The poet achieves a symmetricality in the poem by alluding to the salutary qualities of the living stone in the first part and those of the gushing marble in the second.[41] More important than the principle of structural balance here, though, is the typological bridge established through Andreas's commandment to the marble in lines 1498 and following and Christ's commandment to the stone in 706 and following. In the narrative portions of the poem the author links Andreas both to Matthew and to Christ. The phrase 'halgan stefne' (with a holy voice) first describes Matthew (56b), then Andreas (537b, 1399b, 1456a); and the term 'wigendra hleo' (protector of warriors), which Andreas applies to the disguised Christ (506a), both the narrator (896b, 1450b) and God (1672b) apply to Andreas. They reserve the term for Andreas, however, until he perceives his role clearly and knows that Christ has been with him.

Apart from his conversation with Christ, Andreas's conversations with the devil form the most important part of the poem, since only there does his alignment with Christ become absolute and his entrance into the communion of saints sealed. A devil appears in *Andreas*, as he does in the other saints' lives, when his machinations have proven fruitless or his followers' faith has been in some way subverted. After the Mermedonians fail to kill a young boy for their food because of God's intervention (lines 1135 and following), the 'hellehinca' (hell-limper [1171a]) blames Andreas. The Mermedonians torture Andreas horribly but to no avail, and he prays Christ-like to God in lines 1281 and following. The typological identification grows stronger with Andreas's increased strength, and when Satan's followers viciously attack Andreas again in lines 1334–40 – 'hie oncneo-won / Cristes rode // on his mægwlite' (they recognized the Cross of Christ on his face [1337–8a]). Bearing the sign of the Cross, the *sphragis*, as Thomas D. Hill points out, means that the person so blessed is Satan's direct antagonist from that point on.[42] Satan realizes this in the poem, begins chanting a song of sorrow ('hearmleoð' [1342b]) to his warriors, and eventually must confront his old foe directly:

> Þu þe, Andreas,   aclæccræftum
> lange feredes;   hwæt, ðu leoda feala
> forleolce ond forlærdest!   Nu leng ne miht
> 1365 gewealdan þy weorce;   þe synd witu þæs grim
> weotud be gewyrhtum.   Þu scealt werigmod,
> hean, hroðra leas,   hearm þrowigan,
> sare swyltcwale;   secgas mine
> to þam guðplegan   gearwe sindon,
> 1370 þa þe æninga   ellenweorcum
> unfyrn faca   feorh ætþringan.
> Hwylc is þæs mihtig   ofer middangeard,
> þæt he þe alyse   of leoðubendum,
> manna cynnes,   ofer mine est?

> You for a long time, Andreas, have proceeded in magical arts; lo, you have misled and mistaught many people! No longer now can you perform your work; for you torments are decreed, grim according to your deeds. Sad in mind, dejected, bereft of comfort, you must suffer malice, grievous torment of death; my warriors are prepared for the battle-play, those who at once with bold deeds very soon will drive out your life. Who is so mighty over the earth of mankind that he might loose you from limb-fetters against my goodwill?

The patent irony of these lines vitiates their intended effect, of course, and the devil in *Andreas* seems little more than a hackneyed imitation of his traditional self.[43] But the blatant irony creating such a pale reflection of the robust demons seen in other poems operates in this one to underscore iconographic technique: irony in the first part of the poem emphasizes the distance that Andreas must travel in order to achieve sanctity; irony in the second highlights the unclosable gap between Satan and God. Repetition plays its role even here, for the last, ludicrous phrase of Satan's speech – 'ofer mine est' (against my goodwill) – echoes God's use of the same phrase when he comforts Andreas:[44] 'Ne magon [the Mermedonians] ond ne moton / ofer mine est // þine lichoman / lehtrum scyldige // deaðe gedælan, / ðeah ðu drype þolige, // mirce manslaga' (The Mermedonians, guilty of wickedness, cannot and are not able to consign your body to death against my goodwill, though you suffer a stroke, dark, wicked blows [lines 1215–18a]). Satan, recognizing a defeat that was preordained, finally turns 'on fleame' (in flight [1386a]), leaving Andreas to make the speech in lines 1400 and following that marks his induction into the communion of saints.

Repetition, then, serves in *Andreas* to create the typological superstructure, bringing that aspect of the hagiographic mode to the surface of the poem. It also intensifies irony, which supplants minute stylistic differences and highlights the contrast between the dryht of heaven on the one hand and fallible humanity and the dryht of hell on the other. As Andreas approaches clearer perception, the irony disperses, and he becomes closely identified with Christ and the already sanctified Matthew. The irony turned on the devil, however, cannot be dispersed because of his permanent separation from truth; it helps to spell out his final defeat in the poem.

As different from the other verse saints' lives as they are among themselves, *Andreas* emerges from the Old English poetic canon as perhaps the most unusual example of hagiography. The poet burdens his work with a full panoply of traditional heroic conventions, which critics, with a nod in passing to *Elene*, describe as the most extensive in the genre;[45] and the poem's stylistic, structural, and thematic affinities with *Beowulf* have precipitated a number of studies on its relationship to that Old English masterpiece.[46] Additionally, the fantastic elements in the poem – the cannibalism, the speaking stone, the flood – occasion epithets revealing wonder in even the most sympathetic critics. But despite the poem's idiosyncrasies, it does employ direct discourse much as the other lives do, by establishing a fixed icon in Christ's, in God's, and in Matthew's uses of certain phrases, which Andreas must then appropriate and understand as he moves towards alignment with the godhead. The words-deeds theme is as strong here as elsewhere in Old English poetic hagiography, and direct discourse again expresses a spiritual odyssey. It, together with the central themes of moving from darkness to light, from blindness to perception, and of recognizing a dying world's need for spiritual refreshment, dramatizes the mysterious nature of the Christian faith. The emphasis on typology is not arbitrary; it encourages the reader to see that by immersing himself in the pattern of

Christianity, by believing in and obeying Christ, he delivers himself from the ravages of time and history, becoming one with the Saviour. By accepting Christ's commands, he comes to speak Christ's words and perform his deeds in a revivifying, ennobling ritual of repetition.[47]

Conclusion

Although hagiography has received the attention of some major scholars in this century, chiefly Gordon Hall Gerould,[1] Hippolyte Delehaye,[2] Charles W. Jones,[3] and Theodor Wolpers,[4] the focus has never been on the aesthetics of the Old English branch of the genre. This particular branch is too small and the scope of the work these scholars undertake too large to accommodate in any detail five vernacular poems.[5] But even essays with a more limited focus, such as Rosemary Woolf's[6] and Raymon S. Farrar's,[7] are not sufficiently limited to delineate specifically the stylistic or aesthetic principles of Old English poetic hagiography. Woolf treats the Anglo-Saxon Latin and vernacular, prose and verse traditions from a basically historical standpoint, and Farrar concentrates on representative Old English lives, which do not include *Guthlac A*, *Guthlac B*, *Juliana*, *Elene*, and *Andreas*. Though Farrar makes a valuable contribution to the study of saints' lives by stressing their typological function,[8] he ultimately deals with the stable structure of hagiography generally and asserts that the genre's continuity 'is primarily ideological and only secondarily literary.'[9]

The several critics who do almost exclusively assess the literary qualities of the individual Old English lives tend to dismiss any overriding continuity in the genre, at least in this particular manifestation, and concentrate instead on how the poem under consideration transcends the strictures and limitations of the traditional life. *Andreas*, because it is so odd, *Guthlac A*, because it focuses on 'one element of a typical life,'[10] and *Guthlac B*, because it reviews the saint's life quickly and settles on the saint's death,[11] all detach themselves from the tradition. And, of course, *Juliana* and *Elene* are similarly removed, since they lack the standard conventions listed conveniently by Farrar.[12]

Understandably, this polarization of literary historian and literary critic has left the Old English verse saint's life essentially undefined: a vision necessarily expansive would certainly pass quickly over a body so small, and another vision, as necessarily restricted, might just as surely miss the uniform backdrop of a body seemingly so varied. The problem appears to be that when we have searched for conventions at all, we have expected conventions of content rather than of method. And, to be sure, not one of the five poems has the standard introduction, the standard apology for rhetorical ineptitude, the standard reference to the authority of the life, or the standard catalogues of virtues, miracles, prophecies, and posthumous marvels, although each makes use of certain features of the exordial tradition.[13]

But while the individual quality of the Old English life sets it apart from its continental progenitor, that quality does not negate the possibility of a vernacular convention or tradition replacing a Latin one. As we have seen, the act of paraphrase itself, though part of a venerable rhetorical tradition, can give rise to stylistic features unique to the paraphrase. And stylistic and rhetorical analysis reveals that the Old English poems make use of language in a way that their Latin sources do not: whereas the Latin and even some Old English authors such as Ælfric may use direct discourse for specific purposes, the Old English poems give it an architectonic stature it usually does not have. The Old English poems also tend to organize the technical features of rhetoric and poetry to underline a central theme – the addition of appropriate topoi is a good example of this tendency. Because the themes themselves (for example, steadfastness, delusion, death) do seem so different, it is easy to assume that the lives all function differently. But their use of language and style and their tendency to visualize the material of the life iconographically make them methodologically more alike than different.

We have had to ask a range of questions to arrive at this perception. How do the lives relate to the Latin tradition? To each other? How do they function within a larger cultural context? What characteristic modes of thought do they manifest? Is there an organizing principle behind their use of those modes? Having pursued these questions, we can now summarize the conventions that seem particular to the Old English lives.

The Old English life, instead of relating the entire life of a saint and thus embracing a broad, historically determined set of conventions, centres on the moment of greatest emotional and spiritual turmoil for the saint. It distils the fact of sainthood into the particulars of an individual moment or event so that a certain Christian truth can be told. Focusing on truth in this way is perhaps not unique to the Old English life, since hagiography generally, as Jean Leclercq observes, 'advances a moral thesis and a religious idea,'[14] but the Old English life goes further in trimming away extraneous fact or religious fantasy than does the Latin life. It tends to highlight the moral that usually derives from the climactic encounter with the devil, and it also paradoxically individualizes a saint while preserving his place in Christ's body.

A uniform set of methodological conventions supports this first unusual aspect of the Old English verse saint's life: all the poems manifest an interest in the words-deeds theme; all tend to concentrate a great deal of meaning in direct discourse; each tends to visualize its subject-matter iconographically, consistently juxtaposing a confusion or lack of focus in the dryht of hell or in the mutable world to a perfect symmetry and harmony in the dryht of heaven or in the real world; the lives generally use irony for differentiating the dryht of heaven from the other two realms; all the poems emphasize immediate readiness to obey as a concomitant of holy living; each portrays the saint as Satan's nemesis; and thus each explicitly conflates the saint and Christ when the moment of greatest spiritual victory arrives. The first two conventions need no further comment. The Introduction makes clear the importance of the first; the entire book, the importance of the second. The remaining five points, however, do demand elaboration.

In the discussion of *Juliana* we discovered perhaps the most clear-cut use of stylistic variation to differentiate characters and observed that Cynewulf seems to exploit a principle of juxtaposition similar to that seen in medieval iconographic paintings – such as the illustrations in the Cædmon manuscript – where the saved dryht of heaven is symmetrically represented, while its condemned counterpart in hell appears in a state of asymmetrical chaos. The same principle operates in various ways in the other four poems as well. In *Guthlac A* the poet depicts the fiends opposing the saint as physically unattached to a specific place and as 'lyftlacende' (floating in the air [line 146a]), thus literally expressing their inability to gain Guthlac's spot of ground and metaphorically expressing their failure to match their otherwise imposing discourse with significant action. Guthlac, on the other hand, remains fixed in his physical place, in his faith, and in the qualities of his discourse, thus personifying *stabilitas*, a characteristic monastic virtue, which he 'exemplifies in his rigorous refusal to move despite the assaults of supernatural foes.'[15] The principle of chaos versus symmetry in *Elene* appears predominantly in Judas's early dialogue. He does not integrate the iconographic style, represented by indirect discourse, into his personal style and eventually loses rhetorical control. And in *Guthlac B* the principle appears in Beccel's inept use of variation and in his other linguistic fallibilities, all of which make him fall short of the saintly ideal.

The fourth convention of poetic hagiography, the use of irony, functions in four of the five lives as a subsidiary means for differentiating the two dryhts. In *Juliana*, for example, irony interacts with other features of Affri-

canus's dialogue to undermine what he says. But in *Andreas* the presence
of irony becomes the primary, not the secondary index of character. First
surrounding the mutable Andreas and then the devil, irony here implies a
failure to align understanding with discourse and removes the speaker from
communion with God. Though irony and the other stylistic deviations in
the poems may, to a modern reader, give the saints' lives variety and alleviate some tedium, such variety finally associates the speaker using it with
spiritual misunderstanding and death. 'Quid enim mutabilitas,' Gregory
pointedly queries, 'nisi mors quædam est?'

The fifth convention, present to a degree in the Latin sources but stressed
more in the Old English poems, is a presence of, or an insistence upon,
immediate preparedness to do God's will. The *Andreas* poet makes some
use of this topos,[16] and a phrase important in that poem's typology – 'ic
beo sona gearu' (I will be immediately prepared [line 72b])[17] – appears verbatim in *Juliana* (49b, 365b, 398b) and in *Elene* (85b, 222b) and in concept
in *Guthlac A* (89a) and in *Guthlac B* (889b). The willingness of the godly
to submit themselves immediately and completely to the Lord's will is a
prerequisite for entrance into his presence.

Finally, and perhaps most importantly, come the last two conventions of
Old English verse hagiography. Since aspiring saints have induction into
the general Communion as an ultimate goal, the poets representing the
lives must signal the approaching typological identification with Christ in
some way. They do so first by making the saint take on Christ's traditional
function as a tormentor of demons. Juliana performs this function when
she interrogates the devil; Judas, when he faces the old foe; Guthlac, when
he thwarts the demons in both poems;[18] and Andreas, when he displays the
sphragis and puts the humiliated Satan to flight. Second, the poets actually
conflate the saints with Christ so that the identity becomes clear, the victory certain, and the induction absolute.

The conflation invariably occurs at the point of greatest spiritual victory,
and the devil himself most often makes the identification. In *Guthlac A*,
however, the poet does so, when he expresses wonder over the saint's having to endure more pain:

Hwæt þæt wundra sum

```
        monnum þuhte    þæt he ma wolde
        afrum onfengum    earme gæstas
520     hrinan leton    7 þæt hwæþre gelomp.
        Wæs þæt gen mara    þæt he middangeard
        sylfa gesohte    7 his swat ageat
        on bonena hond;    ahte bega geweald,
        lifes 7 deaðes,    þa he lustum dreag
```

525   eaðmod on eorðan   ehtendra nið.
         Forþon is nu arlic   þæt we æfæstra
         dæde demen,   secgen dryhtne lof
         ealra þara bisena   þe us bec fore
         þurh his wundra geweorc   wisdom cyþað.

Lo, that seemed a wonder to men, that he would let the wretched
spirits touch him more with their eager grips, and yet that happened. It was yet greater that he himself sought the earth and shed
his blood at the hands of slayers; he had power over both life and
death when he, gentle on the earth, gladly suffered the hatred of
persecutors. Therefore, it is now fitting that we should glorify the
deeds of the righteous, say praise to the Lord for all the examples by
which books make wisdom known to us through his wondrous
works.

The *Guthlac A* poet significantly aligns Christ and Guthlac after line
348b,[19] just prior to the saint's final, victorious speech.

Explicit conflation in the remaining four lives occurs as an addition to or
an elaboration of their Latin sources. In chapter 2 I discussed this aspect of
Juliana and in chapter 4 the same feature in *Guthlac B*. Cynewulf alters his
source for *Elene* so that the clear distinction between Judas and Christ in
the devil's speech is obscured in the Old English. The first lines from each
account will illustrate the point:

> Quis iterum hic est, qui non permittet me suscipere animas meo-
> rum? O Jesu Nazarene, omnes traxisti ad te: ecce et lignum tuum
> manifestasti adversum me. O Juda! quid hoc fecisti?   (Strunk, 52)

> Who is this who once again will not allow me to receive my own
> souls? Jesus, Nazarene, you have drawn all men to you; lo, you
> have uncovered your Cross in order to harm me. Judas, why did
> you do this?   (Allen and Calder, 66)

The Old English devil does not so markedly shift his attention from Christ
to Judas, and in lines 905b–7a and 915b–16a he directs parallel complaints
at the two figures:

> Hwæt is þis, la, manna   þe minne eft
> þurh fyrngeflit   folgaþ wyrdeð,
> iceð ealdne nið,   æhta strudeð?

905   Þis is singal sacu;   sawla ne moton,

manfremmende   in minum leng
æhtum wunigan;   nu cwom elþeodig
þone ic ær on firenum   fæstne talde,
hafað mec bereafod   rihta gehwylces,
910   feohgestreona;   nis ðæt fæger sið.
Feala me se hælend   hearma gefremede,
niða nearolicra,   se ðe in Nazareð
afeded wæs;   syððan furþum weox
of cildhade   symle cirde to him
915   æhte mine;   ne mot ænige nu
rihte spowan.[20]

Lo, what man is this who again through ancient strife destroys my
retinue, increases the old enmity, robs my possessions? This is perpetual strife; sinful souls can no longer dwell in my possession; now
a stranger has come, has bereft me of each of rights, of treasures;
that is not a fair experience. The Lord has inflicted many harms,
grievous enmities on me, he who was reared in Nazareth; as soon as
he grew from childhood, he always turned my possessions to himself; now I cannot succeed in any right.

And in *Andreas*, the devil's conflation of the saint and Christ has no counterpart in the Latin source.[21] He addresses Andreas thus:

Hwæt hogodest ðu, Andreas,   hidercyme þinne
on wraðra geweald?   Hwær is wuldor þin,
þe ðu oferhigdum   upp aræfdest,
þa ðu goda ussa   gilp gehnægdest?
1320   Hafast nu þe anum   eall getihhad
land ond leode,   swa dyde lareow þin;
cyneþrym ahof,   þam wæs Crist nama,
ofer middangeard,   þynden hit meahte swa.
Þone Herodes   ealdre besnyðede,
1325   forcom æt campe   cyning Iudea,
rices berædde,   ond hine rode befealg,
þæt he on gealgan his   gast onsende.
Swa ic nu bebeode   bearnum minum,
þegnum þryðfullum,   ðæt hie þe hnægen,
1330   gingran æt guðe.   Lætað gares ord,
earh attre gemæl,   in gedufan
in fæges ferð;   gað fromlice,
ðæt ge guðfrecan   gylp forbegan.

What did you think, Andreas, about your coming here into the power of hostile ones? Where is your glory, which you raised up in arrogance when you subdued the pride of our gods? You have now claimed for yourself alone all the land and the people, as your teacher did; he assumed royal dignity, who was named Christ, over the earth, while it could be so. Herod deprived him of life, overcame the King of the Jews in battle, deprived him of his kingdom, and committed him to the Cross, so that he sent his spirit forth on the gallows. So now I command my children, glorious thanes, that they, youths at battle, should humble you. Let the spear's point, the shaft stained with poison, drive into the heart of the doomed one; go boldly so that you might beat down the pride of the warrior.

In all five poems the poets juxtapose this major convention with important developments in the poems' iconography, and the saints' immutable discourse becomes fixed as the stylistic analogue of the Christ-saint figural connection.

The Old English verse saints' lives have enjoyed modest but vigorous scholarly attention in recent years, and the interest in them has produced admirable results. Obscurities have been clarified, and we are now better prepared to view these poems as works of consummate skill and art, despite their appearance to some as tedious exercises in the Anglo-Saxon version of Christian didacticism. But from the intricacies of the separate lives we can now move to the genre as a whole. By looking closely at a characteristic feature of all the lives – their use of *sermo humilis* and their emphasis on direct discourse – we can allow conclusions and emphases to emerge from each poem so that a pattern can form and a wider understanding of the subject develop. And by setting the poems in a broad cultural context, we may now better see their creators' relationship to a genre: just as rhetoricians and iconographers modified and adapted older, classical forms of their crafts to their distinctly Christian, didactic purposes, so did the Old English poets adapt continental models to their particular situation. More uniformity than diversity thus informs the Old English verse lives. While the individual poets give prominence to their own visions of earthly and transcendent reality, they work within an established, intricate tradition of vernacular poetic hagiography.

Abbreviations
Notes
Bibliography
Index

Abbreviations

Notes

PREFACE

1 The percentage of direct discourse in each poem is as follows:
   Guthlac A   36% (298 of 818 lines)
   Juliana   63% (459 of 730 lines)
   Elene   41% (538 of 1321 lines)
   Guthlac B   35% (188 of 560 lines)
   Andreas   47% (806 of 1722 lines)
   Except in *Guthlac A*, where I allot lines 6–29 instead of just 6–10 to the angel,
   my designation of direct discourse follows *The Anglo-Saxon Poetic Records*, ed
   George Philip Krapp and Elliott Van Kirk Dobbie (New York: Columbia Uni-
   versity Press 1931–53).
2 'Der Dialog in der altgermanischen erzählenden Dichtung' *Zeitschrift für
   deutsches Altertum* 46 (1902) 189–284, espec 198
3 *Ballad and Epic: A Study in the Development of the Narrative Art* (1907; repr
   New York: Russell & Russell 1967) 198
4 *The Larger Rhetorical Patterns in Anglo-Saxon Poetry* (1935; repr New York:
   AMS Press 1966) 101–6
5 *The English Language in Medieval Literature* (London: Methuen 1979) 157
6 Scholars tentatively agree that *Guthlac A* is earliest and *Andreas* is latest in the
   group, but no one is certain. On *Guthlac A* and *Guthlac B* see Jane Roberts, ed
   The Guthlac Poems of the Exeter Book (Oxford: Clarendon Press 1979) 70–1,
   and on *Andreas* consult Kenneth R. Brooks, ed *Andreas and the Fates of the
   Apostles* (Oxford: Clarendon Press 1961) xxi–xxii. For Cynewulf's poems see
   Rosemary Woolf, ed *Juliana* (1954; repr New York: Appleton-Century-Crofts
   1966) 5–7, and Pamela Gradon, ed *Cynewulf's Elene* (1958; repr New York:
   Appleton-Century-Crofts 1966) 22–3.

7 R.M. Wilson estimates the proportion of hagiography that may be lost to us in *The Lost Literature of Medieval England* (London: Methuen 1952) 85–103.

INTRODUCTION

1 In the preface to his *Saints' Legends* (Boston: Houghton Mifflin 1916), vii, Gordon Hall Gerould comments on the difficulty of his task 'since no such study has hitherto been made for any of the European literatures.'
2 '*Juliana*,' in Daniel G. Calder *Cynewulf* (Boston: Twayne 1981) 75–103; 'Theme and Strategy in *Guthlac B*' *Papers on Language and Literature* 8 (1972) 227–42; '*Guthlac A* and *Guthlac B*: Some Discriminations,' in *Anglo-Saxon Poetry: Essays in Appreciation for John McGalliard* ed Lewis E. Nicholson and Dolores Warwick Frese (Notre Dame: University of Notre Dame Press 1975) 65–80
3 'Cynewulf's Multiple Revelations' *Medievalia et Humanistica* 3 (1972) 257–77
4 'Cynewulf's *Elene*: Sources and Structure' *Neophilologus* 54 (1970) 65–76, rev and repr as '*Elene* and the *Dream of the Rood*' in *The Construction of Christian Poetry in Old English* (Carbondale: Southern Illinois University Press 1975) 85–98
5 'The Diet and Digestion of Allegory in *Andreas*' *Anglo-Saxon England* 1 (1972) 147–58
6 For an outline of the genre see Hippolyte Delehaye, sj *The Legends of the Saints* trans V.M. Crawford (Notre Dame: University of Notre Dame Press 1961).
7 Augustine *Confessions* trans William Watts, ed W.H.D. Rouse, Loeb Classical Library (1912; repr 1968) I, 112
8 Ibid, I, 284
9 Erich Auerbach *Literary Language and Its Public in Late Latin Antiquity and in the Middle Ages* trans Ralph Manheim (Princeton: Princeton University Press 1965) 65. Though Auerbach writes primarily about the Latin tradition, more than one critic has intimated a relationship between the Old English lives and Scripture. Without mentioning *sermo humilis*, Catharine A. Regan, in 'Evangelicism as the Informing Principle of Cynewulf's "Elene," ' *Traditio* 29 (1973) 29, implies a connection between it and the Old English lives. She observes: 'It seems reasonable to assume that the monk must have approached saints' lives meditatively, as he approached Scripture, because of the firm habit of meditation he had formed through extensive daily practice.' In *The Art and Background of Old English Poetry* (London: Edward Arnold 1978), 117, Barbara C. Raw makes the link explicit: 'Cynewulf's style is very much closer to that of prose than of verse, particularly in *Juliana*, and this may be an indica-

tion not, as is sometimes suggested, of late date, but of informality, the *sermo humilis* of Augustine transferred into Old English.'

10 In *Corpus Christianorum* CXXIIIA, 142–3. The translation is by Gussie Hecht Tannenhaus, 'Concerning Figures and Tropes,' in *Readings in Medieval Rhetoric* ed Joseph M. Miller et al (Bloomington: Indiana University Press 1973) 97.

11 On the importance of Isidore's work to the early English see J.D.A. Ogilvy *Books Known to the English, 597–1066* (Cambridge, Mass: Mediaeval Academy of America 1967) 166–70.

12 *Etymologiarum sive originum libri xx* ed W.M. Lindsay (Oxford: Clarendon Press 1911) II. i. The translation is by Dorothy V. Cerino, 'The Etymologies, II. 1–15: "Concerning Rhetoric," ' in *Readings in Medieval Rhetoric* 80–1.

13 *Aesthetique Studien zur angelsächsischen Poesie* (Breslau: W. Koebner 1883)

14 'Adaptation of Classical Rhetoric in Old English Literature,' in *Medieval Eloquence: Studies in the Theory and Practice of Medieval Rhetoric* ed James J. Murphy (Berkeley and Los Angeles: University of California Press 1978) 173–97; 'Knowledge of Rhetorical Figures in Anglo-Saxon England' *Journal of English and Germanic Philology* 66 (1967) 1–20; 'Learned Rhetoric in Old English Poetry' *Modern Philology* 63 (1966) 189–201

15 'Adaptation of Classical Rhetoric' 174

16 Ibid

17 Ibid, 178

18 Blake *The English Language* 141

19 Geoffrey Shepherd 'Scriptural Poetry,' in *Continuations and Beginnings* ed Eric G. Stanley (London: Thomas Nelson 1966) 7

20 See Ogilvy *Books Known to the English* 59.

21 *Patrologia Latina* 14.142. The translation is from St Ambrose, *Hexameron, Paradise, and Cain and Abel* trans John J. Savage (New York: Fathers of the Church 1961) 16.

22 E.R. Curtius *European Literature and the Latin Middle Ages* trans Willard R. Trask (Princeton: Princeton University Press 1953) 148

23 See Ogilvy *Books Known to the English* 102, 113.

24 Curtius *European Literature* 94

25 See James L. Rosier 'Death and Transfiguration: *Guthlac B*,' in *Philological Essays: Studies in Old and Middle English Language and Literature in Honour of Herbert Dean Meritt* ed James L. Rosier (The Hague: Mouton 1970) 82–92.

26 Curtius *European Literature* 176–8

27 See Thomas D. Hill 'Two Notes on Patristic Allusion in *Andreas*' *Anglia* 84 (1966) 161–2.

28 Respectively, 'Toward a Unified Approach to Old English Poetic Composition' *MP* 73 (1975–6) 219–28; and 'Rhetoric in England: The Age of Ælfric, 970–1020' *Communication Monographs* 44 (1977) 390–403

29 On manifestations of both classical Latin and native Germanic traditions in Old English poetry consult Walter H. Beale 'Rhetoric in the Old English Verse Paragraph' *Neuphilologische Mitteilungen* 80 (1979) 133–42.

30 All quotations from *Beowulf* are from F. Klaeber, ed *Beowulf and the Fight at Finnsburg* 3rd edn (Lexington: D.C. Heath 1950). Unless otherwise noted, translations from the Old English are my own.

31 See 'Criteria for Style Analysis' *Word* 15 (1959) 154–74, and 'Stylistic Context' *Word* 16 (1960) 207–18, repr in *Essays on the Language of Literature* ed Seymour Chatman and Samuel R. Levin (Boston: Houghton Mifflin 1967) 412–30 and 431–41 respectively.

32 See also Berel Lang, ed *The Concept of Style* (Philadelphia: University of Pennsylvania Press 1979); Stanley B. Greenfield *The Interpretation of Old English Poems* (London and Boston: Routledge and Kegan Paul 1972) 111; Herbert Pilch 'Syntactic Prerequisites for the Study of Old English Poetry' *Language and Style* 3 (1970) 51; Roman Jakobson 'Linguistics and Poetics,' in *Style in Language* ed Thomas A. Sebeok (Cambridge: MIT Press 1960) 375; Harry R. Warfel 'Syntax Makes Literature' *College English* 21 (1960) 251–5; and W. Nelson Francis 'Syntax and Literary Interpretation,' in *Essays on the Language of Literature* ed Chatman and Levin, 209–16.

33 Riffaterre 'Criteria for Style Analysis' 416; and Greenfield *The Interpretation of Old English Poems* 114

34 'Zur Wortstellung und -betonung im Altgermanischen' *Beiträge zur Geschichte der deutschen Sprache und Literatur* 57 (1933) 1–109

35 *The Meter of 'Beowulf'* (Oxford: Oxford University Press 1958)

36 'Some Aspects of the Technique of Composition of Old English Verse' *Transactions of the Philological Society* (1952) 1–14

37 'The Old English Epic Style,' in *English and Medieval Studies Presented to J.R.R. Tolkien* ed Norman Davis and C.L. Wrenn (London: George Allen and Unwin 1962) 13–26

38 'The Art of Old English Verse Composition' *Review of English Studies* 21 (1970) 129–42, 257–66

39 Ibid, 130–1

40 See Slay 'Some Aspects of Composition' 6, n 1.

41 'The Art of Old English Verse Composition' 131

42 Ibid, 261–2. See also Greenfield *The Interpretation of Old English Poems* 112.

43 'The Art of Old English Verse Composition' 264

44 'Poetic Language and Old English Metre,' in *Early English and Norse Studies Presented to Hugh Smith* ed Arthur Brown and Peter Foote (London: Methuen 1963) 150–71

45 'Old English Poetry: Alliteration and Structural Interlace' *Language and Style* 6 (1973) 196–205. Curiously, Lewis does not cite Quirk's article.

46 'Poetic Language' 150–1

47 Ibid, 155
48 Ibid, 160
49 Ibid, 171
50 'The Interlace Structure of *Beowulf'* *University of Toronto Quarterly* 37 (1967) 1–17
51 Lewis fails to note LePage's 'Alliterative Patterns as a Test of Style in Old English Poetry' JEGP 58 (1959) 434–41, an essay especially germane to his topic. See also Paull F. Baum 'The Meter of the *Beowulf'* MP 46 (1948–9) 73–91, 145–62, likewise germane and likewise absent from Lewis's essay.
52 Lewis 'Alliteration and Structural Interlace' 199
53 Ibid, 200
54 *The Interpretation of Old English Poems* 117. The translation is Greenfield's.
55 Ibid, 120
56 Ibid
57 Ibid
58 Ibid, 122
59 Ibid
60 'Earmcearig' appears only in *The Wanderer* and in *The Seafarer*, line 14: 'Hu ic earmcearig / iscaldne sæ' (How I wretched the ice-cold sea). As Lewis notes, 'earmcearig' and 'eðle' in *The Seafarer* interact 'as reciprocal situational and emotional aspects of the Seafarer's loneliness' ('Alliteration and Structural Interlace' 196–7). Wretchedness and cold normally belong together.
61 See Frederic G. Cassidy and Richard N. Ringler, eds *Bright's Old English Grammar and Reader* 3rd edn (New York: Holt, Rinehart and Winston 1971) 273–4. Alfred Reszkiewicz describes a syntactic analogue to this stylistic option in 'Split Constructions in Old English,' in *Studies in Language and Literature in Honour of Margaret Schlauch* ed M. Brahmer et al (Warsaw: Polish Scientific Publishers 1966) 313–26.
62 The next widest separation is one line. See lines 3b–4a, 37–8, and 111b–12a. Otherwise the two parts of the verb appear in the same line or half-line. See 26b, 56a, 58a, 64a, 70a, 72b, 73a.
63 Thirty-nine per cent of *Beowulf* is in direct discourse (1232 of 3182 lines). For a discussion of Beowulf's fifteen speeches and their relationship to the poem's structure see Brian A. Shaw 'The Speeches in *Beowulf*: A Structural Study' *Chaucer Review* 13 (1978) 86–92.
64 Greenfield *The Interpretation of Old English Poems* 130–1
65 See Stanley B. Greenfield's discussion of the coast-guard–Beowulf exchange in 'Of Words and Deeds: The Coastguard's Maxim Once More,' in *The Wisdom of Poetry: Essays in Early English Literature in Honor of Morton W. Bloomfield* ed Larry D. Benson and Siegfried Wenzel (Kalamazoo, Mich: Medieval Institute Publications 1982) 45–51.
66 Peter Clemoes 'Action in *Beowulf* and Our Perception of It,' in *Old English*

Poetry: Essays on Style ed Daniel G. Calder (Berkeley and Los Angeles: University of California Press 1979) 166. Robert Levine, 'Direct Discourse in *Beowulf*: Its Meaning and Function' (PH D diss, Berkeley 1963) 196, notes that 'because his actions match his words, Beowulf is a fully heroic figure.'

67 'Direct Discourse in *Beowulf*' 60–1

68 On the heroic in the poem see J.R.R. Tolkien 'The Homecoming of Beorhtnoth Beorhthelm's Son' *Essays and Studies* 6 (1953) 14; Edward B. Irving, Jr 'The Heroic Style in "The Battle of Maldon" ' *Studies in Philology* 58 (1961) 457–67; George Clark '*The Battle of Maldon*: A Heroic Poem' *Speculum* 43 (1968) 52–71; and Thomas D. Hill 'History and Heroic Ethic in *Maldon*' *Neophilologus* 54 (1970) 291–6.

69 Intimations of the idea occur in Bernard F. Huppé's *Doctrine and Poetry: Augustine's Influence on Old English Poetry* (Albany: State University of New York Press 1959), 237–8, and in Morton W. Bloomfield's 'Patristics and Old English Literature: Notes on Some Poems,' in *Studies in Old English Literature in Honor of Arthur G. Brodeur* ed Stanley B. Greenfield (Eugene: University of Oregon Press 1963), 38. N.F. Blake gives the theory full treatment and credence in 'The Battle of Maldon,' *Neophilologus* 49 (1965) 332–45, and J.E. Cross's 'Oswald and Byrhtnoth: A Christian Saint and a Hero Who Is a Christian,' *English Studies* 46 (1965) 93–109, puts the whole matter to rest. He states simply that 'Byrhtnoth did not gain a martyr's crown, although, as Professor Bloomfield rightly suggests, there may well have been some who considered that he should have done. As critics explaining the poem however we are not concerned with these. We should listen to the opinion of only one man, the poet, as it is revealed or implied within the poem' (94). Critics viewing *Maldon* as hagiography subscribe to an analogical fallacy.

70 See Stanley B. Greenfield *A Critical History of Old English Literature* (New York: New York University Press 1965) 99–101.

71 Irving 'Heroic Style in *Maldon*' 460

72 'Flyting in *The Battle of Maldon*' NM 71 (1970) 201–2

73 Quotations from *Maldon* are from vol. 6 of the ASPR, *The Anglo-Saxon Minor Poems* ed E.V.K. Dobbie (New York: Columbia University Press 1942).

74 For the Old Norse parallel to this hapax legomenon and a study of the Viking's speech as an example of foreign dialect, see Fred C. Robinson 'Some Aspects of the *Maldon* Poet's Artistry' *JEGP* 75 (1976) 26ff.

75 Anderson 'Flyting in *Maldon*' 200–1

76 George Clark 'The Hero of *Maldon*: Vir pius et strenuus' *Speculum* 54 (1979) 272

77 See F.L. Cross, ed *The Oxford Dictionary of the Christian Church* 2nd edn (Oxford: Oxford University Press 1974) 833.

78 All quotations from the Vulgate are from *Biblia Sacra* 4 vols (Milwaukee:

Bruce 1955), and translations of it from *The Holy Bible* (Rheims 1582 and Douay 1609 version; 1899; repr Rockford, Ill: Tan Books 1971).

79 Quoted in Auerbach *Literary Language* 27 (my translation). The continental Germans also show a predictable interest in words and deeds. See lines 1–5 of the Old Saxon *Heliand*, where we learn that while on earth, Christ performed many miracles 'mid uuordun endi mid uuercun' (with words and with deeds [*Heliand und Genesis* ed Otto Behaghel, 8th edn, rev Walter Mitzka (Tübingen: Max Niemeyer Verlag 1965) 4]).

80 Marcia L. Colish *The Mirror of Language: A Study of the Medieval Theory of Knowledge* rev edn (Lincoln and London: University of Nebraska Press 1983) 3

81 For a discussion of the communion of saints see Charles W. Jones *Saints' Lives and Chronicles in Early England* (Ithaca, NY: Cornell University Press 1947) 62–3.

82 See George S. Metes 'Word-Order Variation as a Stylistic Feature in the Old English *Andreas*' (PH D diss, Wisconsin 1972) 36.

83 *PL* 75.1004; my trans

84 See Keith A. Tandy 'Verbal Aspect as a Narrative Structure in Ælfric's *Lives of Saints*,' in *The Old English Homily and Its Background* ed Paul E. Szarmach and Bernard F. Huppé (Albany, NY: State University of New York Press 1978) 181–202.

85 Ibid, 188

86 Ibid, 199

87 Text and translation are from *Ælfric's Lives of Saints* ed Walter W. Skeat, EETS, OS no 94 (1890; repr Oxford: Oxford University Press 1966) II, 126–7.

88 Text and translation are from *Bede's Ecclesiastical History of the English People* ed Bertram Colgrave and R.A.B. Mynors (Oxford: Clarendon Press 1969) 214–15.

89 See Ruth Waterhouse 'Ælfric's Use of Discourse in Some Saints' Lives' *ASE* 5 (1976) 83–103.

90 Ibid, 90

91 Ibid, 91, 103

92 Cf the Old English and Latin St Christopher in *Three Old English Prose Texts* ed Stanley Rypins, EETS, OS no 161 (Oxford: Oxford University Press 1924), and the Old English and Latin Apollonius of Tyre in *The Old English Apollonius of Tyre* ed Peter Goolden (Oxford: Oxford University Press 1958).

93 For a discussion of the major alterations of the source see my article 'Oppressed Hebrews and the Song of Azarias in the Old English *Daniel*' *SP* 77 (1980) 213–26.

94 See Gertrud Schiller *Iconography of Christian Art* trans Janet Seligman (Greenwich, Conn: New York Graphic Society 1971) I, 1, and Albert C. Moore *Iconography of Religions* (Philadelphia: Fortress Press 1977) 27.

95 *The Cædmon Manuscript of Anglo-Saxon Biblical Poetry* ed Sir Israel Gollancz (Oxford: Oxford University Press 1927) 3, 16, 17. For a good discussion of the juxtaposition of serenity and chaos in the art of the Middle Ages see Adolf Katzenellenbogen 'The Image of Christ in the Early Middle Ages,' in *Life and Thought in the Early Middle Ages* ed Robert S. Hoyt (Minneapolis: University of Minnesota Press 1967) 66–84.

96 See Jean H. Hagstrum *The Sister Arts: The Tradition of Literary Pictorialism and English Poetry from Dryden to Gray* (Chicago: University of Chicago Press 1958), and Mario Praz *Mnemosyne: The Parallel between Literature and the Visual Arts* (Princeton: Princeton University Press 1970).

97 Jackson J. Campbell 'Some Aspects of Meaning in Anglo-Saxon Art and Literature' *Annuale Mediaevale* 15 (1974) 5–45. See especially 44–5. See also Robert D. Stevick, 'A Formal Analog of *Elene*' *Studies in Medieval and Renaissance History* ns (1982) 47–104, who explores the identicality of geometric structures in folio 94v of the Lindisfarne Gospels and Cynewulf's *Elene*. He observes that 'the design of the decorative page will help us understand the formal plan of the poem, not as its direct source (though that would not be impossible), but as a creation in another medium whose form has its source in the same procedural technique and is developed in accordance with the same esthetic principles' (48).

98 See André Grabar *Christian Iconography: A Study of Its Origins* (Princeton: Princeton University Press 1968) 11.

99 Ibid, 33

100 See, for example, Thomas D. Hill 'Old English Poetry and the Sapiential Tradition' (PH D diss, Cornell 1967) 59; Peter Clemoes *Rhythm and Cosmic Order in Old English Christian Literature* (Cambridge: Cambridge University Press 1970) 15; and Alvin A. Lee 'Old English Poetry, Mediaeval Exegesis and Modern Criticism' *Studies in the Literary Imagination* 8 (1975) 67.

101 *Studies in the Literary Imagination* 8 (1975) 15–46

102 Ibid, 20–1. For a fuller treatment of the relationship between hagiography and iconography, consult Earl's doctoral dissertation, 'Literary Problems in Early Medieval Hagiography' (Cornell 1971).

CHAPTER ONE: *GUTHLAC A*

A version of this chapter was read at the sixth annual Rocky Mountain Conference on British Studies, Colorado Springs, 25–7 October 1979.

1 Compare these statements to that in *Juliana*, lines 55–7: 'næfre þu þæs swiðlic / sar gegearwast, // þurh hæstne nið, / heardra wita, // þæt þu mec onwende / worda þissa' (never, through violent hatred, will you prepare such severe pain of hard torments that you might turn me from these words), and

see my discussion of them in chap 2, p 47, above. All quotations of *Guthlac A* are from Roberts, ed *The Guthlac Poems of the Exeter Book.*

2 See Greenfield *A Critical History of Old English Literature* 119. He writes: 'From beginning to end [of *Guthlac A*] there is emphasis upon the virtuous individual vs. the sinful crowd, upon earthly transience vs. heavenly permanence, upon ineffectual words vs. significant deeds.' But he concentrates his discussion on the beorg symbol as thematic focal point for the poem.

3 'The Prologue of the Old English "Guthlac A"' *Medieval Studies* 23 (1961) 304.

4 'Saints' Lives' in *Continuations and Beginnings* ed Eric G. Stanley (London: Thomas Nelson 1966) 56

5 Shook argues that the central theme of the poem concerns angelology. See 'The Burial Mound in *Guthlac A*' MP 58 (1960) 1, and 'The Prologue of "Guthlac A,"' espec 294–9.

6 'Guthlac A: An Interpretation' MS 33 (1971) 57

7 'Some Discriminations' 68

8 Ibid, 69

9 *Form and Style in Early English Literature* (London: Methuen 1971) 22–3

10 As noted above, Lipp, 'Guthlac A: An Interpretation' 52, and Calder, 'Some Discriminations' 69, discern only five sections in the prologue, viewing lines 60–80 as a single unit.

11 Since Paul F. Reichardt deals effectively with the nature theme, it is not necessary to trace its development here. See 'Guthlac A and the Landscape of Spiritual Perfection' *Neophilologus* 58 (1974) 331–8.

12 Cynewulf exploits the technique of physically separating a word pair normally collocated in a different way in *Elene*. See chap III, pp 63–4.

13 Since, as S.K. Das observes, *Guthlac A* symbolically recreates the 'corruption of First Man and the Temptation of Christ' (*Cynewulf and the Cynewulf Canon* [Calcutta: University of Calcutta Press 1942] 233; see also Lee *Guest-Hall of Eden* [New Haven: Yale University Press 1972] 109), light and darkness have special importance in the poem's iconography, beyond their general association with goodness and evil. In Christian iconographic paintings light (in the form of the glory, nimbus, and aureole) is traditionally associated with sanctity. Guthlac's movement towards the light and away from the darkness first encompassing his beorg also functions within the iconographic tradition, for Christ is sometimes associated with black and darkness in pictures of the Temptation. See Clara Erskine Clement *A Handbook of Christian Symbols and Stories of the Saints* (Boston: Ticknor 1886) 2, 9.

14 Changes in Guthlac's place on earth also occur after line 348. Initially referred to as 'bimiþen fore monnum' (hidden before men [147a]) and 'dygle stowe' (secret place [159a, 215a]), it then becomes 'leofestan // earde on eorðan' (the dearest place on earth [427b–8a]), while the plain becomes 'grenan wong' (the

green plain [477a, 746a]) and 'sigewong' (the victory plain [742a]). Additionally, the term 'leofestan earde' is then applied to heaven (655b–56a).

15 In her discussion of the nature theme in *Guthlac A* Toby Langen observes that 'from the time of Jesus' walking on the water and calming the storm, Christians have considered closeness to or power over nature emblematic of holiness. We have recapitulations of both events in saints' lives, and close relationships with birds are commonplace' ('A Commentary on the Two Old English Poems on St. Guðlac' [PH D diss, Washington 1973] 66). See further Zacharias P. Thundyil, *Covenant in Anglo-Saxon Thought* (Madras: Macmillan Co of India 1972) 185, 189, who states that 'the *communio sanctorum* of the Apostles' Creed was understood by the early Church not only to mean communion of saints but communion of holy things' (185). Jean Daniélou, *From Shadows To Reality* trans Dom Wulstan Hibberd (London: Burns and Oates 1960) 15, alludes to the typological significance of having power over animals. Adam, a type of Christ, had such power in Paradise.

16 Two auxiliary features of the envelope are the repetition of the word 'gecorene' (chosen [lines 59b, 797a]), the first instance referring to 'the few,' the second to the saint, and the echo of 'Stod se dygle stow / dryhtne in gemyndum' (The secret place stood in the mind of God [215]) in 'Stod se grena wong / in Godes wære' (The green plain stood in God's keeping [746]). In the latter case 'the difference between intent (*gemyndum*) and keeping (*wære*) is the difference between plan and accomplishment' (Langen 'A Commentary' 70).

17 *Old English Verse* (London: Hutchinson University Library 1972) 130. See also Calder, 'Some Discriminations' 71, who agrees with Shippey but argues that no progress should be visible since 'Guthlac has not yet been supremely triumphant.'

18 For an analysis of this speech see chap 2, pp 46–7.

19 See chap 3, pp 65ff.

20 See Bruce Mitchell and Fred C. Robinson *A Guide to Old English* rev edn (Toronto: University of Toronto Press 1982) 114–15, and Stephen A. Barney *Word-Hoard: An Introduction to Old English Vocabulary* (New Haven: Yale University Press 1977) 10.

21 Isidore defines *anaphora* as follows: 'Anaphora est repetitio eiusdem verbi per principia versuum plurimorum' (Anaphora is the repetition of the same word at the beginnings of many verses [*Etymologia* I. xxxvi. 8]; my trans).

22 Peah occurs only one time outside direct discourse (line 516b), when the poet expresses wonder at Guthlac's having to endure additional torments.

23 Conditional gif clauses appear four times in the narrative portions of the poem: lines 34a, 195b, 236a, 433a.

24 Sustained rhyme (more than two full lines) occurs in line 24–5, 75–7, 729–30, 808–10, each time reinforcing spiritual truth. For a discussion of rhyme in the

poem see Jane Roberts 'A Metrical Examination of the Poems *Guthlac A* and *Guthlac B' Proceedings of the Royal Irish Academy* 71 (1971) 106–8.

25 Two other points, demonstrating progress in the poem, pertain to Guthlac's final speech. The demons accuse the saint of 'oferhygd' (pride [line 269a]) in their first speech; now Guthlac does the same to them (661a). Secondly, Guthlac applies the word 'idel' to the demons' words both here (662) and in his second speech (308b). A progression is implicit, since through the first instance of the word the poet merely tells us that the demons speak without real force, and by the second instance he has shown that to be true.

26 Kemp Malone, in *A Literary History of England* ed Albert C. Baugh (New York: Appleton-Century-Crofts 1948) 73

27 Woolf *Juliana* 19

CHAPTER TWO: *JULIANA*

A version of this chapter was read at the Fifth Ohio Conference on Medieval and Renaissance Studies, Cleveland, 12–14 October 1978.

1 Calder *Cynewulf* 93. For a slight elaboration of Calder's argument see R. Barton Palmer 'Characterization in the Old English *Juliana' South Atlantic Bulletin* 41.4 (1976) 10–21.

2 Calder *Cynewulf* 94

3 Ibid, 79

4 Formal features characterizing direct discourse in this poem do not generally characterize the narrative portions, which comprise 271 of the 730 lines. For instance, variational chiasmus occurs outside direct discourse only twice (lines 1–3, 579–80), and as Claes Schaar points out (*Critical Studies in the Cynewulf Group* [1949; repr New York: Haskell House 1967] 126–8), dialogue tends to consist of complex, narrative of compound sentences. Additionally, the words gedwola and soð (discussed on pp 57ff above) never occur in the poem's narrative sections.

5 All quotations from *Juliana* are from Woolf's edition. I have taken the liberty of changing ꞹ to w and ȝ to g in the Old English.

6 Cassiodorus defines *parison* in 'In psalterium expositio,' PL LXX, col 287, as 'equality of sentence parts.' For a discussion of this figure see Dorothy M. Jehle 'Latin Rhetoric in the Signed Poems of Cynewulf' (PH D diss, Loyola of Chicago 1973) 49.

7 Das, *Cynewulf and the Cynewulf Canon* 106, comments as follows on lines 51–3: 'The juxtaposition of the *sæmran gode, deofolgield, hæðenfeoh* 51–53 with *soðne god, gæsta Hleo* 47–49 is a stroke of art; for these represent the contradicting agencies at work behind the two conflicting elements of the poem

noted above, namely, God and the dark ministers of hell; in other words, Christianity and paganism. Thus, the poet identifies the devils with the heathen gods.'

8 Schaar *Critical Studies in the Cynewulf Group* 191. Schaar notes other chiastic arrangements in the Cynewulfian poems, but variational chiasmus is the most striking stylistic device and can be easily noticed by the reader. Isidore defines *chiasmus* under the Latin term *antimetabole*, which is 'conversio verborum, quae ordine mutato contrarium efficit sensum' (a reversal of words, which produces a contrary sense by changed order [see *Etymologia* II. xxi. 11]; my translation).

9 See George S. Tate 'Chiasmus as Metaphor: The "Figura Crucis" Tradition and "The Dream of the Rood" ' *NM* 79 (1978) 114–25.

10 Cynewulf uses initial stress on finite verbs eight times in the first twenty-five lines of the poem, where it is appropriate to the subject matter (5, 6, 11, 14, 15, 16, 17, 22), but otherwise concentrates it in direct discourse. Juliana uses it six times in her confrontations with the human antagonists (49, 53, 111, 181, 212, 223), while they employ it only twice apiece (Affricanus: 99, 144; Eleusius: 194, 198).

11 'Tunc Juliana prudenti pertractans consilio dixit ad eos: Euntes dicite Eleusio: Si credideris Deo meo, et adoraveris Patrem et Filium et Spiritum Sanctum, accipiam te maritum. Quod si nolueris, quaere tibi aliam uxorem' (William Strunk, ed *The Juliana of Cynewulf* [London and Boston: D.C. Heath 1904] 34). Michael J.B. Allen and Daniel G. Calder translate: 'When you return, say to Eleusius, "If you believe in my God and worship the Father, the Son and the Holy Spirit, I will accept you as a husband; if not, look for another wife" ' (*Sources and Analogues of Old English Poetry: The Major Latin Texts in Translation* [Cambridge: D.S. Brewer 1976] 123). I will use Strunk's edition of the Latin source and the Allen and Calder translation of it throughout the text.

12 See Das's comments on these lines, *Cynewulf and the Cynewulf Canon* 155.

13 Roberta Frank 'Some Uses of Paronomasia in Old English Scriptural Verse' *Speculum* 47 (1972) 221

14 Das, *Cynewulf and the Cynewulf Canon* 142, discusses the effect of rhyme in lines 149–52.

15 *Juliana* 17

16 Ludwig Borinski, *Der Stil König Alfreds: eine Studie zur Psychologie der Rede* (Leipzig: Sächsische Forschung-institute 1934) 63, notes that Old English has a 'Tendenz zur kurzen Satzkern' (quoted in David Carkeet 'Aspects of Old English Style' *Language and Style* 10 [1977] 174).

17 Arthur G. Brodeur, *The Art of Beowulf* (Berkeley and Los Angeles: University of California Press 1969) 39, appropriately observes that variation 'could be a dangerous instrument in the hands of an inferior poet: it could impart on the

one hand an effect of sheer redundancy, on the other an unpleasing jerkiness of pace; it could stiffen the flow of style, and clog the stream of thought.'

18 See Isidore *Etymologia* II. xx. 4. See also Jehle, 'Latin Rhetoric in the Signed Poems of Cynewulf' 54, who refers to Aquila Romanus for a definition of this figure: '*Tautologia*, he says, results when a noun or any word is explained by many words.'

19 *The Use of Swa in Old English* (Baltimore: Johns Hopkins University Press 1932) 58. Cf 'Sie ðæt on cyninges dome swa deað swa lif swa he him forgifan wille' (Be it in the king's judgment, as well death as life as he will grant him [*Laws of King Alfred* 7, cited in Bosworth and Toller *An Anglo-Saxon Dictionary* (London: Oxford University Press 1898) Sv 'swa,' VI 2(a)]).

20 Ericson *The Use of Swa in Old English* 60

21 We may note further Cynewulf's famous swa passage in *Christ* II (lines 591–6a) and Peter Clemoes's comment on it: Cynewulf 'uses rhythm to create outward pattern ... he exploits the structure of the verse to organize his presentation of every man's absolute choice between heaven and hell as a tight, rhetorically figured series of antitheses' (*Rhythm and Cosmic Order* 11).

22 *Juliana* 17

23 The Latin reads as follows: 'Per misericordes deos Appollinem Dianam, quod si permanseris in his sermonibus, feris te tradam' (Strunk, 35): 'By the merciful gods, Apollo and Diana, if you persist in speaking like this, I will hand you over to wild beasts' (Allen and Calder, 123).

24 'Concerning Figures and Tropes' trans Tannenhaus, in *Readings in Medieval Rhetoric* ed Miller et al, 113. The Latin reads: 'Synchisis est hyperbaton ex omni parte confusum'; see *Corpus Christianorum* CXXIIIA, 159.

25 Bartlett *The Larger Rhetorical Patterns in Anglo-Saxon Poetry* 101

26 Das *Cynewulf and the Cynewulf Canon* 157

27 The Latin reads 'Dic, dulcissima mea Juliana, quomodo me tanto tempore delusisti? Quis te persuasit colere alienum Deum? Convertere ad me et declina omnes cruciatus qui tibi parati sunt si sacrificare nolueris' (Strunk, 35): 'Tell me, my sweetest Juliana, why have you mocked me for so long? Who persuaded you to worship a strange god? Turn back to me and escape all the torments prepared for you if you refuse to sacrifice' (Allen and Calder, 124).

28 Cynewulf varies the chiastic figure in other portions of the poem as well (eg, 4b–6a). Jehle comments: 'This slight delay in completing the *chiasmus* prevents monotony and recalls Quintilian's statement that figures are no longer an ornament to style when used immoderately' ('Latin Rhetoric in the Signed Poems of Cynewulf' 51).

29 Das *Cynewulf and the Cynewulf Canon* 171. See 158ff for an explanation of intonation, and see 155–65 for the important sound elements which converge in line 168.

30 Ibid, 171

31 On religious laughter in *Juliana* see Calder *Cynewulf* 81. For the use of the comic in saints' lives see Curtius *European Literature* 428.

32 The Latin source reads: 'Ecce principium quæstion is: accede, et sacrifica magnæ Dianæ, et liberaberis de tormentis. Quod si nolueris, per magnum deum Apollinem, non tibi parcam' (Strunk, 36): 'Look, this was just the beginning of the test. Give in; sacrifice to the great Diana and you will be freed from torment. But if you refuse, by the great god Apollo, I won't spare you' (Allen and Calder, 124).

33 George A. Smithson, *The Old English Christian Epic* University of California Publications in Modern Philology 1 (1910) 321, 356, 372, characterizes the demon's speeches as 'tedious digressions.'

34 See Jehle, 'Latin Rhetoric in the Signed Poems of Cynewulf' 59–75, who notes several figures in the devil's speeches. Among them are anaphora, synchisis, tautologia, schesis onomaton, zeugma, and parison.

35 Frank 'Some Uses of Paronomasia' 210

36 *Critical Studies in the Cynewulf Group* 191–2

37 Ibid, 124

38 Eric G. Stanley 'Old English Poetic Diction and the Interpretation of *The Wanderer, The Seafarer* and *The Penitent's Prayer,*' Anglia 73 (1953) 413–66; repr in *Essential Articles for the Study of Old English Poetry* ed Jess B. Bessinger, Jr, and Stanley Kahrl (Hamden, Conn: Archon Books 1968) 458–514; see espec 487. See also Anderson *Cynewulf: Structure, Style, and Theme in His Poetry* (London and Toronto: Associated University Presses 1983) 71–2; Anderson observes that the long catalogues in the devil's dialogue in *Juliana* serve an artistic function they do not have in the Latin source. Lines 289–315a, for example, 'prepare us for the Gregorian analysis of temptation and sin that follows (345–417a)' (72).

39 In her study of 'Figures of Evil in Old English Poetry,' *Leeds Studies in English* 8 (1975), 5, Joyce M. Hill notes that 'one of the ways ... in which those guilty of mortal sin manifested their spiritual corruption was in their perverted imitation of the good. Their motivation for this behaviour was envy, and pride in their own worth. Satan imitated God, but subsequent sinners imitated Satan himself, and if unrepentant, earned for themselves the same fate as him: a state of everlasting exile and perpetual banishment from God's sight. Anglo-Saxon poets followed Christian tradition in presenting Satan, Adam and Eve, and Cain in varying degrees as imitators, and the *Beowulf* poet added a fifth in Grendel.' For a discussion of the devil's penchant for masquerading as an angel, see J.M. Evans '*Genesis B* and Its Background' RES 14 (1963) 7–9.

40 On the relation of the demon to Satan, Rosemary Woolf observes that he 'is only slightly less terrified of his *fæder* in hell than he is of the saint herself. The clear implication is that the punishment in hell is not restricted to men who have failed to satisfy God, but is also inflicted on devils who have failed to

satisfy Satan.' See 'The Devil in Old English Poetry' RES 4 (1953) 1–12; repr in *Essential Articles* 164–79; see 171.

41 The Latin reads: 'Domina mea Juliana, dimitte me; jam amplius noli homini-
bus me ridiculum facere; non enim potero postea homines convincere. Patrem
meum superasti, me vinxisti, quid adhuc vis? Dicunt increduli Christianos misericordes esse, tu autem in me ferox visa es' (Strunk, 43): 'My lady Juliana, let
me go. Don't make me even more ridiculous now to men, for afterwards I'll be
unable to conquer them. You have conquered my father; you have bound me.
What more do you want? The unbelievers say the Christians are merciful, but
you seem ferocious to me' (Allen and Calder, 128).

CHAPTER THREE: *ELENE*

1 Commentators who view Elene's treatment of Judas judgmentally have fallen
victim to the tendency of approaching the poem's first part from a simple, single perspective. From Judas's standpoint, Elene's actions are, of course, cruel
and brutal, and Rosemary Woolf seems justified in remarking that the saint's
heroic resolve sounds false ('Saints' Lives' 47). But if we view the poem from
the simultaneous perspective of an achieved and an aspiring saint, both Elene's
heroic resolve and our sympathetic response to Judas justify themselves. For
reactions akin to Woolf's see Regan, 'Evangelicism as the Informing Principle
of Cynewulf's "Elene" ' *Traditio* 29 (1973) 34–5, who grants the validity of
Woolf's remarks about Elene but questions whether our sympathetic response
to Judas is unintentional. See also James Doubleday, 'The Speech of Stephen
and the Tone of *Elene*,' in *Anglo-Saxon Poetry* ed Nicholson and Frese, 121–2,
who justifies his dubious political reading of the poem by concentrating on
Elene's harsh treatment of Judas. For a reversal of the positions represented by
Woolf, Regan, and Doubleday see Campbell, 'Cynewulf's Multiple Revelations.' He defends Elene's treatment of Judas, since she figurally represents the
Church, which had to ' "snibben" evil wherever it found it' 266–7). Campbell
does not satisfactorily deal with our sympathetic response to Judas, however.
2 The initial ambiguity of the poem has been accounted for by Thomas Hill,
'Sapiential Structure and Figural Narrative in the Old English "Elene" ' *Traditio* 27 (1971) 162–3, and by Regan, 'Evangelicism as the Informing Principle of
"Elene" ' 33, in terms of the polysemous nature of the text. Both see Elene
and Judas as figural representatives of the Christians and Jews respectively.
3 On paronomasia see Frank 'Some Uses of Paronomasia' 210.
4 All quotations from *Elene* are from Pamela Gradon, ed *Cynewulf's Elene*. I
have taken the liberty of changing ƿ to w and ȝ to g.
5 Frank 'Some Uses of Paronomasia' 221
6 The oppositions in *Elene* are variously discussed by Smithson, *The Old English
Christian Epic* 312; Greenfield, *A Critical History of Old English Literature*

114; Robert Stepsis and Richard Rand, 'Contrast and Conversion in "Elene" '
NM 70 (1969) 273–82; Gardner, *'Elene* and the *Dream of the Rood'* 85–98;
Calder, *Cynewulf* 104–38; Regan, 'Evangelicism as the Informing Principle of
"Elene" ' 30; and Anderson, *Cynewulf* 114.

7 *Cynewulf* 160

8 Ibid, 161

9 For an alternative stylistic reading of this speech see W.A.M. Van der Wurf
   'Cynewulf's *Elene*: The First Speech to the Jews' *Neophilologus* 66 (1982) 301–
   12.

10 The entire speech in Latin lacks the obvious structural divisions of the Old
   English: 'Cognovi de sanctis libris propheticis, quia fuistis dilecti Dei; sed quia
   repellentes omnem sapientiam, eum qui volebat de maledicto vos redimere ma-
   ledixistis, et eum qui per sputum oculos vestros illuminavit immundis potius
   sputis injuriastis, et eum qui mortuos vestros vivificabat in mortem tradidistis,
   et lucem tenebras existimastis et veritatem mendacium, pervenit in vos male-
   dictum quod est in lege vetra scriptum. Nunc autem eligite ex vobis viros, qui
   diligenter sciunt legem vestram, ut respondeant mihi de quibus interrogavero
   eos' (Charles W. Kent, ed *Elene: An Old English Poem* [Boston: Ginn 1889]
   29–30). For a translation of the whole of the *Acta Quiriaci*, consult Allen and
   Calder *Sources and Analogues of Old English Poetry* 60–80. They translate
   Elene's speech as follows: 'I have learned from the prophets' holy books that
   you were God's chosen ones. Rejecting all wisdom, however, you cursed Him
   who wanted to redeem you from the curse; you wronged Him who with His
   spit brought light to your eyes, spitting filthily instead on Him; you betrayed
   into death the man who brought life to your dead; you assumed the light was
   darkness and the truth a lie; accordingly, the curse which is written in your
   law has come upon you. Now from among yourselves choose men who know
   your law well, so they can answer the questions I shall ask them' (62). I will
   use the Kent edition of the Latin and the Allen and Calder translation of it
   throughout.

11 Elene has thirteen speeches in all, seven long speeches containing ten lines or
   more and six short speeches containing nine lines or less. See the chart on p
   86.

12 Compare Juliana's use of asyndetic sentence structure in *Juliana*, line 217, and
   my comment on it in chap 2, p 48.

13 In *A Literary History of England* ed Baugh, 25–9. For a fuller treatment of the
   device see Richard A. Lewis 'Plurilinear Alliteration in Old English Poetry'
   Texas Studies in Literature and Language 16 (1975) 589–602.

14 'Studies in Anglo-Saxon Literary Styles' (PH D diss, Virginia 1968) 18

15 For a discussion of anticipation and recapitulation in Old English see Mitchell
   and Robinson *A Guide to Old English* 63–4.

16 See speeches 1 (lines 288–9), 2 (364–5), 5 (643–4), 6 (670–1), 12 (686–7), 13 (852–3), and the discussion on p 73.

17 See Schaar *Critical Studies in the Cynewulf Group* 188–9.

18 For a discussion of what the elaboration implies see Gardner '*Elene* and the *Dream of the Rood*' 92–3, and Hill 'Sapiential Structure and Figural Narrative in the Old English "Elene" ' 169–70.

19 See Varda Fish 'Theme and Pattern in Cynewulf's *Elene*' NM 76 (1975) 5. See also Stevick, 'A Formal Analog of *Elene*' 99, who cautions that 'any putative three-part narrative may have to be reduced to two parts (those concerning Constantine and Elene-Judas), to which a one-section addition [the epilogue] has been made.'

20 Of this speech Schaar notes: 'The chiasmus is here placed at the end of the queen's speech and the rhetorical artifice, along with the expanded half-lines, give an emphatic close to the queen's menaces' (*Critical Studies in the Cynewulf Group* 189).

21 Hill 'Sapiential Structure and Figural Narrative in the Old English "Elene" ' 169; Campbell 'Cynewulf's Multiple Revelations' 269; Fish 'Theme and Pattern in Cynewulf's *Elene*' 17

22 For a much later use of antithetical 'dialects' in one character, see the morality play *Mankind* and W.A. Davenport's discussion of it in *Fifteenth-Century English Drama: The Early Moral Plays and Their Literary Relations* (Cambridge: D.S. Brewer 1982) 36ff. Davenport observes that Mankind can initially speak in both a lofty and a low dialect, showing us, 'in stylistic terms, the range of [spiritual] possibilities for Mankind' (39).

23 Stepsis and Rand, 'Contrast and Conversion in "Elene" ' 281, note some of Cynewulf's additions to his Latin source. They do not discuss this passage, however. On Cynewulf's amplifications of the Latin see Gardner '*Elene* and the *Dream of the Rood*' 86, and Schaar, *Critical Studies in the Cynewulf Group* 25, who states that 'the style of Cynewulf's poem is much fuller than that of the Latin legends.' On the demon's speeches in *Juliana* see chap 2 above, pp 55ff.

24 Campbell 'Cynewulf's Multiple Revelations' 268. See Gardner '*Elene* and the *Dream of the Rood*' 92–3; Doubleday 'The Speech of Stephen and the Tone of *Elene*' 121; and Regan 'Evangelicism as the Informing Principle of "Elene" ' 31, for suggested explanations for the mixed style of Judas's dialogue.

25 'Typology and Iconographic Style in Early Medieval Hagiography' 26

26 In discussing this aspect of Judas's initial 'person,' Hill writes that 'Judas seems to be fully aware of the significance of Christ's death on the Cross and to accept his father's and grandfather's Christian views without any specific reservations, and at the same time is resolutely determined to prevent Elene from finding the Cross "þy læs toworpen sien / frod fyrngewritu ond þa

fæderlican / lare forleton" (430–32). This sharp contrast between Judas' apparent acceptance of a Christian understanding of the significance of the Cross,
and his resolute efforts to keep Elene from finding it, is particularly noticeable
since a word or a phrase would have been enough to obviate the difficulty'
('Sapiential Structure and Figural Narrative in the Old English "Elene" ' 163).

27 For instances of the imperative mood in direct discourse in the poem see the
chart on p 86 above.

28 See Kent, 36–8, and Allen and Calder, 63–4.

29 Anderson *Cynewulf* 148

30 Campbell 'Cynewulf's Multiple Revelations' 269. See also Stanley, 'Old English
Poetic Diction,' in *Essential Articles* ed Bessinger and Kahrl, 469, who speaks of
the 'parabolical diction' of this passage.

31 'Bread and Stone: Cynewulf's "Elene" 611–18' *NM* 76 (1975) 552–3

32 On prolepsis in the passage see Hill 'Sapiential Structure and Figural Narrative
in the Old English "Elene" ' 172–3, and Regan 'Evangelicism as the Informing
Principle of "Elene" ' 39.

33 Kent, 41. 'When someone in solitary confinement has loaves set before him,
will he eat stones?' (Allen and Calder, 64)

34 For a discussion of Affricanus's speech see chap 2, pp 51–2.

35 Antistrophe, which involves the repetition of words at the ends of clauses, is a
term not found in Isidore, Cassiodorus, or Bede. Martianus Capella and Aquila
Romanus, however, do include it in their discussions. See Jehle 'Latin Rhetoric
in the Signed Poems of Cynewulf' 149.

36 Six uses of ic in ten lines represent the highest concentration of the pronoun in
the entire poem. The next-highest concentration (five) occurs in Judas's speech
from the pit, lines 699–708.

37 Gordon Whatley 'Cynewulf and Troy: A Note on "Elene" 642–61' *NQ* 218
(1973) 204

38 The Latin source says simply: 'Obsecro vos, educite me, et ego ostendam vobis
crucem Christi' (Kent, 45): 'I implore you, take me out and I will show you
Christ's Cross' (Allen and Calder, 65).

39 Anderson *Cynewulf* 148

40 *Critical Studies in the Cynewulf Group* 190. Kent, 6, calls Judas's prayer 'a
most remarkable production.'

41 Schaar, *Critical Studies in the Cynewulf Group* 122, notes the consummate
artistry of these lines, and Shippey elaborates, concentrating on the differences
between the Old English and the Latin: 'One notes that the order is now chiastic, i.e. that the two *gif*-clauses are at beginning and end, with the two main
clauses in the centre, while furthermore a quite new distinction has been introduced, the contrast of *woruld* and *wuldor*, earth and Heaven, both supplying
arguments for Christ's status as the Son of God. The result is a rather striking
double argument and reassertion of the main point. But this has been con-

structed by Cynewulf, quite deliberately, on the basis of what may have been the Latin author's mistake or at best infelicity! Similar arrangements are not uncommon' (*Old English Verse* 167).

42 The third instance of indirect discourse in Judas's dialogue also occurs after his conversion and also employs plurilinear alliteration; see lines 1188–95.

43 Alarik Rynell, 'Parataxis and Hypotaxis as a Criterion of Syntax and Style' *Lunds Universitets Årsskrift* NF avd 1, Bd 48, Nr 3 (1952) 44, points out that parataxis can make a narrative 'more lively and animated, dynamic and dramatic, emotional and impassioned' than hypotaxis, which tends to produce a more 'complicated and abstract, more calm and static, more logical and dispassionate' effect.

44 Raw *The Art and Background of Old English Poetry* 46

45 Ellen F. Wright, 'Cynewulf's *Elene* and the "Singal Sacu" ' NM 76 (1975) 547, talks of the difficulty of conversion, and Fish, 'Theme and Pattern in Cynewulf's *Elene*' 22–3, points out that even Cynewulf's confinement is verbal. His conversion is to a poet of the spirit rather than of the letter.

CHAPTER FOUR: *GUTHLAC B*

1 'Death and Transfiguration' 84. Das contends that *Guthlac B*, like *Guthlac A*, is 'expressly built upon the conception of the Fall of Man as its basis' (*Cynewulf and the Cynewulf Canon* 232).

2 Rosier 'Death and Transfiguration' 84

3 Ibid, 85

4 See Calder 'Theme and Strategy in *Guthlac B*' 234.

5 Ibid

6 Thomas D. Hill 'The First Beginning and the Purest Earth: *Guthlac B*, Lines 1–14,' *Notes and Queries* 28 (1981) 387–9

7 *Felix's Life of Saint Guthlac* ed Bertram Colgrave (Cambridge: Cambridge University Press 1956). All quotations of Felix are from this edition. I will use Colgrave's facing-page translation throughout this chapter.

8 All quotations of *Guthlac B* are from Roberts, ed *The Guthlac Poems of the Exeter Book*.

9 Thomas D. Hill 'The Typology of the Week and the Numerical Structure of the Old English *Guthlac B*' MS 37 (1975) 531–6

10 J. Richard Stracke, 'Eþelboda: *Guthlac B*, 1003' MP 74 (1976–7) 194, shows that the dictionary definition of eþelboda as 'native preacher' is inaccurate: 'The poet consistently uses eþel not for a literal native land but for the state by which man metaphorically lives with God.'

11 'Death and Transfiguration' 88

12 Ibid, 86

13 Ibid, 86–8

14 Ibid, 89

15 Ibid, 90

16 Emile Mâle *The Gothic Image: Religious Art in France of the Thirteenth Century* trans Dora Nussey (1913; repr New York: Harper and Row 1958) 5

17 D.W. Robertson, Jr *A Preface to Chaucer: Studies in Medieval Perspectives* (Princeton: Princeton University Press 1962) 121–2

18 Jerome Mazzaro *Transformations in the Renaissance English Lyric* (Ithaca and London: Cornell University Press 1970) 10ff

19 Roberts 'A Metrical Examination' 107

20 E. de Bruyne *L'Esthetique du Moyen Age* (Louvain: Édition de l'institut Supériéur de Philosophie 1947) 135. See also Robertson *A Preface to Chaucer* 114ff.

21 Roberts 'A Metrical Examination ' 107. She notes that 'the repeated forms are all within dip portions of the lines.'

22 In constructions where separations occur between auxiliary and infinitive or linking verb and complement, a maximum of one line divides the parts. See, for example, lines 831 ('ac he on þam lande / lifgan moste,' but he could live in that land) and 1315b–16a ('sweg wæs on lyfte // gehyred under heofonum,' the sound was in the air heard under the heavens). See also 948a, 971b, 993b–4, 1057b–8, 1061b–2, 1114–15, 1134, 1145b–6, 1154b–6, 1201b–2, 1225b–6, 1317.

23 The syntactic and rhetorical flourishes adorning the Old English poem have relevance to meaning and are unique to the vernacular account of Guthlac's death. The Latin original lacks the stylistic features of the Old English: 'Fili mi, languoris mei causa est, ut ab his membris spiritus separetur; finis autem infirmitatis meae erit octavus dies, in quo, peracto huius vitae cursu, debeo dissolvi et esse cum Christo; expedit enim, sarcina carnis abiecta, agnum Dei sequi' (152–4); 'My son, the cause of my sickness is that my spirit is leaving this body; and the end of my sickness will be on the eighth day when, having finished the course of this life, I must be released and be with Christ; for it is fitting that I should put off the burden of the flesh and follow the Lamb of God' (153–5). Felix tends to use direct discourse to convey information, not to develop major thematic interests.

24 Gordon Hall Gerould observes that the vernacular lines 'give Guthlac's consoling reply, which contains some of the noblest and tenderest poetry in Old English' ('The Old English Poems on St. Guthlac and Their Latin Source' *Modern Language Notes* 37 [1917] 88). The Latin source reads as follows: 'Fili mi, tristitiam ne admittas; non enim mihi labor est ad Dominum meum, cui servivi, in requiem venire aeternam' (My son, do not give way to sadness, for it is no hardship to me to enter on eternal rest with my Lord whom I have served [154, 155]).

25 *Critical Studies in the Cynewulf Group* 183

26 Calder 'Theme and Strategy in *Guthlac B*' 234–5

27 Cf lines 858a and 863a ('deopra firena,' of deep sins); 864b and 871b ('feond rixade,' the enemy ruled; 'deað ricsade,' death ruled); 934b and 943b ('neah geþrungen,' thronged near, closely assailed); and 942b and 954b ('wæs þam bancofan, wæs se bancofa,' the body was).

28 Two subsidiary points should be made. The poet indicates Guthlac's strength, as Cynewulf does Elene's, through the use of the imperative mood here (lines 1064a, 1077a) and in his third speech (1171b, 1175b, 1178b, 1182b, 1192b). And the differences between saint and servant are symbolized in their use of the verb to be, which seems to index their respective spiritual attainments: Guthlac employs the existentially certain 'ic eom' twice (1077b, 1268b), Beccel, not at all.

29 The Latin source for this speech reads: 'Fili mi, quia tempus nunc propinquat, ultima mandata mea intende. Postquam spiritus hoc corpusculum deseruerit, perge ad sororem meam Pegam, et dicas illi, quia ideo aspectum ipsius in hoc saeculo vitavi, ut in aeternum coram Patre nostro in gaudio sempiterno ad invicem videamur. Dices quoque, ut illa corpus meum inponat in sarcofago et in sindone involvat, quam mihi Ecgburh mittebat. Nolui quidem vivens ullo lineo tegmine corpus meum tegere, sed pro amore dilectae Christi virginis, quae haec munera mihi mittebat, ad volvendum corpus meum reservare curavi' (My son, since my time now draws near, listen to my last commands. After my spirit has left this poor body, go to my sister Pega and tell her that I have in this life avoided her presence so that in eternity we may see one another in the presence of our Father amid eternal joys. Tell her also to place my body in the coffin and wrap it in the cloth which Ecgburh sent me. While I was alive I was unwilling to cover my body with any linen vestment, but out of affection for the virgin beloved of Christ who sent me this gift, I have taken care to keep it to wrap my body in [154–6, 155–7]).

30 The Latin source for lines 1227–69a reads: 'Fili mi, de hac re sollicitari noli; quod enim vivens ulli hominum indicare nolue, nunc tibi manifestabo. A secundo etenim anno, quo hanc heremum habitare coeperam, mane vespereque semper angelum consolationis meae ad meum colloquium Dominus mittebat, qui mihi misteria, quae non licet homini narrare, monstrabat, qui duritiam laboris mei caelestibus oraculis sublevabat, qui absentia mihi monstrando ut praesentia praesentabat. O fili, haec dicta mea conserva, nullique alii nuntiaveris, nisi Pegae aut Ecgberhto anachoritae, si umquam in colloquium eius tibi venire contigerit, qui solus haec sic fuisse cognoscet' (My son, do not be troubled about this thing, which while I was alive I was unwilling to tell anyone; but now I will make it clear to you. From the second year that I began to inhabit this desert place, every morning and evening the Lord has sent an angel to talk with me for my consolation, who showed me mysteries which it is not lawful for man to utter, who relieved the hardness of my toil with heavenly

oracles, and who revealed to me things which were absent as though they were present. O, my son, keep these words of mine and tell them to no one except to Pega or Ecgberht the anchorite, if ever you should happen to converse with him, for he alone will know that such things have happened to me [156, 157]).

31 This variation parallels Affricanus's technique in *Juliana* (see chap 2, pp 49ff, above), but the stylistic similarity does not give us a moral equation of Beccel and Affricanus. Instability in *Guthlac B*, unlike that in *Juliana*, connotes human fallibility, not evil.

32 See n 30 above.

33 Blanche Colton Williams *Gnomic Poetry in Anglo-Saxon* (1914; repr New York: AMS Press 1966) 63–4

34 On the literary echo in medieval literature generally, see Gradon *Form and Style in Early English Literature* 152–211, espec 152–3 and 160–1. On the literary echo in Cynewulf's poetry consult Schaar *Critical Studies in the Cynewulf Group* 235ff, and Robert E. Diamond 'The Diction of the Signed Poems of Cynewulf' *Philological Quarterly* 38 (1959) 234.

35 Langen, 'A Commentary' 85, points out that Beccel's grief parallels Guthlac's disease. It too has a sudden onset (line 1008) and is hot (1019–20) and swelling (1009). She concludes that the poet undoubtedly 'considers Beccel's frame of mind to share other qualities of disease, to be in effect worldly.'

36 See the Introduction, p 19.

37 See Leonard H. Frey 'Exile and Elegy in Anglo-Saxon Christian Epic Poetry' *JEGP* 62 (1963) 298–9, and Calder 'Theme and Strategy in *Guthlac B*' 237.

CHAPTER FIVE: *ANDREAS*

1 Constance B. Hieatt 'The Harrowing of Mermedonia: Typological Patterns in the Old English "Andreas" ' *NM* 77 (1976) 59

2 *From Shadows to Reality* 40

3 Lee *Guest-Hall of Eden* 109

4 Hieatt 'The Harrowing of Mermedonia' 52

5 Hill 'Figural Narrative in *Andreas' NM* 70 (1969) 261–73; Walsh 'The Baptismal Flood in the Old English *Andreas*: Liturgical and Typological Depths' *Traditio* 33 (1977) 137–58

6 Brooks *Andreas and the Fates of the Apostles* xxvi

7 C.L. Wrenn *A Study of Old English Literature* (New York: W.W. Norton 1967) 129

8 Brooks *Andreas and the Fates of the Apostles* xxvii, and Lee *Guest-Hall of Eden* 83. Woolf, 'Saints' Lives' 51–2, also comments on the curious nature of this poem.

9 'Figural Narrative in *Andreas*' 269

10 'The Living Stone and the Patriarchs: Typological Imagery in *Andreas*, Lines 706–810' *JEGP* 72 (1973) 167–74

11 '*Andreas*: Mermedonian Cannibalism and Figural Narration' *NM* 75 (1974) 74–8. See further James W. Earl 'The Typological Structure of *Andreas*,' in *Old English Literature in Context* ed John D. Niles (Cambrige: D.S. Brewer 1980) 66–89.

12 'Figural Narrative in *Andreas*' 271

13 Hieatt 'The Harrowing of Mermedonia' 51. For a view of the poem that minimizes its hagiographical and typological features, see Edward B. Irving, Jr 'A Reading of *Andreas*' *ASE* 12 (1983) 215–37.

14 See pp 36ff above.

15 Eric G. Stanley '*Beowulf*,' in *Continuations and Beginnings* 138

16 The distribution of stressed finite verbs is as follows:
God   1212b, 1438b
Christ   291b, 612b, 720b (indirect discourse), 1413b (indirect discourse)
Andreas   762b, 789b, 904b, 909b, 1282b, 1295b
Thanes   865b
Mermedonians   1568b, 1604b

17 Chiasmus occurs in lines 1213 (God); 279–80 (Christ); 356, 434b–5a, 902–3a (Andreas). See Schaar, *Critical Studies in the Cynewulf Group* 200ff, who points out the lack of variety in all features of the poem's style.

18 Andreas uses the figure in lines 429–33a.

19 See line 615a (Christ).

20 See line 760 (Andreas).

21 See lines 25b–9a.

22 See lines 393–4 (Andreas) and 963b–4 (Christ).

23 See lines 103–4, 174–5, 216, 1441 (God); 279–80, 292–3a, 424b–5a (Christ); 1193–4 (Andreas); 866–7, 869–70, 887–8 (Thanes). Das, *Cynewulf and the Cynewulf Canon* 191, is incorrect in saying that rhyme 'is merely sporadic' in *Andreas*. But even though the author of the poem 'more than most other Anglo-Saxon poets seems to have been fond of rime' (Arthur G. Brodeur 'A Study of Diction and Style in Three Anglo-Saxon Narrative Poems,' in *Nordica et Anglica: Studies in Honor of Stefan Einarsson* ed Allan H. Orrick [The Hague: Mouton 1968] 104), he does not use it in a discernibly systematic way.

24 Bartlett *The Larger Rhetorical Patterns in Anglo-Saxon Poetry* 104, and Metes 'Word Order Variation as a Stylistic Feature in the Old English *Andreas*' 87–91

25 Besides lines 305–6, which Bartlett mentions as the exception, see 601–2 and 631, which introduce speeches by Christ and show sv order, and 896, which introduces a speech by Andreas and has vs word order.

26 Thomas Rendall, 'Bondage and Freeing from Bondage in Old English Religious Poetry' *JEGP* 73 (1974) 510, points out one of the poet's techniques for empha-

sizing the link between Andreas and Christ: 'By a stress upon the bondage motif not found in either the original *Acts* or the Old English prose version of this
saint's life, the *Andreas* poet is able to parallel Andreas' rescue of his fellow
missionary Matthias with Christ's salvation of man.'

27 'The Diet and Digestion of Allegory in *Andreas*' 150–1

28 Ibid, 154

29 The breakdown in irony coincides with certain developments in the sea voyage,
which Lee describes in *Guest-Hall of Eden*, 93.

30 All quotations of *Andreas* are from Brooks's edition, *Andreas and the Fates of
the Apostles*.

31 'The Diet and Digestion of Allegory in *Andreas*' 148–9

32 Bruce F. Kawin *Telling It Again and Again: Repetition in Literature and Film*
(Ithaca: Cornell University Press 1972) 45

33 On archetypes, repetition, and the abolition of profane time see Mircea Eliade
Cosmos and History: The Myth of the Eternal Return trans Willard R. Trask
(New York: Harper and Row 1959) 35.

34 Hill 'Two Notes on Patristic Allusion in *Andreas*' 156–62

35 Franz Blatt, ed *Die lateinischen Bearbeitungen der Acta Andreae et Matthiae
apud anthropophagos* (Giessen and Copenhagen: Verlag von Alfred Töpelmann
1930) 37. I will use the Allen and Calder translation throughout the text
(*Sources and Analogues of Old English Poetry* 15–34).

36 Predictably, the connection between God and Christ grows more explicit as the
poem progresses. In lines 926ff Christ uses two phrases also used by God: 'in
gramra gripe' 951a–cf 217a), and 'þeh ðu drype ðolie' (955b–cf 1217b).

37 The Latin source reads as follows: 'obsecro te, domine iesu christe magister
bone, quoniam sicut nobis precepisti omnia dereliquimus et secuti sumus te.
Propterea si tu sic mihi hec talia preparasti, et ad escam me dedisti ad devoran-
dum iniquissimis istius civitatis, non effugio preceptum tuum, fiat non sicut
ego volo, sed sicut tu vis, paratus sum enim omnia pro te sustinere, set tantum
deprecor clementiam tuam, ut concedas mihi maxime lumen oculorum meo-
rum, ut vel videam qualiter isti exerpeant caro mea' (Blatt, 35): 'Lord Jesus
Christ, good Master, I am praying to you because we left everything and followed you, just as you told us. That is why, if you have prepared these tortures for me and surrendered me to this city's wicked people to be devoured as
food, I will not run away from your command. May it not be as I want, but as
you do; for I am ready to suffer everything for your sake. Only most of all I
pray you of your mercy that you grant me the light of my eyes so I may see
how they tear my flesh' (Allen and Calder, 16).

38 Andreas is introduced as 'se halga wer' (the holy man [line 168b]) and is not
referred to as 'se halga' until 359a.

39 Greenfield, *A Critical History of Old English Literature* 105–6, similarly analyses this passage.

40 Brodeur's evaluation of variation in *Andreas* especially pertains here: 'The poet's use of variation reveals none of that consciousness of its possibilities as a structural element which marks the superiority of *Beowulf* over all others; for him its value is momentary, and in his hands it tends to slow the action' ('A Study of Diction and Style in Three Anglo-Saxon Narrative Poems' 104).

41 Greenfield *A Critical History of Old English Literature* 107

42 'The *Sphragis* as Apotropaic Sign: *Andreas* 1334–44' *Anglia* 101 (1983) 147–51

43 Das *Cynewulf and the Cynewulf Canon* 230

44 The devil also repeats a phrase used by Andreas of Christ, augmenting the irony of his discourse and the typology of the poem: he says that Andreas speaks 'wordum wrætlicum' (with wondrous words [line 1200a–cf 630a]).

45 Wrenn *A Study of Old English Literature* 129; Gerould *Saints' Legends* 86; Charles W. Kennedy *The Earliest English Poetry* (London: Oxford University Press 1943) 267; Shippey *Old English Verse* 119

46 See especially R.M. Lumiansky 'The Contexts of O.E. "Ealuscerwen" and "Meoduscerwen" ' *JEGP* 48 (1949) 116–26; Leonard J. Peters 'The Relationship of the Old English *Andreas* to *Beowulf*' *PMLA* 66 (1951) 844–63; Hans Schabram 'Andreas und Beowulf. Parallelstellen als Zeugnis für literarische Abhängigkeit' *Nachrichten der Giessener Hochschulgesellschaft* 34 (1965) 201–18; Lee C. Overholster 'A Comparative Study of the Compound Use in *Andreas* and *Beowulf*' (PH D diss, Michigan 1971); David Hamilton '*Andreas* and *Beowulf*: Placing the Hero,' in *Anglo-Saxon Poetry* ed Nicholson and Frese, 81–98. Helen C. White also mentions the connection in her chapter 'The Saint's Legend as a Literary Type,' in *Tudor Books of Saints and Martyrs* (Madison: University of Wisconsin Press 1963) 21.

47 The *Andreas* poet uses the phrase 'eft swa ær' (again as it was before) three times (lines 1274a, 1341a, 1476a), thus underscoring the importance of repetition in the poem. Cf *Guthlac A* 390a.

CONCLUSION

1 *Saints' Legends*

2 *The Legends of the Saints*

3 *Saints' Lives and Chronicles in Early England*

4 *Die englische Heiligenlegende des Mittelalters* (Tübingen: Max Neimeyer Verlag, 1964)

5 Gerould and Wolpers provide the most extended treatments. See *Saints' Legends* 59–94, and *Die englische Heiligenlegende des Mittelalters* 111–30.

6 'Saints' Lives'

7 'Structure and Function in Representative Old English Saints' Lives' *Neophilologus* 57 (1973) 83–93

8 Ibid, 88–9

9 Ibid, 84. For other historical treatments of the saint's life consult Benjamin P. Kurtz *From St. Antony to St. Guthlac* University of California Publications in Modern Philology 12 (1926) 103–46, and Bertram Colgrave 'The Earliest Saints' Lives Written in England' *Proceedings of the British Academy* 44 (1958) 35–60.

10 Lipp *'Guthlac A*: An Interpretation' 46. See also Kathleen E. Dubs, '*Guthlac A* and the Acquisition of Wisdom' *Neophilologus* 65 (1981) 607–13, who tries to remove the poem 'from the constraints of the hagiographic tradition' (612).

11 See Rosier 'Death and Transfiguration,' Greenfield *The Interpretation of Old English Poems* 135, and Kurtz *From St. Antony to St. Guthlac* 146.

12 'Structure and Function' 90–2

13 Consult Margaret Bridges 'Exordial Tradition and Poetic Individuality in Five Old English Hagiographic Poems' ES 60 (1979) 361–79.

14 *The Love of Learning and the Desire for God* trans Catharine Misrahi (New York: Fordham University Press 1961) 200

15 Thomas D. Hill 'The Middle Way: *Idel-Wuldor* and *Egesa* in the Old English *Guthlac A*' RES 30 (1979), 182

16 See chap 5, p 119, above.

17 See also line 1567 and 1579, as well as 214, 234, 1153, and 1369.

18 Shook, 'The Burial Mound in *Guthlac A*' 9, notes that the demons who once tortured the saint are now tortured by him. See also *Guthlac B*, lines 894ff.

19 For the importance of this half-line, see chap 1, p 33, above.

20 See chap 3, pp 87ff, for further discussion of this speech.

21 See Allen and Calder *Sources and Analogues of Old English Poetry* 29.

Bibliography

PRIMARY SOURCES

Allen, Michael J.B., and Daniel G. Calder, trans and eds *Sources and Analogues of Old English Poetry: The Major Latin Texts in Translation* Cambridge: D.S. Brewer 1976

Ambrose, Saint *Hexaemeron.* PL 14

– *Hexameron, Paradise, and Cain and Abel* Trans John J. Savage. New York: Fathers of the Church 1961

Augustine, Saint *Confessions* Trans William Watts, ed W.H.D. Rouse. Loeb Classical Library. 1912; repr 1968, vol 1

Bede *De schematibus et tropis. Corpus Christianorum* CXXIIIA

– *Bede's Ecclesiastical History of the English People* Ed Bertram Colgrave and R.A.B. Mynors. Oxford: Clarendon Press 1969

Behaghel, Otto, ed *Heliand und Genesis* 8th edn rev by Walter Mitzka. Tübingen: Max Niemeyer Verlag 1965

Biblia Sacra 4 vols. Milwaukee: Bruce 1955

Blatt, Franz, ed *Die lateinischen Bearbeitungen der Acta Andreae et Matthiae apud anthropophagos* Giessen and Copenhagen: Verlag von Alfred Töpelmann 1930

Bosworth, Joseph, and T. Northcote Toller *An Anglo-Saxon Dictionary* London: Oxford University Press 1898

Brooks, Kenneth R., ed *Andreas and the Fates of the Apostles* Oxford: Clarendon Press 1961

Cassiodorus, Magnus Aurelius *In psalterium expositio* PL 70

Colgrave, Bertram, ed *Felix's Life of Saint Guthlac* Cambridge: Cambridge University Press 1956

Cynewulf *Cynewulf's Elene* Ed Pamela Gradon. 1958; repr New York: Appleton-Century-Crofts 1966

- *Elene: An Old English Poem* Ed Charles W. Kent. Boston: Ginn 1889
- *Juliana* Ed Rosemary Woolf. 1954; repr New York: Appleton-Century-Crofts 1966
- *The Juliana of Cynewulf* Ed William Strunk. London and Boston: D.C. Heath 1904
Gollancz, Sir Israel, ed *The Cædmon Manuscript of Anglo-Saxon Biblical Poetry: Junius XI: in The Bodleian Library* London: Oxford University Press 1927
Goolden, Peter, ed *The Old English Apollonius of Tyre* Oxford: Oxford University Press 1958
Gregory the Great *Moralium libri, sive expositio in librum b. job.* PL 75–6
    ly Bible Rheims 1582 and Douay 1609 version, 1899; repr Rockford, Ill: Tan s 1971
    of Seville *Etymologiarum sive originum libri xx* Ed W.M. Lindsay. 2 vols. Oxford: Clarendon Press 1911
Klaeber, F., ed *Beowulf and the Fight at Finnsburg* 3rd edn. Lexington, Mass: D.C. Heath 1950
Krapp, George, and Elliot Van Kirk Dobbie, eds *The Anglo-Saxon Poetic Records* 5 vols. New York: Columbia University Press 1931–53
Miller, Joseph, et al, eds *Readings in Medieval Rhetoric* Bloomington: Indiana University Press 1973
Roberts, Jane, ed *The Guthlac Poems of the Exeter Book* Oxford: Clarendon Press 1979
Rypins, Stanley, ed *Three Old English Prose Texts.* EETS, os no 161. Oxford: Oxford University Press 1924
Skeat, Walter W., ed *Ælfric's Lives of Saints.* EETS, os nos 76, 82, 94, 114. 1881–1900. 4 vols in 2, repr Oxford: Oxford University Press 1966, vol II

SECONDARY SOURCES

Anderson, Earl R. 'Flyting in *The Battle of Maldon*' NM 71 (1970) 197–202
- *Cynewulf: Structure, Style, and Theme in His Poetry* London and Toronto: Associated University Presses 1983
Auerbach, Erich *Literary Language and Its Public in Late Latin Antiquity and in the Middle Ages* Trans Ralph Manheim. Princeton: Princeton University Press 1965
Barney, Stephen A. *Word-Hoard: An Introduction to Old English Vocabulary* New Haven: Yale University Press 1977
Bartlett, Adeline C. *The Larger Rhetorical Patterns in Anglo-Saxon Poetry* 1935; repr New York: AMS Press 1966
Baugh, Albert, ed *A Literary History of England* New York: Appleton-Century-Crofts 1948
Baum, Paull F. 'The Meter of the *Beowulf*' MP 46 (1948–9) 73–91, 145–62.

Beale, Walter H. 'Rhetoric in the Old English Verse Paragraph' NM 80 (1979) 133–42

Bjork, Robert E. 'Oppressed Hebrews and the Song of Azarias in the Old English *Daniel*' SP 77 (1980) 213–26

Blake, N.F. 'The Battle of Maldon' *Neophilologus* 49 (1965) 332–45

– *The English Language in Medieval Literature* London: Methuen 1979

Bliss, A.J. *The Meter of 'Beowulf'* Oxford: Oxford University Press 1958

Bloomfield, Morton W. 'Patristics and Old English Literature: Notes on Some Poems' In *Studies in Old English Literature in Honor of Arthur G. Brodeur* Ed Stanley B. Greenfield. Eugene: University of Oregon Press 1963, 36–43

Bolton, W.F. 'The Background and Meaning of *Guthlac*' JEGP 61 (1962) 595–603

Bonner, Joshua 'Toward a Unified Critical Approach to Old English Poetic Composition' MP 73 (1975–6) 219–28

Bridges, Margaret 'Exordial Tradition and Poetic Individuality in Five Old English Hagiographic Poems' ES 60 (1979) 361–79

Brodeur, Arthur G. 'A Study of Diction and Style in Three Anglo-Saxon Narrative Poems' In *Nordica et Anglica*: *Studies in Honor of Stefan Einarsson* Ed Allan H. Orrick. The Hague: 1968, 97–114

– *The Art of Beowulf* Berkeley and Los Angeles: University of California Press 1969

Calder, Daniel G. 'Theme and Strategy in *Guthlac B*' PLL 8 (1972) 227–42

– '*Guthlac A* and *Guthlac B*: Some Discriminations' In *Anglo-Saxon Poetry*: *Essays in Appreciation for John McGalliard* Ed Lewis Nicholson and Dolores Warwick Frese. Notre Dame: University of Notre Dame Press 1975, 65–80

– 'The Study of Style in Old English Poetry: a Historical Introduction' In *Old English Poetry: Essays on Style* Ed Daniel G. Calder. Berkeley and Los Angeles: University of California Press 1979, 1–65

– *Cynewulf* Boston: Twayne 1981

Campbell, A. 'The Old English Epic Style' In *English and Medieval Studies Presented to J.R.R. Tolkien* Ed Norman Davis and C.L. Wrenn. London: George Allen and Unwin 1962, 13–26

Campbell, Jackson J. 'Learned Rhetoric in Old English Poetry' MP 63 (1966) 189–201

– 'Knowledge of Rhetorical Figures in Anglo-Saxon England' JEGP 66 (1967) 1–20

– 'Cynewulf's Multiple Revelations' *Medievalia et Humanistica* 3 (1972) 257–77

– 'Some Aspects of Meaning in Anglo-Saxon Art and Literature' *Annuale Mediaevale* 15 (1974) 5–45

– 'Adaptation of Classical Rhetoric in Old English Literature' In *Medieval Eloquence*: *Studies in the Theory and Practice of Medieval Rhetoric* Ed James J. Murphy. Berkeley and Los Angeles: University of California Press 1978, 173–97

Campbell, Joseph *The Hero with a Thousand Faces* 2nd edn. Princeton: Princeton University Press 1968

Carkeet, David 'Aspects of Old English Style' *Language and Style* 10 (1977) 173–89

Cassidy, Frederic G., and Richard N. Ringler, eds *Bright's Old English Grammar and Reader* 3rd edn. New York: Holt, Rinehart and Winston 1971

Casteen, John '*Andreas*: Mermedonian Cannibalism and Figural Narration' *NM* 75 (1974) 74–8

Cherniss, Michael D. *Ingeld and Christ* The Hague: Mouton 1972

Clark, George '*The Battle of Maldon*: A Heroic Poem' *Speculum* 43 (1968) 52–71

– 'The Hero of *Maldon*: Vir pius et strenuus' *Speculum* 54 (1979) 257–82

Clement, Clara Erskine *A Handbook of Christian Symbols and Stories of the Saints* Boston: Ticknor 1886

Clemoes, Peter *Rhythm and Cosmic Order in Old English Christian Literature* Cambridge: Cambridge University Press 1970

– 'Action in *Beowulf* and Our Perception of It' In *Old English Poetry: Essays on Style* Ed Daniel G. Calder. Berkeley and Los Angeles: University of California Press 1979, 147–68

Colgrave, Bertram 'The Earliest Saints' Lives Written in England' *Proceedings of the British Academy* 44 (1958) 35–60

Colish, Marcia L. *The Mirror of Language: A Study of the Medieval Theory of Knowledge* Rev edn. Lincoln and London: University of Nebraska Press 1983

Cross, F.L., ed *The Oxford Dictionary of the Christian Church* 2nd edn. Oxford: Oxford University Press 1974

Cross, J.E. 'Oswald and Byrhtnoth: A Christian Saint and a Hero Who Is a Christian' *ES* 46 (1965) 93–109

Curtius, Ernst R. *European Literature and the Latin Middle Ages* Trans Willard R. Trask. Princeton: Princeton University Press 1953

Daniélou, Jean *From Shadows to Reality* Trans Dom Wulstan Hibberd. London: Burns and Oates 1960

Das, S.K. *Cynewulf and the Cynewulf Canon* Calcutta: University of Calcutta Press 1942

Davenport, W.A. *Fifteenth-Century English Drama: The Early Moral Plays and Their Literary Relations* Cambridge: D.S. Brewer 1982

De Bruyne, Edgar *L'Esthetique du Moyen Age* Louvain: Edition de l'institut Supérieur de Philosophie 1947

Delehaye, Hippolyte, SJ *The Legends of the Saints* Trans V.M. Crawford. Notre Dame: University of Notre Dame Press 1961

Diamond, Robert E. 'The Diction of the Signed Poems of Cynewulf' *PQ* 38 (1959) 228–41

Doubleday, James F. 'The Allegory of the Soul as Fortress in Old English Poetry' *Anglia* 88 (1970) 503–8

– 'Two Part Structure in Old English Poetry' *Notre Dame English Journal* 8 (1973) 71–9

– 'The Speech of Stephen and the Tone of *Elene*' In *Anglo-Saxon Poetry: Essays in Appreciation for John McGalliard* Ed Lewis E. Nicholson and Dolores Warwick Frese. Notre Dame: Notre Dame University Press 1975, 116–23

Dubs, Kathleen E. '*Guthlac A* and the Acquisition of Wisdom' *Neophilologus* 65 (1981) 607–13

Earl, James W. 'Literary Problems in Early Medieval Hagiography' PH D diss, Cornell 1971

– 'Typology and Iconographic Style in Early Medieval Hagiography' *Studies in the Literary Imagination* 8 (1975) 15–46

– 'The Typological Structure of *Andreas*' In *Old English Literature in Context* Ed John D. Niles. Cambridge: D.S. Brewer 1980, 66–89

Eliade, Mircea *Cosmos and History: The Myth of the Eternal Return* Trans Willard R. Trask. New York: Harper and Row 1959

Ericson, Eston Everett *The Use of Swa in Old English* PH D diss, Johns Hopkins. Baltimore: Johns Hopkins University Press 1932

Evans, J.M. '*Genesis B* and Its Background' *RES* 14 (1963) 1–16, 113–23

Fakundiny, Lydia 'The Art of Old English Verse Composition' *RES* 21 (1970) 129–42, 257–66

Farrar, Raymon S. 'Structure and Function in Representative Old English Saints' Lives' *Neophilologus* 57 (1973) 83–93

Fish, Varda 'Theme and Pattern in Cynewulf's *Elene*' *NM* 76 (1975) 1–25

Francis, W. Nelson 'Syntax and Literary Interpretation' In *Essays on the Language of Literature* Ed Seymour Chatman and Samuel R. Levin. Boston: Houghton Mifflin 1967, 209–16

Frank, Roberta. 'Some Uses of Paronomasia in Old English Scriptural Verse' *Speculum* 47 (1972), 207–26

Frey, Leonard 'Exile and Elegy in Anglo-Saxon Christian Epic Poetry' *JEGP* 62 (1963) 293–302

Gardner, John 'Cynewulf's *Elene*: Sources and Structure' *Neophilologus* 54 (1970) 65–76. Rev and repr '*Elene* and the *Dream of the Rood*' In *The Construction of Christian Poetry in Old English* Carbondale: Southern Illinois University Press 1975, 85–98

Garnett, James M. 'The Latin and the Anglo-Saxon *Juliana*' *PMLA* 14 (1899) 279–98

Gerould, Gordon Hall *Saints' Legends* Boston and New York: Houghton Mifflin 1916

– 'The Old English Poems on St. Guthlac and Their Latin Source' *MLN* 37 (1917) 77–89

Grabar, André *Christian Iconography: A Study of Its Origins* Princeton: Princeton University Press 1968

Gradon, Pamela *Form and Style in Early English Literature* London: Methuen 1971

Greenfield, Stanley B. 'Syntactic Analysis and Old English Poetry' *NM* 64 (1963) 373–8

– *A Critical History of Old English Literature* New York: New York University Press 1965

– 'Grammar and Meaning in Poetry' *PMLA* 82 (1967) 377–87

– 'Grendel's Approach to Heorot: Syntax and Poetry.' In *Old English Poetry: Fif-*

teen Essays Ed Robert P. Creed. Providence: Brown University Press 1967,
275–84
– *The Interpretation of Old English Poems* London and Boston: Routledge and
Kegan Paul 1972
– 'Of Words and Deeds: The Coastguard's Maxim Once More' In *The Wisdom of
Poetry: Essays in Early English Literature in Honor of Morton W. Bloomfield*
Ed Larry D. Benson and Siegfried Wenzel. Kalamazoo, Mich: Medieval Institute
Publications 1982 45–51
Hagstrum, Jean H. *The Sister Arts: The Tradition of Literary Pictorialism and Eng-
lish Poetry from Dryden to Gray* Chicago: University of Chicago Press 1958
Hamilton, David B. 'Studies in Anglo-Saxon Literary Styles' PH D diss, Virginia 1968
– 'The Diet and Digestion of Allegory in *Andreas*' ASE 1 (1972) 147–58
– '*Andreas* and *Beowulf*: Placing the Hero' In *Anglo-Saxon Poetry: Essays in
Appreciation for John McGalliard* Ed Lewis E. Nicholson and Dolores Warwick
Frese. Notre Dame: Notre Dame University Press 1975, 81–98
Hart, Walter M. *Ballad and Epic: A Study in the Development of the Narrative
Art* 1907; repr New York: Russell and Russell 1967
Heusler, Andreas 'Der Dialog in der altgermanischen erzählenden Dichtung' *Zeit-
schrift für deutsches Altertum* 46 (1902) 189–284
Hieatt, Constance B. 'The Harrowing of Mermedonia: Typological Patterns in the
Old English "Andreas"' NM 77 (1976) 49–62
Hill, Joyce M. 'Figures of Evil in Old English Poetry' *Leeds Studies in English*
8 (1975) 5–19
Hill, Thomas D. 'Two Notes on Patristic Allusion in *Andreas*' Anglia 84 (1966)
156–62
– 'Old English Poetry and the Sapiential Tradition' PH D diss, Cornell 1967
– '"Figural Narrative in *Andreas*"' NM 70 (1969) 261–73
– 'History and Heroic Ethic in *Maldon*' Neophilologus 54 (1970) 291–6
– 'Sapiential Structure and Figural Narrative in the Old English "Elene"' *Traditio*
27 (1971) 159–77
– 'The Typology of the Week and the Numerical Structure of the Old English
Guthlac B' MS 37 (1975) 531–6
– 'The Middle Way: *Idel-Wuldor* and *Egesa* in the Old English *Guthlac A*' RES 30
(1979) 182–7
– 'The First Beginning and the Purest Earth: *Guthlac B*, Lines 1–14' NQ 28 (1981)
387–9
– 'The *Sphragis* as Apotropaic Sign: *Andreas* 1334–44' Anglia 101 (1983) 147–51
Huppé, Bernard F. *Doctrine and Poetry: Augustine's Influence on Old English
Poetry* Albany: State University of New York Press 1959
– 'The Concept of the Hero in the Early Middle Ages' In *Concepts of the Hero in*

the Middle Ages and the Renaissance Ed Norman T. Burns and Christopher J.
Reagan. Albany: State University of New York Press 1975 1–26

Irving, Edward B., Jr 'The Heroic Style in *The Battle of Maldon*' SP 58 (1961)
457–67

– 'A Reading of *Andreas*' ASE 12 (1983) 215–37

Isaacs, Neil D. *Structural Principles in Old English Poetry* Knoxville: University of
Tennessee Press 1968

Jakobson, Roman 'Linguistics and Poetics' In *Style in Language* Ed Thomas A.
Sebeok. Cambridge: MIT Press 1960, 350–77

Jehle, Dorothy M. 'Latin Rhetoric in the Signed Poems of Cynewulf' PH D diss,
Loyola of Chicago 1973

Jones, Charles W. *Saints' Lives and Chronicles in Early England* Ithaca: Cornell
University Press 1947

Katzenellenbogen, Adolf 'The Image of Christ in the Early Middle Ages' In *Life and
Thought in the Early Middle Ages* Ed Robert S. Hoyt. Minneapolis: University
of Minnesota Press 1967, 66–84

Kawin, Bruce F. *Telling It Again and Again: Repetition in Literature and Film*
Ithaca: Cornell University Press 1972

Kennedy, Charles W. *The Earliest English Poetry* London: Oxford University Press
1943

Kintgen, Eugene 'Echoic Repetition in Old English Poetry, Especially *The Dream of
the Rood*' NM 75 (1974) 202–23

Kolve, V.A. *The Play Called Corpus Christi* Stanford: Stanford University Press
1966

Kuhn, Hans 'Zur Wortstellung und -betonung im Altgermanischen' *Beiträge zur
Geschichte der deutschen Sprache und Literatur* 57 (1933) 1–109

Kurtz, Benjamin P. *From St. Antony to St. Guthlac* University of California Publications in Modern Philology 12 (1926) 103–46

Lang, Berel, ed *The Concept of Style* Philadelphia, Penn: University of Pennsylvania Press 1979

Langen, Toby 'A Commentary on the Two Old English Poems on St. Guthlac' PH D
diss, Washington 1973

Leclercq, Jean *The Love of Learning and the Desire for God. A Study of Monastic
Culture* Trans Catharine Misrahi. New York: Fordham University Press 1961

Lee, Alvin A. *The Guest-Hall of Eden: Four Essays on the Design of Old English
Poetry* New Haven: Yale University Press 1972

– 'Old English Poetry, Mediaeval Exegesis and Modern Criticism' *Studies in the
Literary Imagination* 8 (1975) 47–73

Lehmann, Winfred P. *The Development of Germanic Verse Form* Austin: University of Texas Press 1956

Le Page, R.B. 'Alliterative Patterns as a Test of Style in Old English Poetry' *JEGP* 58 (1959) 434–41

Leslie, R.F. 'Analysis of Stylistic Devices and Effects in Anglo-Saxon Literature' In *Stil und Formprobleme in der Literatur* Ed Paul Bockman. Heidelberg: Carl Winter Universitätsverlag 1956, 129–36

Levine, Robert 'Direct Discourse in *Beowulf*: Its Meaning and Function' PH D diss, Berkeley 1963

Lewis, Richard A. 'Old English Poetry: Alliteration and Structural Interlace' *Language and Style* 6 (1973) 196–205

– 'Plurilinear Alliteration in Old English Poetry' *TSLL* 16 (1975) 589–602

Leyerle, John 'The Interlace Structure of *Beowulf*' *UTQ* 37 (1967) 1–17

Lipp, Frances R. '*Guthlac A*: An Interpretation' *MS* 33 (1971) 46–62

Lumiansky, R.M. 'The Contexts of O.E. "Ealuscerwen" and "Meoduscerwen" ' *JEGP* 48 (1949) 116–26

Mâle, Emile *The Gothic Image: Religious Art in France of the Thirteenth Century* Trans Dora Nussey. 1913; repr New York: Harper and Row 1958

Mazzaro, Jerome *Transformations in the Renaissance English Lyric* Ithaca and London: Cornell University Press 1970

Merbot, Reinhold *Aestethique Studien zur angelsächsischen Poesie* Breslau: W. Koebner 1883

Metes, George Sorin 'Word-Order Variation as a Stylistic Feature in the Old English *Andreas*' PH D diss, Wisconsin 1972

Mitchell, Bruce, and Fred C. Robinson *A Guide to Old English* Rev edn. Toronto: University of Toronto Press 1982

Moore, Albert C. *Iconography of Religions* Philadelphia: Fortress Press 1977

Ogilvy, J.D.A. *Books Known to the English, 597–1066* Cambridge, Mass: Mediaeval Academy of America 1967

Overholster, Lee C. 'A Comparative Study of the Compound Use in *Andreas* and *Beowulf*' PH D diss, Michigan 1971

Palmer, R. Barton 'Characterization in the Old English "Juliana" ' *South Atlantic Bulletin* 41, no 4 (1976) 10–21

Peters, Leonard 'The Relationship of the Old English *Andreas* to *Beowulf*' *PMLA* 66 (1951) 844–63

Pilch, Herbert 'Syntactic Prerequisites for the Study of Old English Poetry' *Language and Style* 3 (1970) 51–61

Praz, Mario *Mnemosyne: The Parallel between Literature and the Visual Arts* Princeton: Princeton University Press 1970

Quirk, Randolph 'Poetic Language and Old English Metre' In *Early English and Norse Studies Presented to Hugh Smith* Ed Arthur Brown and Peter Foote. London: Methuen 1963, 150–71

Raw, Barbara C. *The Art and Background of Old English Poetry* London: Edward Arnold 1978

Regan, Catharine A. 'Evangelicism as the Informing Principle of Cynewulf's "Elene" ' *Traditio* 29 (1973) 27–52

Reichardt, Paul F. *'Guthlac A* and the Landscape of Spiritual Perfection' *Neophilologus* 58 (1974) 331–8

Reinsma, Luke 'Rhetoric in England: The Age of Ælfric, 970–1020' *Communication Monographs* 44 (1977) 390–403

Rendall, Thomas 'Bondage and Freeing from Bondage in Old English Religious Poetry' *JEGP* 73 (1974) 497–512

Reszkiewicz, Alfred 'Split Constructions in Old English' In *Studies in Language and Literature in Honour of Margaret Schlauch* Ed M. Brahmer et al. Warsaw: Polish Scientific Publishers 1966, 313–26

Riffaterre, Michael 'Criteria for Style Analysis' *Word* 15 (1959) 154–74. Repr in *Essays on the Language of Literature* Ed Seymour Chatman and Samuel R. Levin. Boston: Houghton Mifflin 1967, 412–30

– 'Stylistic Context' *Word* 16 (1960) 207–18. Repr in *Essays on the Language of Literature* Ed Seymour Chatman and Samuel R. Levin. Boston: Houghton Mifflin 1967, 431–41

Roberts, Jane 'A Metrical Examination of the Poems *Guthlac A* and *Guthlac B*' *Proceedings of the Royal Irish Academy* 71 (1971) 91–137

Robertson, D.W., Jr *A Preface to Chaucer: Studies in Medieval Perspectives* Princeton: Princeton University Press 1962

Robinson, Fred C. 'Some Aspects of the *Maldon* Poet's Artistry' *JEGP* 75 (1976) 25–40

Rosier, James L. 'Death and Transfiguration: *Guthlac B*' In *Philological Essays: Studies in Old and Middle English Language and Literature in Honour of Herbert Dean Meritt* Ed James L. Rosier. The Hague: Mouton 1970, 82–92

Rynell, Alarik 'Parataxis and Hypotaxis as a Criterion of Syntax and Style' *Lunds Universitets Årsskrift* NF avd 1, Bd 48, Nr 3 (1952) 3–59

Schaar, Claes *Critical Studies in the Cynewulf Group* 1949; repr New York: Haskell House 1967

Schabram, Hans 'Andreas und Beowulf. Parallelstellen als Zeugnis für literarische Abhängigkeit' *Nachrichten der Giessener Hochschulgesellschaft* 34 (1965) 201–18

Schiller, Gertrud *Iconography of Christian Art* Trans Janet Seligman. Vol 1. Greenwich, Conn: New York Graphic Society 1971

Shaw, Brian A. 'The Speeches in *Beowulf*: A Structural Study' *Chaucer Review* 13 (1978) 86–92

Shepherd, Geoffrey 'Scriptural Poetry' In *Continuations and Beginnings* Ed Eric G. Stanley. London: Thomas Nelson 1966, 1–36

Shippey, T.A. *Old English Verse*. London: Hutchinson University Library 1972

Shook, Laurence K. 'The Burial Mound in *Guthlac A*' *MP* 58 (1960) 1–10

– 'The Prologue of the Old English "Guthlac A" ' *MS* 23 (1961) 294–304

Slay, Desmond 'Some Aspects of the Technique of Composition of Old English

Verse' *Transactions of the Philological Society* (1952) 1–14

Smithson, George Arnold *The Old English Christian Epic: A Study in the Plot Technique of the Juliana, the Elene, the Andreas, and the Christ in Comparison with the Beowulf and with the Latin Literature of the Middle Ages* University of California Publications in Modern Philology 1 (1910) 303–400

Stanley, Eric G. '*Beowulf*' In *Continuations and Beginnings* Ed Eric G. Stanley. London: Thomas Nelson 1966, 104–41

– 'Old English Poetic Diction and the Interpretation of *The Wanderer, The Seafarer,* and *The Penitent's Prayer' Anglia* 73 (1953) 413–66. Repr in *Essential Articles for the Study of Old English Poetry* Ed Jess B. Bessinger, Jr, and Stanley J. Kahrl. Hamden, Conn: Archon Books 1968, 458–514

Stepsis, Robert, and Richard Rand 'Contrast and Conversion in "Elene" ' *NM* 70 (1969) 273–82

Stevick, Robert D. 'A Formal Analog of *Elene' Studies in Medieval and Renaissance History* ns 5 (1982) 47–104

Stracke, J. Richard '*Eþelboda*: Guthlac B, 1003' *MP* 74 (1976–7) 194–5

Szittya, Penn R. 'The Living Stone and the Patriarchs: Typological Imagery in *Andreas,* Lines 706–81' *JEGP* 72 (1973) 167–74

Tandy, Keith 'Verbal Aspect as a Narrative Structure in Ælfric's *Lives of Saints*' In *The Old English Homily and Its Background* Ed Paul E. Szarmach and Bernard F. Huppé. Albany: State University of New York Press 1978, 181–202

Tate, George S. 'Chiasmus as Metaphor: The "Figura Crucis" Tradition and "The Dream of the Rood" ' *NM* 79 (1978) 114–25

Thundyil, Zacharias P. *Covenant in Anglo-Saxon Thought* Madras: Macmillan Company of India 1972

Tolkien, J.R.R. 'The Homecoming of Beorhtnoth Beorhthelm's Son' *Essays and Studies* 6 (1953) 1–18

Van der Wurf, W.A.M. 'Cynewulf's *Elene*: The First Speech to the Jews' *Neophilologus* 66 (1982) 301–12

Walsh, Marie M. 'The Baptismal Flood in the Old English *Andreas*: Liturgical and Typological Depths' *Traditio* 33 (1970) 137–58

Warfel, Harry R. 'Syntax Makes Literature' *College English* 21 (1960) 251–5

Waterhouse, Ruth 'Ælfric's Use of Discourse in Some Saints' Lives' *ASE* 5 (1976) 83–103

Wentersdorf, Karl P. '*Guthlac A*: The Battle for the *Beorg' Neophilologus* 62 (1978) 135–42

Whatley, Gordon 'Cynewulf and Troy: A Note on "Elene" 642–61' *NQ* 218 (1973) 203–5

– 'Bread and Stone: Cynewulf's "Elene" 611–618' *NM* 76 (1975) 550–60

White, Helen C. *Tudor Books of Saints and Martyrs* Madison: University of Wisconsin Press 1963

Williams, Blanche Colton *Gnomic Poetry in Anglo-Saxon* 1914; repr New York: AMS Press 1966

Wilson, R.M. *The Lost Literature of Medieval England* London: Methuen 1952

Wittig, Joseph 'Figural Narrative in Cynewulf's *Juliana*' ASE 4 (1975) 37–55

Wolpers, Theodor *Die englische Heiligenlegende des Mittelalters* Tübingen: Max Niemeyer Verlag 1964

Woolf, Rosemary 'Saints' Lives' In *Continuations and Beginnings* Ed Eric G. Stanley. London: Thomas Nelson 1966 37–66

– 'The Devil in Old English Poetry' RES 4 (1953) 1–12. Repr in *Essential Articles for the Study of Old English Poetry* Ed Jess B. Bessinger, Jr, and Stanley J. Kahrl. Hamden, Conn: Archon Books 1968, 164–79

Wrenn, C.L. *A Study of Old English Literature* New York: W.W. Norton 1967

Wright, Ellen F. 'Cynewulf's *Elene* and the "Singal Sacu" ' NM 76 (1975) 538–49

General Index

Index of Lines

Single words, half-lines, and lines cited in the notes but not discussed are not indexed.

McMaster Old English Studies and Texts